Praise for *Unwinding Anxiety*

"One of the hardest things about tacklin
behind it. Judson Brewer has given us a
and hacks that anyone can use to feel be

—B. J. FOGG, PHD, *NEW YORK TIMES-*

"*Unwinding Anxiety* provides a step-by-step guide to Judson Brewer's personally designed, clinically proven path that can alleviate your mind from anxiety, obsessive thinking, addiction, and more. It guides your brain to rewire in helpful ways as it inspires your mind to understand its inner processes more deeply and to live with more freedom, gratitude, interpersonal connection, and joy."

—DANIEL J. SIEGEL, MD, *NEW YORK TIMES*–BESTSELLING AUTHOR OF *AWARE*

"You cannot thrive if you're perpetually anxious. It's that simple. Judson Brewer has given us a plan that can help us overcome our anxious thoughts, feelings, and habits to create true well-being. It is absolutely game-changing."

—ARIANNA HUFFINGTON, *NEW YORK TIMES*–BESTSELLING AUTHOR OF *THRIVE*

"Grounded in the best of current science and totally user-friendly, *Unwinding Anxiety* reveals how a powerful set of mindfulness tools can free us from the worry that rules our lives. This is the most helpful and informative book on anxiety I've read!"

—TARA BRACH, PHD, AUTHOR OF *RADICAL ACCEPTANCE*

"In a world that can be overwhelming, Judson Brewer has created a plan to stop the overwhelm. He shows us accessible ways to stop worry in its tracks and mindfulness techniques that can redirect our energy in positive, healing ways. It's exactly what we need right now."

—U.S. REPRESENTATIVE TIM RYAN (D-OH)

"An incredibly relatable and practical guide to anxiety. Judson Brewer's research has contributed greatly to our understanding of why anxiety is so hard to shake. This book gives us the tools to break free. Anxiety is at the root of so many of the habits we want to change. *Unwinding Anxiety* will not only help you deal with anxiety, but will also help you find freedom from the behaviors that hold you back."

—KELLY MCGONIGAL, PHD, AUTHOR OF *THE JOY OF MOVEMENT*

"Brewer weaves together science from his lab and stories from his clinic to expertly illustrate how anxiety develops, becomes a habit loop, and why our anti-anxiety strategies continue to fail us. *Unwinding Anxiety* provides actionable steps that you can implement into your own life to stop this cycle. Compellingly written, this compassionate book is full of insights that couldn't have come at a better time."

—JEWEL

"This may be the only book on anxiety you'll ever need. Drawing on his lab's latest neuroscience and clinically proven techniques, Dr. Brewer ingeniously reveals why anxiety loops are so hard to break. Showing clearly how and why worry is so addictive, he guides you in how to shift through the gears to break the old habits that keep anxiety going, and to unwind the rope that's been coiled around your life. With new insights on every page, this is evidence-based psychological science at its best."

—MARK WILLIAMS, EMERITUS PROFESSOR OF CLINICAL PSYCHOLOGY, UNIVERSITY OF OXFORD, COAUTHOR OF *MINDFULNESS*

"In *Unwinding Anxiety* neuroscientist Judson Brewer offers a brilliant breakthrough: brain-based methods for lessening our anxiety-driven habits. And anxiety, after all, is the common cold of our emotional life."

—DANIEL GOLEMAN, AUTHOR OF *EMOTIONAL INTELLIGENCE*

"Judson Brewer has written a relatable, introspective guide to overcoming anxiety. Backed by research and experience, *Unwinding Anxiety* is an exploration of how anxiety grows in our brains and offers a key to unwinding those habitual thought patterns. Much more than relaying research and science, this book offers user-friendly, practical steps to the possibility of managing worry!"

—SHARON SALZBERG, AUTHOR OF *LOVINGKINDNESS* AND *REAL CHANGE*

UNWINDING ANXIETY

NEW SCIENCE SHOWS HOW TO BREAK THE CYCLES OF WORRY AND FEAR TO HEAL YOUR MIND

JUDSON BREWER, MD, PhD

Avery
an imprint of Penguin Random House
New York

AVERY
an imprint of Penguin Random House LLC
penguinrandomhouse.com

First trade paperback edition 2022

Illustrations by Julia Miroshnichenko

The Library of Congress has cataloged the hardcover edition of this book as follows:

Names: Brewer, Judson, author.
Title: Unwinding anxiety: new science shows how to break the cycles of worry and fear to heal your mind / Judson Brewer, MD, PhD.
Description: New York: Avery, Penguin Random House LLC, 2021. | Includes index.
Identifiers: LCCN 2020041047 (print) | LCCN 2020041048 (ebook) | ISBN 9780593330449 (hardcover) | ISBN 9780593330456 (ebook)
Subjects: LCSH: Anxiety. | Habit breaking. | Change (Psychology). | Mindfulness (Psychology).
Classification: LCC BF575.A6 B74 2021 (print) | LCC BF575.A6 (ebook) | DDC 152.4/6—dc23
LC record available at https://lccn.loc.gov/2020041047
LC ebook record available at https://lccn.loc.gov/2020041048

ISBN (paperback) 9780593421406

Printed in the United States of America

9th Printing

Book design by Patrice Sheridan

To Amazon Addict

• • •

Contents

PART 2 Updating Your Brain's Reward Value: Second Gear 103

PART 3 Finding That Bigger, Better Offer for Your Brain: Third Gear 157

Introduction

ANXIETY IS EVERYWHERE. It always has been. But in the last several years, it has come to dominate our lives in a way that it perhaps never has.

My own history with anxiety goes back much further. I'm a doctor—a psychiatrist, to be precise. Only after years of struggling to help my patients overcome their anxiety and continually feeling like I was missing something important in their treatment did I connect the dots between anxiety, my lab's neuroscience research on habit change, and my own panic attacks. And that's when everything changed. I had a lightbulb moment when I realized that one of the reasons so many people fail to see that they have anxiety is the way it hides in bad habits. Now I think many more people are unavoidably aware of their anxiety, whether or not they are trying to conquer a habit.

I never planned to become a psychiatrist. In fact I had no idea what type of doctor I wanted to be when I started medical school. I just knew that I wanted to bring together my love of science with my desire to help people. Combined MD/PhD programs are set up so that you spend the first couple of years in medical school, learning all of the facts and concepts. After that, you switch to your PhD years, focusing on a specific scientific field and learning how to do research. Then you go back to the wards and finish your third and fourth years of medical school before heading off to residency to specialize in a particular field of medicine.

When I started medical school, I wasn't dead set on becoming a certain kind of doctor. I was simply fascinated by the complexity and beauty of human physiology and cognition and wanted to learn how this human system of ours worked. Typically, the first two years of medical school give medical students the time and space to start leaning toward a field they might want to specialize in. Then they confirm this decision during their hospital ward rotations in the third and fourth years. It takes eight or so years to complete a combined MD/PhD program, so I figured that I had plenty of time to discover what called to me, and just focused on learning everything I could. It took me four years to complete my PhD, which was just enough time for me to forget everything I had learned in my first two years of medical school.

So when I finished my PhD and went back to pick up where I had left off in medical school, I chose psychiatry as my first ward rotation so I could relearn everything I had forgotten about how to interview patients while I was off in PhD land. I had never thought of becoming a psychiatrist, as they generally aren't portrayed positively in the movies, and in medical school I had heard the joke that psychiatry is for "the lazies and the crazies"—that is to say, you become a psychiatrist if you yourself are lazy or crazy. But that psychiatry rotation opened my eyes to what I could later look back on and say was a confluence of serendipity and timing. What I learned was that I absolutely loved being on the wards and really connected to the struggles of my psychiatric patients. I could see myself being perfectly happy trying to help them understand their minds so that they could more effectively work with their problems. While I loved most of my other ward rotations, nothing called to me quite as much as psychiatry, so that's the medical specialty that I chose.

When I graduated from medical school and started my residency training at Yale, I found that not only was psychiatry a good fit for me, but I developed an even deeper connection to my patients who struggled with addictions. I had started meditating at the beginning of medical school and had continued doing so on a daily basis during my eight years of MD/PhD training. As I learned more about my addicted patients' struggles, I realized that they were talking about the same types of struggles that I had learned about in my own meditation training—those connected feelings of craving, clinging, grasping. To my surprise, I found we shared a language and a struggle.

Residency was also the period when I started having my own panic attacks, fueled by lack of sleep and the feeling that I didn't know anything, combined with the uncertainty of being on call and never knowing when my beeper was going to go off in the middle of the night and what train wreck was going to be on the other end when I called the nursing station. All of this took a collective toll on my psyche. Talk about being able to empathize with my anxious patients! Fortunately, my meditation practice helped here as well. I was able to use my mindfulness skills to ride out full-blown panic attacks that would wake me from sleep. Better yet, and I didn't know why at the time, these skills helped me not to add fuel to the fire of panic: I learned to work with anxiety and panic so that I didn't worry or freak out about having more panic attacks, which kept anxiety at bay and kept me from developing a true panic disorder. I also started to learn that I could teach people to become aware of uncomfortable feelings (rather than habitually avoiding them); I could give them a way to handle and work with their emotions that wasn't simply prescribing them a pill.

Toward the end of my residency, I realized that virtually nobody was researching the science of meditation. Here was what seemed like a hidden gem, something that had helped me with extreme anxiety (and possibly could help my patients as well), and nobody was exploring why or how well it worked. So over the next decade, I threw myself into creating a program to help people overcome their harmful habits—which are strongly connected to and even driven by anxiety. In fact, anxiety is in and of itself a harmful habit. Now it is an epidemic. This book is the result of all that research.

In the movie *The Martian,* Matt Damon's character has an "oh shit" moment when he realizes that he's stranded on Mars. During a windstorm, all of his buddies hightail it back to the safety of their spaceship and leave him for dead. He sits down in his little Martian outpost, wearing his cute little NASA hoodie, and tries to cheer himself up with a rousing speech: "In the face of overwhelming odds, I'm left with only one option. I'm going to have to science the shit out of this," says Matt.

Taking up Matt Damon's inspiration, in this book I have scienced the shit out of anxiety.

There are loads of books out there about these topics—thick ones and thin ones, some with catchy titles, fantastic stories, and secret methods or "hacks" for success. But not all of them are, shall we say, overflowing with actual brain science.

I can promise you there is plenty of science in this book. And it's actual science, based on studies my lab has done over many years and with real participants (first at Yale, now at Brown University). I've also published the papers that other people read and write books about, so we're covered there, too.

I've been doing research for decades and I've loved learning and discovering new things. But I'd have to say, the single most interesting and important connection that I've made is the link between anxiety and habits—why we learn to get anxious, and how even that becomes a habit. Making that connection has answered the question of why we worry, which has satisfied some of my scientific curiosity about anxiety, but more important, it has been critical for helping my patients understand and work with their own anxiety.

You see, anxiety hides in people's habits. It hides in their bodies as they learn to disconnect from these feelings through myriad different behaviors. Seeing this connection, I could now help my patients understand how they had formed habits around everything from drinking too much alcohol to stress-eating to procrastinating as a way to deal with anxiety. I could also help them see why they were struggling so much and failing to overcome both anxiety and their other habits. Anxiety would feed the other behaviors, which would then perpetuate their anxiety, until all would spiral out of control, landing them in my office.

One of the main things I've learned is that in psychiatry, the maxim "the less you know, the more you say" is applicable. In other words, the less you understand about a topic or situation, the more you fill that void with words. More words don't equal a better interpretation or more insight for your patients. In fact, when you don't know what you are talking about, the more words you use, the greater the chances are that you will dig yourself into a hole, and when you find yourself in a hole, stop digging, right?

It was a painful lesson to learn, but I realized that "the less you know, the more you say" applied to me as much as to anyone. Imagine that! I *wasn't* some exception to the rule, where I could go on spouting nonsense as if the more I talked, the more it helped my patients. If I did precisely the opposite—that is, I kept my mouth shut, tried out some of that Zen "don't know" mind, and waited until I saw some clear connection instead of trying to sound like a psychiatrist—I could actually really help people.

The "less is more" adage applies to domains outside of psychiatry as well—like science. As I spoke less and listened more, I realized that the concepts I was developing concerning habit change kept boiling down and down, simplifying themselves as they went. But as a scientist, I had to be careful not to believe my own hype. The concepts were simple, but did they actually work? And could they work in settings beyond my outpatient clinic? So back in 2011, when my first big clinical trial for smoking cessation showed a whopping *five times* greater quit rate for my program than the "gold standard" treatment, I started exploring how we could use those "weapons of mass distraction" (smartphones) to help people overcome bad habits. I scienced the shit out of that, too, finding that we could get remarkable results, in real clinical trials. And by remarkable, I mean a 40 percent reduction in craving-related eating in people who are obese/overweight, a 63 percent reduction in anxiety in people with Generalized Anxiety Disorder (and close to that level of benefit with anxious doctors), and so on. We even showed that app-based training could target specific brain networks related to smoking. Yes, with an app!

The results of my clinical psychiatry practice, research, and concept distillation make up this book, which I hope will be a useful and pragmatic guide to changing how you understand anxiety so that you can work with it effectively—and as a bonus, break all those unhelpful habits and addictions.

PART 0

Understanding Your Mind

A problem can't be solved by the same consciousness that created it.

—INTERNET MEME ATTRIBUTED TO ALBERT EINSTEIN

(YOU MAY BE wondering why I'm calling the beginning of this book Part 0 instead of Part 1. It's because Part 1 is what happens once you understand what is going on. Part 0 is all about what happens before you are even conscious of being anxious.)

Keep this in mind as you read: Part 0 will teach you the psychology and neuroscience of how anxiety gets set up, giving you the framework with which to start working with it. Part 1 will show you how to identify anxiety triggers (and what anxiety itself triggers). Part 2 will help you understand why you get stuck in cycles of worry and fear and how to update your brain's reward networks so that you can get unstuck. Part 3 will teach you simple tools that tap into your brain's learning centers to break anxiety cycles (and other habits) for good.

CHAPTER 1

Anxiety Goes Viral

ANXIETY IS LIKE pornography. It's hard to define, but you sure know it when you see it.

Unless of course, you can't see it.

In college, I was a type A go-getter who loved a challenge. I grew up in Indiana as one of four kids of a single mother, and when it came time to pick a college, I applied to Princeton because my college counselor told me I'd never get in. When I arrived on campus (sight unseen), I felt like a kid in a candy store: I was blown away by all of the opportunities that I was exposed to and wanted to do everything. I tried out for an a cappella singing group (and was rightfully rejected), joined the crew team (for a semester), played in the orchestra (becoming co-chair of its governing body my senior year), led backpacking trips for the outdoor program, rode for the cycling team (another relatively short stint), learned how to rock-climb (religiously spending hours at the climbing wall several times a week), joined a whimsical running group called the Hash House Harriers, and much more. I loved my college experience so much that I stayed on campus each summer, where I cut my teeth in the lab learning how to do research. Oh, and I supplemented my chemistry degree with a certificate in music performance to round out my education. Four years went by like a blur.

As I was nearing the end of my senior year, preparing to head to medical school, I made an appointment to see the doctor at student health, because despite all of my activity, I was feeling distinctly unhealthy. I was getting severe bloating and stomach cramps, accompanied by a dash-for-the-bathroom urgency to relieve my bowels like I'd never had before. It got so bad that I had to plan my daily running routes to make sure I was within pooping distance of a bathroom. When I explained my symptoms to the doctor (this was pre-Google, so I couldn't just come in having smugly self-diagnosed myself), he asked inquisitively if I could possibly be stressed or anxious. I blurted out something to the effect of no way, that was impossible, because I exercised every day, ate healthfully, played the violin, and on and on. While he patiently listened, my anxiety-denying mind spat out a (hardly) plausible possibility: I had recently led a backpacking trip, so I must not have correctly purified my water (though I'm pretty careful with this kind of stuff, and nobody else on the trip got sick).

"It must be giardiasis," an amoebic infection that you get from drinking unpurified water in wilderness settings that manifests as severe diarrhea, I posited to the doctor as convincingly as possible. Yes, he knew what giardiasis was (he was a doctor, after all), and no, my symptoms didn't sound quite like actual giardiasis. I didn't want to see what was staring me in the face: I was so stressed out that my anxiety was showing up in my body, because my mind was either ignoring the anxiety or in frank denial of it. Anxious? No way. Not me.

After I spent about ten minutes trying to convince the doctor that I couldn't possibly be anxious, nor did I have something that the doctor called irritable bowel syndrome (which manifests itself with the exact symptoms I had just described to him), he shrugged his shoulders and wrote me a prescription for the antibiotic that would supposedly clear my guts of *Giardia*, the theoretical cause of my diarrhea.

Of course my symptoms continued, until I finally learned that anxiety is quite a shape-shifter, ranging from a little bit of nervousness before a test to full-blown panic attacks to even the bowel-emptying blowouts that forced me to keep the locations of all the public restrooms in Princeton, New Jersey, in my head.

The online dictionary defines anxiety as "a feeling of worry, nervousness, or unease, typically about an imminent event or something with an uncertain outcome." This encompasses, well, just about anything. Since any event that is about to happen is imminent and the only thing we *can* be certain about is that things are uncertain, anxiety can rear its head in just about any place, situation, or time of day. We can have a little pinprick of anxiety when a colleague in a meeting puts up a slide about the company's quarterly results, or a shot of anxiety when those results are followed by said colleague saying that there will be layoffs in the coming weeks and the powers that be aren't sure just how many people will lose their jobs.

Some people wake up with anxiety in the morning, that nervousness prodding them awake like a hungry cat, followed by unshakable worry that spins them more and more awake (no coffee needed) and builds throughout the day because they can't figure out why they are anxious. This is the case for my patients with Generalized Anxiety

Disorder (GAD), who wake up anxious, worry their way through the day, and then continue their binge-worrying late into the night, fueled by thoughts of *Why can't I get to sleep?* Other folks have panic attacks that come out of the blue or (as happens with me) that wake them from sleep in the middle of the night. Still others worry about specific things or themes, yet oddly are unaffected by other events or categories that one would think should drive them bonkers.

And of course it would be very un-psychiatrist-like of me to not mention that there is quite a lengthy list of anxiety disorders. Despite my medical training, I'm a bit hesitant to label things as disorders or conditions myself, because as you'll see shortly, a lot of this stuff shows up simply from a slight misalignment of one of our brain's natural (and generally helpful) processes. It's like labeling "being human" as a condition. When "conditions" happen, I think of the mind/brain as more akin to a violin string that has gone slightly out of tune. In this situation, we don't label the instrument as defective and throw it away, but instead listen to what is wrong and tighten (or loosen) the strings a bit so we can continue making music. Yet for diagnostic and billing purposes, anxiety disorders run the orchestral gamut from specific phobias (e.g., fear of spiders) to obsessive-compulsive disorder (e.g., constant worrying about germs and resultant constant handwashing) to Generalized Anxiety Disorder (which is basically what it sounds like: excessive worry about everyday things).

What flips the switch from everyday anxiety to "disorder" is somewhat in the eye of the diagnostician. For example, to meet a threshold for a diagnosis of GAD, someone must have excessive anxiety and worry about a "variety of topics, events, or activities," and this must occur "more often than not for at least six months and is clearly excessive." I love that last part: "clearly excessive." Maybe I slept through the medical school lecture on how to determine exactly when worry moves from insufficiently to clearly excessive and signals that it's time to pull out my prescription pad or call in the meds.

Because anxiety generally lives internally rather than manifesting itself as a big growth on the side of someone's head, I have to ask my patients a bunch of questions to see how their anxiety shows up. I certainly didn't know that I was anxious back in college until I put two and two together and finally connected my keeping track of all the bathrooms on my running route to worrying. Per the medical manuals, some of the typical symptoms of anxiety include edginess, restlessness, tiring easily, impaired concentration, irritability, increased muscle aches, and difficulty sleeping. But as you can clearly see, these symptoms by themselves don't pin a THIS PERSON IS ANXIOUS sign on your back for everyone to read. Critically, similar to my experience denying that I was anxious in college, I have to help my patients make the link between these manifestations and what's going on inside their head before we can move forward.

To help highlight how differently anxiety can show up in a person's life, let me give you two examples from high-powered, put-together women.

My wife, Mahri, a forty-year-old college professor who is beloved by her students and internationally known for her research, can't remember when her anxiety came of age. It wasn't until she was in graduate school and had a conversation on this topic with her sister and cousin that she started recognizing family mannerisms as manifestations of anxiety. Putting a label on what seems quirky in isolation but is blazingly clear as a pattern was a lightbulb moment for her. She put it this way: "Anxiety was so subtle that it wasn't until we could name it in our family that we could recognize it in ourselves." She noticed that her grandmother, her mother, and her aunt all had some level of anxiety, and that this had been the case for as long as she could remember. For example, when Mahri was a kid, her mom would get caught up in excessive planning as a way to try to control her situations. This was especially evident when they were going on a trip. Mahri hated getting ready for traveling because her mom's anxiety would show up in the form of snapping (irritability) at her, her father, and her sister.

Only when Mahri could recognize anxiety in her family members did she realize that she had it as well. In a not-so-formal, before-breakfast interview for this book, she reflected about what anxiety feels like to her: "It is a low-grade feeling that has no object in itself. It attaches to any particular situation or thought that it can. It's as though my mind is looking for something to be anxious about. It's a feeling that I would previously have labeled as nervousness about certain things. It was hard to disconnect from my life experiences, because I thought it was just attached to legitimate life changes and circumstances." Yes, this is a key characteristic of generalized anxiety: our mind picks an innocuous object and starts worrying about it. For many, anxiety is a wildfire in the wilderness that starts with the strike of a match at dawn and is fueled by everyday experiences, burning brighter and stronger as the day unfolds.

At the end of our conversation as we headed to breakfast, Mahri added, "People who don't know me wouldn't suspect that this is something that I'm always working with." Shrink training or not, I can attest to that: she comes across as cool as a cucumber to her colleagues and college students. Yet both she and I can sense the times when she's anxious, often being clued in by her focusing on something in the future and starting to plan. It's as though her brain picks an object or period that has a bit of inherent uncertainty (e.g., the weekend), starts to rev up simply because it lacks form, and then with each mental planning stroke tries to mold that clay into a familiar shape. To artists, a block of clay says possibility. To travelers, a weekend promises adventure. To the nervous, that lack of structure screams anxiety. Mahri and I have a running joke in which I ask her some variation of "Have you planned this morning to plan this afternoon to plan for the evening?"

In contrast to the slow burn of generalized anxiety, some people have intermittent periods of panic. Consider Emily, Mahri's college roommate (a good friend of ours who is married to one of my best friends from medical school—they inadvertently introduced Mahri and me). As an attorney, Emily works on high-level political issues, including international negotiations. When she was in law school, she started having panic attacks. I asked her to explain what those were like for her. In an email response, she described them:

> It was the summer between my second and third years of law school, when I was fortunate enough to have scored a summer associate position at a big law firm. As a summer associate, you are often invited to the homes of firm partners for dinner with their families, and a few other "summers" and full-time associates. It is supposed to be a bonding experience, and lets you see what personal life is like for those who worked at the firm. After one of these dinners in July, which was indeed enjoyable, I came home and went to bed, falling asleep easily. About two hours later, however, I jolted awake, heart pounding, sweating, gasping for air. I had no idea what was wrong—I couldn't remember

having any sort of bad dream or anything. I quickly got out of bed and walked around, trying to stop it. I was so worried that I called my husband, who was working an overnight shift at the emergency department of a hospital, and begged him to come home, which he did. My symptoms eventually eased, and I realized I would survive, but I still didn't quite understand what had happened.

As I returned to law school for my final year that fall, with a full-time job offer from the firm in hand, I relaxed and didn't have any other incidents that I can remember. But by the next summer, the panic attacks returned—almost always the same as before, jolting me awake just a few hours after falling asleep easily. I was studying for the bar exam, which is a miserable experience, and simultaneously my parents, who had been married for thirty years (happily, as far as I knew), suddenly announced they were getting divorced. In addition, as I started my new job at the law firm, working some very long hours, an older associate whose office was right next to mine decided to "haze" me and treat me like his property, lecturing me about how I had no control over my life because the firm basically owned me, and how grateful I should be for this opportunity. This horrible combination of events/circumstances, seemingly stripping me of control over what I understood to be my life, led to a series of panic attacks over a six-month time period. I saw a therapist for a few sessions and did my own research, and by this point recognized what was happening. Once I knew what it was [panic attacks], I felt like I had more control. I would tell myself, "You feel like you're going to die, but you won't. This is your brain playing games with you. *You* decide what happens next." I learned how to deep-breathe my way out of an attack and focus my thoughts intensely on the very act of calming down.

Now, not everyone has the Mr. Spock–like superhuman reasoning and focus of Emily, yet in contrast to Mahri's description of the slow burn of generalized anxiety, Emily's story shows how anxiety can be like a tea kettle, heating up and heating up until it blows—often in the middle of the night. And critically for both Emily and Mahri, it wasn't until they could name their particular variety of anxiety that they could start working with it.

Whether someone is a bona fide physician or simply Dr. Google, the bottom line here is that anxiety, clinical or otherwise, is a bit of a sticky wicket to diagnose. We all get anxious—it's a part of life—yet how we deal with it is critical. If we don't know how anxiety shows up or why, we might get caught up in temporary distractions or short-term fixes that actually feed it, creating bad habits in the process (have you ever eaten ice cream or cookies when you're stressed?). Or we might spend our whole lives adding to our anxiety by trying to cure it (*why can't I just find why I'm anxious and fix it?*). That's what this book is all about.

Together, we'll explore how anxiety grew out of our brain's very basic survival mechanisms, how it can even become a self-perpetuating habit, and what you can do to change your relationship to it so that it unwinds on its own. Here's the bonus: in the process, you'll also learn about how it can set other habits in motion (and how to work with them as well).

Anxiety is not new: In a letter to John Adams back in 1816, Thomas Jefferson wrote: "There are indeed gloomy & hypochondriac minds, inhabitants of diseased bodies, disgusted with the present, &

despairing of the future; always counting that the worst will happen, because it may happen. To these I say how much pain have cost us the evils which have never happened!" While I'm not even close to a historian, I can imagine Jefferson had quite a bit to be anxious about, from helping to birth a new country to living with his hypocritical attitude toward slavery. (He wrote that "all men are equal," that slavery was a "moral depravity" and a "hideous blot," that it presented a great threat to the survival of the new American nation, but he also enslaved more than six hundred people over his lifetime.)

In our modern world, with technological advances helping to provide a more stable food supply and the United States now being about a quarter of a millennium old, we might expect that there is less to worry about. BC—that is, before COVID-19—the Anxiety and Depression Association of America estimated that 264 million people worldwide had an anxiety disorder. In a study that now seems ancient because the data were collected between 2001 and 2003, the National Institute of Mental Health reported that 31 percent of U.S. adults experience an anxiety disorder sometime in their lives, and that 19 percent of the population had an anxiety disorder within the past year. Over the past two decades, things have only gotten worse. In 2018, the American Psychological Association surveyed a thousand U.S. adults about their sources and levels of anxiety. The APA found that 39 percent of Americans reported being more anxious than they were in 2017, and an equal amount (39 percent) had the same level of anxiety as the last year. That's nearly 80 percent of the population.

Where is all of this anxiety coming from? The same APA poll found that 68 percent of respondents reported worries about health and safety made them somewhat or extremely anxious. Some

67 percent of folks reported finances as their source, followed by politics (56 percent) and interpersonal relationships (48 percent). In their "Stress in America" survey (2017), the APA found that 63 percent of Americans felt that the future of the nation was a large source of stress, and 59 percent checked the box that "the United States is at the lowest point they can remember in history." Remember, this was back in 2017, three years before COVID-19 hit.

Based on observations that mental illness tends to be more common in regions of the United States that also have a lower socioeconomic status, some have wondered whether less wealthy countries—where basic needs such as steady sources of food, clean water, and safety might be substantial stressors—would have higher rates of anxiety. To address this question, a study published in *JAMA Psychiatry* in 2017 looked at rates of Generalized Anxiety Disorder across the globe. Ready for this? Lifetime prevalence was highest in high-income countries (5 percent), lower in middle-income countries (2.8 percent), and lowest in low-income countries (1.6 percent). The authors opined that individual differences in the tendency to worry may show up more under conditions of relative wealth and stability found in high-income countries. Speculation proliferates as to why this is. For example, having our basic needs met may provide more idle time to let our survival brains look for something to be threatened by or worried about, leading some to dub this population the "worried well." Yet people with GAD are far from healthy: half of the individuals in this study reported severe disability in one or more life domains. I think of my patients with GAD as Olympians in the endurance "sport" of anxiety—they can worry longer and harder than anyone else on the planet.

With the emergence of the COVID-19 pandemic, early estimates report (surprise!) that anxiety levels skyrocketed. A cross-sectional survey of people in China from February 2020 found the prevalence of GAD to be 35.2 percent—and this was relatively early in the grand scheme of the pandemic. A report from the United Kingdom from late April 2020 reported that "mental health had deteriorated" compared with pre-COVID-19 trends. A study in the United States in April 2020 found that 13.6 percent of respondents reported severe psychological distress. That's a whopping 250 percent increase compared to 2018, where only 3.9 percent reported this level of woe.

You only have to look as far as your own experience or social media feed to confirm this for yourself. Large-scale disasters such as the COVID-19 pandemic are almost always accompanied by increases in a broad range of mental disorders, including substance use and anxiety. For example, nearly 25 percent of New Yorkers reported increasing their alcohol use after the 9/11 attack back in 2001, and six months after the 2016 Fort McMurray wildfire (the costliest disaster in Canadian history), area residents showed a spike to 19.8 percent in Generalized Anxiety Disorder symptoms.

Anxiety isn't a loner. It tends to hang out with friends. That same *JAMA* study from 2017 found that 80 percent of people with GAD experienced another lifetime psychiatric disorder, most commonly depression. A recent study from my lab found something similar: 84 percent of individuals with GAD presented with comorbid disorders.

And anxiety doesn't just come out of the blue. It is born.

CHAPTER 2

The Birth of Anxiety

ANXIETY IS A strange beast.

As a psychiatrist, I learned that anxiety and its close cousin, panic, are both born from fear. As a behavioral neuroscientist, I know that fear's main evolutionary function is helping us survive. In fact, fear is the oldest survival mechanism we've got. Fear teaches us to avoid dangerous situations in the future through a brain process called negative reinforcement.

For example, if we step out into a busy street, turn our head, and see a car coming right at us, we instinctively jump back onto the safety of the sidewalk. That fear reaction helps us to learn quickly that streets are dangerous and to approach them with caution. Evolution made this really simple for us. So simple that we need only three elements in situations like this to learn: an environmental cue, a behavior, and a result. In this case, walking up to a busy street (the environmental cue) is our signal to look both ways before crossing (the behavior). Crossing the street uninjured (the result) teaches us to remember to repeat the action again in the future. We share this survival tool with all animals. Even the sea slug, a creature with the most "primitive" nervous system known in science (twenty thousand neurons total, as opposed to roughly a hundred billion in the human brain), uses this same learning mechanism.

Sometime in the last million years, humans evolved a new layer on top of our more primitive survival brain; neuroscientists call this the prefrontal cortex (PFC). (From an anatomical perspective, this "newer" brain region is located just behind our eyes and forehead.) Involved in creativity and planning, the PFC helps us to think and plan for the future. The PFC predicts what will happen in the future based on our past experience. Yet critically, the PFC needs accurate information to make accurate predictions. If information is lacking, our PFC plays out different versions of what might happen to help us choose the best path forward. It does this by running simulations based on previous events in our lives that are most similar. For example, trucks and buses are similar enough to cars that we can safely assume we should look both ways to avoid any fast-moving vehicle.

Enter anxiety.

Anxiety is born when our PFCs don't have enough information to accurately predict the future. We saw this with COVID-19, when it exploded onto the world stage in early 2020. As would be true of any newly discovered virus or pathogen, scientists raced to study the characteristics of COVID-19 in order to find out precisely how contagious and deadly it was so that we could act appropriately. Yet especially in the early days of discovery, uncertainty abounded. Without accurate information, our brains found it easy to spin stories of fear and dread, based on the latest reports that we had heard or read. And because of the way our brains are wired, the more shocking the news—increasing our sense of danger and feelings of fear—the more likely our brains are to remember it. Now add elements of fear and uncertainty—the illness or death of family members; the prospect of losing your job; hard decisions about whether or not to send your kids to school; concerns about how to safely reopen the economy; and so on—and you get a big heap of badness for your brain to try to sort through.

Notice how fear itself does not equal anxiety. Fear is an adaptive learning mechanism that helps us survive. Anxiety, on the other hand, is maladaptive; our thinking and planning brain spins out of control when it doesn't have enough information.

You can get a sense of this simply by looking at how quickly a fear response happens. If you step into a busy street and a car bears down on you, you reflexively jump back onto the sidewalk. In this situation you don't have time to think. Processing all of that information (car, speed, trajectory, etc.) in your PFC takes much too long, and making a decision about what to do ("should I step back or will the car swerve around me?") takes even longer. We can break it down into three very different time scales that differentiate reflexes from learning from anxiety:

1. Immediate (milliseconds)
2. Acute (seconds to minutes)
3. Chronic (months to years)

That *immediate reaction* happens at the survival level. We aren't learning anything in this situation; we're simply getting out of harm's way. This has to happen really quickly and instinctually. Jumping back onto the sidewalk is something that happens so quickly that you realize what just happened only after the fact. That's a reaction that starts in your older brain's autonomic nervous system, which acts quickly and outside of your conscious control to regulate all sorts of things, like how much blood your heart pumps or whether your muscles get more blood than your digestive tract. It is lifesaving because when there is an immediate threat, you don't have time to think—thinking is a much slower process. In other words, this fight/flight/freeze reaction keeps you alive long enough to get to the next phase and actually learn from it.

Once you are safely out of harm's way, *that's* when you feel the acute adrenaline rush and start processing what just happened (*acute learning*). The thought that you almost got killed helps you link up stepping out into the street with danger. Your brain might even dredge up a distant memory or two, as your parent's voice pops into your head and you remember the first time your mom or dad scolded you for not looking both ways before crossing the street. The unpleasantness of the fearful physiological reaction helps you learn: put your phone away and look both ways before crossing the street. Notice how quickly learning happens here. You don't need to spend months in therapy trying to decipher whether you have a death wish or were a defiant kid when you were growing up; it's a simple matter of learning to pay attention in dangerous situations. You connect the dots between a busy street and a close encounter with a car; ironically, you rapidly learn what your parents kept trying to teach you when you were a kid. (Notice how much more effective learning from experience is than extrapolating from a concept—our brains are really good at this.) Importantly, like zebras who jump and kick, or dogs who shake their bodies after surviving stressful situations, you need to learn how to safely discharge the excess energy associated with that "I almost died" adrenaline surge, so that it doesn't lead to chronic or post-traumatic stress and anxiety. Simply talking to someone doesn't count here; you may really have to do something physical, like shout, shake, dance, or engage in some type of physical exercise.

Your older and newer brains work well together to help you survive: when you act instinctively (jump out of the street) and learn from those situations (look both ways before crossing), you live long enough to be able to start planning for the future ("I should make sure my kids know that this is a dangerous intersection"). When everything is working well, this is where the PFC shines. The PFC takes information from past experience and projects it into the future as a way to model and predict what might or could happen, so instead of constantly reacting to what is happening right now, you can plan for what's next. This is all well and good as long as you have enough information to make a good prediction. The more certain you can be of what is about to happen, the more you can predict and plan ahead.

Like a seed needing fertile soil, the old survival brain creates the conditions for anxiety to sprout in your thinking brain (*chronic*). This is where anxiety is born. Fear + uncertainty = anxiety. For example, how does it feel the first time that your kids want to walk to school or a few blocks to a friend's house alone? You've carefully taught them safe street crossing, stranger danger, and all the rest. But the moment they are out of sight, what does your mind do? It starts filling with all of the worst-case scenarios.

In the absence of past experience and/or (accurate) information, you will find it really hard to shut off that worry switch and calmly plan for the future. Your thinking/planning brain doesn't have an information switch such that when it runs low on information, it goes into sleep mode until more information is available. Quite the opposite. Anxiety urges you into action. "Go get me some information!" it screams in your ears (oddly, from inside your head). And you find yourself trying to remember all of the spy movies that you've seen so you can secretly tail your kids to make sure they get to their destination safely (without you).

Broadly speaking, it seems that more information should be a good thing (when you can get it). After all, knowing more should help us be more in control, because information is power, right? With the advent of the Internet, there is no shortage of information, yet accuracy gets buried under the volume of the content. When virtually anyone can post anything that they want to and are rewarded not for accuracy, but instead for humor or outrage or shock value, the web quickly fills with so much information that we find it nearly impossible to wade through it all. (Fake news spreads six times faster than real news.) This does the opposite of helping us feel like we are in control. From a scientific standpoint, the impact of having too much information to make choices when planning has been dubbed *choice overload.*

Alexander Chernev and his colleagues at the Kellogg School of Management at Northwestern University even identified three factors that significantly diminish our brain's ability to make choices: higher levels of task difficulty, greater choice set complexity, and (surprise!) higher uncertainty. Life in the age of 24/7 information availability brings with it greater complexity due simply to sheer volume. Getting a bazillion possible articles from a Google search can feel like going to the beach to dip your toe in the water, then looking up and seeing a tidal wave coming right at you. The sense that you can never stay current with the news cycle (because you now can know what is happening anywhere in the world at any time) or even keep up with your social media circle can feel like picking up a glass of water because you are thirsty, feeling the need to drink all of it, and failing to realize that the glass is bottomless.

Not only does information overload feel overwhelming, but then add in the nature of the information: contradictory (and potentially purposely misleading) information naturally leads to higher uncertainty. You don't need me to point out how much our brains hate contradictory stories. Why? They are the epitome of uncertainty (more on the evolutionary origins of this in chapter 4). And unfortunately, complexity and uncertainty will only increase as techniques of manipulation of information become more sophisticated (e.g., deep fakes).

The less certain the information, a state usually accompanied by an urge to editorialize (which adds more to the volume of information to be waded through), the more your PFC starts spinning faster and faster, taking whatever substrate is available as it tries to quickly spit out all possible what-if scenarios for you to ponder. Of course, this hardly counts as planning, but your brain doesn't know any better. The more inaccurate the information your PFC incorporates, the worse the outcome. And as the scenarios become more worst-case (which tends to happen as the PFC starts to go off-line, ironically due to the ramping up of the anxiety), your fight/flight/freeze physiology can get triggered to the point that just thinking about these possible (but highly improbable) situations can make you feel that you're in danger, even though the danger is only in your head. Voilà! Anxiety.

Let's return to the example of letting your kids head out on their first three-block adventure to school or their friend's house. Back in the "olden days" (i.e., before cell phones), our parents had to send us out into the wild and simply wait for us to come home (or call from our friend's house to let them know we'd arrived safely). Now parents can load their children down with every conceivable tracking device before sending them out the door so that they know where their kids are at any moment. And as they can track every step, they can worry about everything along the way. (*She stopped. Why did she stop? Was she talking to a stranger or tying her shoe?*) With each bit of uncertain information, the brain spins out every conceivable what-if scenario. This is the planning brain trying to think through all of the contingencies in an effort to help out. Does this substantively increase the child's safety? Probably not, especially when weighed against the increase in anxiety that it spawns.

Yes, anxiety is an evolutionary add-on. When fear-based learning is paired with uncertainty, your well-intentioned PFC doesn't wait for the rest of the ingredients (e.g., more information). Instead, it takes whatever it's got in the moment, uses worry to whip it together, fires up the adrenaline oven, and bakes you a loaf of bread you didn't ask for: a big hot loaf of anxiety. And in the process of making the loaf, your brain stores a bit of the dough—like sourdough starter—away for later. The next time you plan for something, your brain pulls that anxiety starter out of your mental pantry and adds it as an "essential ingredient" to the mix, to the point where that sour taste overpowers reason, patience, and the process of gathering more information.

LIKE COVID-19, ANXIETY is also contagious. In psychology, the spread of emotion from one person to another is aptly termed *social contagion*. Our own anxiety can be cued/triggered simply by talking to someone else who is anxious. Their fearful words are like a sneeze landing directly on our brain, emotionally infecting our PFC, and sending it out of control as we begin to worry about everything from whether our family members will get sick to how our jobs will be affected. Wall Street is a great example of social contagion. We watch the stock market spike and crash, the stock indexes being an indicator of how feverish our collective anxiety is at the moment. Wall Street even has something known as the Volatility Index (VIX), also known as the fear index, and I bet you won't be surprised that it hit a ten-year high back in March of 2020, as stock traders started to realize what an unprecedented mess the world was in.

When we can't control our anxiety, that emotional fever spikes into panic (defined online as "sudden uncontrollable fear or anxiety, often causing wildly unthinking behavior"). Overwhelmed by uncertainty and fear of the future, our PFCs—the rational thinking parts of our brains—go off-line. Logically, we know that we don't need to store a six-month supply of toilet paper in our basement, but when we're running through the grocery store and see someone's cart piled high with Charmin, their anxiety infects us, and we go into survival mode. Must. Get. Toilet. Paper. Our PFC comes back online only when we're out in the parking lot trying to figure out how to fit all that toilet paper into our car or carry it onto the subway.

So how do we keep our PFCs online in uncertain times? How can we avoid panic? Too many times, I've seen my anxious clinic patients try to suppress or think themselves out of anxiety. Unfortunately, both willpower and reasoning rely on the PFC, which at these critical moments has shut down and isn't available. Instead, I start by teaching them how their brains work so that they can understand how uncertainty weakens their brain's ability to deal with stress, priming it for anxiety when fear hits. Learning that uncertainty triggers anxiety, which in turn can lead to panic, allows them to be on the lookout. And simply knowing that this is their survival brain kicking into high gear (even if it is a little misguided because it doesn't have enough information) helps put my patients a little more at ease.

But this is only the first step. Our brains are constantly asking "what if?" When we log on to social media and scroll for the latest information, all we see is more speculation and fear. Social contagion knows no physical boundaries and can be spread from anywhere in the world. Instead of desperately searching for information, we need to add something more reliable to help us work with our emotions. Ironically, the antidote to panic relies on our survival instincts—leveraging these same learning mechanisms that lead to worry and anxiety in the first place.

To hack our brains and break the anxiety cycle, we must become aware of two things: that we are getting anxious and/or panicking and what results from anxiety/panicking. This helps us see if our behavior is actually helping us survive or in fact is moving us in the opposite direction. Panic can lead to impulsive behaviors that are dangerous; anxiety weakens us mentally and physically and also has more long-term health consequences. Becoming aware of these damaging effects helps our brain's learning system determine the relative worth of behaviors: more valuable (rewarding) behaviors are placed higher in a reward hierarchy in our brain, and thus are more likely to be repeated in the future, while the less valuable (unrewarding) behaviors fall to the bottom (more on this in chapter 10).

Once we are aware of how unrewarding anxiety is, we can then bring in the *bigger, better offer,* or BBO (more on this in chapter 15). Since our brains will choose more rewarding behaviors simply because they feel better, we can practice replacing old habitual behaviors such as worry with those that are naturally more rewarding.

For example, early on in the COVID-19 pandemic, public health officials warned us to stop touching our faces, because we can more easily catch a virus if we've touched a doorknob or contaminated surface and then touch our face. If you notice that you have a habit of touching your face (which many of us do: one study published back in 2015 found that we do this, on average, twenty-six times an hour), you can be on the lookout for when you carry out that behavior. With that trigger, you can step back and notice if you are starting to worry as a mental behavior ("oh no, I touched my face—maybe I'll get sick!"). Instead of panicking, you can take a deep breath and ask yourself, "When was the last time I washed my hands?" Just by taking a moment to pause and ask such a question, you give your PFC a chance to come back online and do what it does best: think ("oh, right! I just washed my hands"). Here you can leverage certainty: if you've just washed your hands, haven't been in public, and so forth, the likelihood that you're going to get sick is pretty low.

Self-awareness also helps to foster good hygiene habits through reinforcement learning: you feel better when you've been in the habit of washing your hands, and you can more easily reassure yourself in the moments when you accidentally or habitually touch your face (or scratch an itch). At the same time, if you're not great at regular handwashing, awareness plus uncertainty gives you a kick in the pants to wash your hands more regularly, or at least wash them when you've just come from a real-world social space; that natural feeling of dis-ease urges you into action. The more you can clearly see the positive feeling and effects of good hygiene and compare them to the negative feeling of uncertainty or anxiety, the more your brain naturally moves toward the former, because it feels better.

Understanding these simple learning mechanisms will help you "keep calm and carry on" (which is how Londoners dealt with the uncertainty of constant air raids in World War II) instead of getting caught in anxiety or panic in the face of uncertainty. At times when your mind starts to spin out in your worry du jour, you can pause and take a deep breath while you wait for your PFC to come back online. Once it's up and running again, you can then compare the feeling of anxiety to that of calmness and think clearly. To our brains, it's a no-brainer. More important, once you are able to tap into your brain's power to overcome anxiety, you can broaden your learning to work with other habitual tendencies as well. It simply takes a little practice so that the bigger, better offers become new habits not just for anxiety, but far beyond.

While anxiety is born from fear, it needs nourishment to grow and flourish. To help you see more clearly what feeds anxiety, you need to know how habits get set up in the first place to help you understand how your mind works.

CHAPTER 3

Habits and Everyday Addictions

HATE TO TELL you this, but you're addicted to something.

When you read the word *addicted*, your first thoughts might be of alcohol, heroin, opioids, or other illicit drugs. You might also think that addiction is something that happens to *other people*. A friend, family member, or coworker who really struggled (or is still struggling) might pop into your head as your brain quickly compares their situation to yours. In fact, I wouldn't be surprised if you said out loud, "No way, I'm not an addict. I just have a few pesky habits that keep sticking around."

I can guess that's your first reaction, because that's exactly what I thought for the longest time. I'm just a normal guy who grew up in the center of normal—Indiana. My mom made sure I ate my vegetables, got an education, and stayed away from drugs. I clearly took her lessons to heart—perhaps even too much?—because here I am, in my forties, and I'm a vegetarian with too many graduate degrees (MD and PhD). Everything a boy could do to make his mom proud. Yet I didn't know the first thing about addiction.

In fact, it wasn't until I was in my psychiatry residency training at Yale that I really learned about addiction. I saw patients addicted to meth, cocaine, heroin, alcohol, cigarettes . . . you name it. Many of them were addicted to multiple substances at the same time, and many had been in and out of rehab. In most cases, these were ordinary, intelligent people who knew all too well the costs of their addiction on their health, their relationships, the people around them—heck, on their lives in general—and yet they could not get back in control. It was often as baffling as it was sad.

Seeing what my patients were going through brought to life the otherwise dry definition of addiction: "continued use despite adverse consequences." Addiction isn't limited to the use of chemicals such as nicotine, alcohol, and heroin. Continued use despite adverse consequences goes way beyond cocaine or cigarettes or any of the really bad things I had avoided. That definition—and let's hear it once again, in case we're in any doubt: "continued use despite adverse consequences"—well, that could mean continued use of *anything.*

This thought brought me up short. While I was treating patients who had ruined their lives with use of the big bad stuff, I also had some nagging questions in my head: "What if the root of addiction isn't in the *substances themselves,* but in a deeper place? What *really* causes addiction?" Could anxiety be a habit, or even an addiction? In other words, how obvious are the adverse consequences of anxiety? Can we get addicted to worrying? On the surface, it seems that anxiety helps us get things done. It seems that worrying helps us protect our children from harm. But does the science back this up?

The joke among psychological researchers is that when we conduct research, we are in fact conducting "me-search." We study our own quirks, foibles, and pathology (conscious or unconscious) in order to gain a way into the wider subject. So I looked inward; and I also started asking friends and coworkers about their habits. Long story short: I found addiction everywhere. And this is what it looked like: Continued shopping despite adverse consequences. Continued pining away for that special someone despite adverse consequences. Continued computer gaming despite adverse consequences. Continued eating despite adverse consequences. Continued daydreaming despite adverse consequences. Continued social media checking despite adverse consequences. Continued worrying despite adverse consequences (yes, as you'll see, worry does have significant adverse consequences). Addiction isn't limited to the so-called hard drugs and addictive substances. It is everywhere. Is this new, or had we missed something?

The answer: this is old *and* new. Let's start with the new.

The rate of change in our world over the last twenty years far outstrips all the changes in the previous two hundred years. Our brains and bodies haven't kept up, and it's killing us.

Let's use where I grew up—Indianapolis, Indiana, the middle of the Midwest, the center of normal—as an example. Back in the 1800s, if I lived on a farm on the prairie and I had a hankering for a new pair of shoes, I'd need to hitch my horse to my wagon, ride into town, talk to the person at the general store about what shoes I wanted (and what size), go back home, wait a couple of weeks for the order to go out to the cobbler and for them to be made, hitch my horse back up to my wagon, go back into town, and (assuming I had the money to pay for the shoes) buy the darn shoes. Now? I can be zipping along in my car, find myself stuck in traffic, and in a fit of frustration, click on an ad that I saw in my email (yes, targeted to me because Google knows I like to buy shoes), and as if by magic, one to two days later (thanks to Amazon Prime), a pair of perfectly fitting shoes shows up on my doorstep.

You don't need to be an addiction psychiatrist to see that the two-minute, two-click fix is more likely to get you to keep buying shoes than the two-month experience.

In the name of convenience and efficiency, the modern world is increasingly designed to create addictive experiences. This holds true for things (like shoes, food, etc.) and behaviors (like watching TV, checking social media, or playing video games). It can even be true for thoughts, like politics, romance, or the need to keep up with the latest news: dating apps and news feeds are increasingly engineered to have itch-inducing features and headlines designed to be "clickbait." Instead of time-honored news agencies delivering a newspaper to your door once a day, letting you decide what to read, modern media conglomerates and start-ups decide what information to deliver to you and when. They can track your every search and click, which give them feedback on which articles have click-worthy stickiness that gets you to scratch that itch. Based on this feedback, they can write more clicky and sticky articles, rather than simply delivering the news. Notice how today more headlines are phrased as questions or partial answers than ten years ago.

On top of this, because almost everything is readily available at a moment's notice through our TVs, laptops, and smartphones, companies can take advantage of any weak moment (boredom, frustration, anger, loneliness, hunger) by offering a simple emotional fix (buy these shoes, eat this food, check this news feed). And these addictions get reified and solidified into habits, so that they don't *feel* like addictions—they just feel like who we are.

How did we get here?

To answer this question, we need to go back a lot further in time than *Little House on the Prairie*. We need to go back to when our brains evolved the ability to learn.

Remember, our brains have old and new components. The new parts facilitate thinking, creativity, decision-making, and so on. But these newer sections are layered on top of the *older* parts of our brain—parts that evolved to help us survive. One example that I gave in chapter 2 was the fight/flight/freeze instinct. Another feature of the "old brain" that I briefly touched on previously is what's known as the *reward-based learning system*. Reward-based learning is based on positive and negative reinforcement. Put simply, you want to do more of the things that feel good (positively reinforcing) and less of the things that feel bad (negatively reinforcing). This ability is so important and evolved so far back that scientists can see it at play in sea slugs—as I mentioned earlier, organisms with only twenty thousand neurons in their entire nervous system (a discovery so big Eric Kandel won the Nobel Prize for it). Imagine that: just twenty thousand neurons. That's a creature similar to a car stripped down to only the essential elements needed to make it go (and stop).

Back in cave-person days, reward-based learning was exceedingly helpful. Since food was hard to come by, our hairy ancestors might come across some food and their stodgy little brains would grunt, "Calories . . . survival!" Cave person tasted the food—yummy—and presto! Cave person survived. When cave person got some sugar or fat, his or her brain not only connected nutrients with survival but also released a chemical called *dopamine*, a neurotransmitter essential for learning to pair places with behaviors. Dopamine acted like a primeval whiteboard, upon which was written: "Remember what you are eating and where you found it." Cave person laid down a context-dependent memory and learned over time to repeat the process. See food, eat food. Survive. Also, feel good. Repeat. Trigger/cue, behavior, reward.

Fast-forward to last night. You weren't feeling so great—you had a bad day at work; your partner said something hurtful; or you recalled the moment your father left your mother for somebody else—and you remembered that Lindt Excellence Extra Creamy Milk Chocolate Bar on the door of your refrigerator. These days, finding food isn't as hard as it was for the cave person, so food has a different role in the (over-) developed world at least. Our modern brains say, *Hey, you can use this dopamine thing for more than remembering where food is. In fact, the next time you feel bad, you can try eating something good, and you'll feel better!* We thank our brains for that great idea and quickly learn that if we eat chocolate or ice cream when we're mad or sad, we feel better. This is the exact same learning process that cave person went through, but now the trigger is different: Instead of a hunger signal coming from our stomach, an emotional signal—feeling sad/mad/hurt/lonely—triggers our urge to eat.

Recall back to when you were a teenager. Remember those rebel kids outside of school smoking? You really wanted to be that cool, so you start smoking. The Marlboro man wasn't a dork, and this was no accident. See cool. Smoke to be cool. Feel good. Repeat. Trigger, behavior, reward. And each time you perform the behavior, you reinforce this brain pathway.

Before you know it—because it's not really a conscious occurrence—the way you deal with an emotion or to assuage stressors becomes a habit.

This is a crucial moment, so please read this slowly: With the same brain mechanisms as that unnamed cave person, we modern geniuses have gone from *learning to survive* to literally *killing ourselves* with these habits. And it's gotten exponentially worse in the last twenty years. Obesity and smoking are among the leading preventable causes of morbidity and mortality in the world. Undeterred by modern medicine, anxiety disorders top the charts as the most predominant psychiatric conditions.

On top of this, people spend most of their time online getting little dopamine hits from clicking on this or that, or liking this or that, or being liked for this or that. Each of these habits and conditions are created by our old brain trying to help us survive in a new world.

And it's not working so well.

I'm not just talking about stress or overeating or shopping or unhealthy relationships or too much time online or that general anxiety we all seem to face all the time. If you ever get caught up in a worry habit loop, you know what I mean:

Trigger: Thought or emotion
Behavior: Worrying
Result/reward: Avoidance, overplanning, etc.

Here, a thought or emotion triggers your brain to start worrying. This results in avoiding the negative thought or emotion, which feels more rewarding than the original thought or emotion.

Let's recap:

Our brains evolved to help us survive. When we were hungry cave people, we used reward-based learning to help us remember where to find food. Now this learning process can be leveraged to trigger cravings and evoke emotions . . . and create habits, compulsive behavior, and addictions.

Companies have understood this for quite a while now.

The food industry spends billions of dollars finding just the right amount of salt, sugar, and crunch to make foods irresistible. Social media companies spend thousands of hours tweaking their algorithms to make sure you are triggered by the perfect photos, videos, and posts to keep you scrolling for hours (while looking at their advertising partners). News outlets optimize their headlines for clickbait. Online retailers design their websites with hooks like "other customers like you also purchased . . ." to keep you searching until you buy. It's everywhere, and it's only going to get more intense and bigger.

And it's worse than you realize: there are additional "addiction maximizers" in play in the modern world.

First, the most crave-ogenic (that is to say, meant to make you crave) type of reinforcement learning is called *intermittent reinforcement*. When an animal is given a reward that isn't on a regular schedule or one that seems random (intermittent), the dopamine neurons in the brain perk up more than usual. Think of a time when someone surprised you with a gift or party. I bet you can remember it, right? That's because *unexpected* rewards fire off dopamine in your brain at a much higher rate than *expected* ones.

Casinos provide one example of how this works in the commercial world. They have dialed intermittent reinforcement in so well that they have a formula/algorithm that has the slot machines "hit" just enough times to get people to keep playing, even though on average everyone loses money (the casino's "winning" formula).

Here's another: Silicon Valley. It turns out that intermittent reinforcement extends to *anything* that alerts you to something new. Remember, this is our *old* brain, using the only tricks that it has to try to survive in today's fast-paced and hyperconnected world. That part of the brain, though, doesn't know the difference between a saber-toothed tiger and a late-night email from your boss. So any kind of alert—from the ancient "You've got mail" of aol.com to a buzz in your pocket for a new like on your social media post—triggers a response in your old brain. Your email, Twitter, Facebook, Instagram, Snapchat, WhatsApp, Trulia 3-bedroom, 2½-bath apartment with granite countertops search filter—anything that claims to help you stay connected is designed for maximum addiction, in part because they *don't* bing, beep, tweet, email, or chirp at regular intervals.

The second everyday addiction maximizer in the modern world is *immediate availability*. Buying those shoes back in the 1800s was a lot of work, and that was a good thing. If I had a hankering for new shoes to celebrate the end of the Civil War, I couldn't just impulsively order them, knowing that they'd show up at my barn the next day. And because the process was arduous and time-consuming and slow and, crucially, *not immediate*, I had to think hard about the costs and benefits. Were the shoes I already had really worn out, or would they work for a little while longer?

Time is critical for allowing all of that excitement to wash over us (oh, new shoes, how fun!), and importantly, go away. Time gives us, well, time to sober up, so that the sweet juiciness of the moment can fade into the reality of the need.

In the modern world, however, you can take care of any need or desire almost instantly. Stressed out? No problem. Cupcakes are right around the corner. Bored? Check out the latest posts on Instagram. Anxious? Watch cute puppy videos on YouTube. "Need" a new pair of shoes (as in see someone with a cute pair of shoes that you have to have)? Just hop on Amazon.

Hate to also tell you this, but . . . your smartphone is nothing more than an advertising billboard in your pocket. What's more, you pay for it to advertise to you constantly.

By combining the reward-based learning built into our old brain with intermittent reinforcement *and* immediate availability, we've created a dangerous formula for modern-day habits and addictions that goes well beyond what we typically think of as substance abuse.

I'm not laying this out just to scare you. I want you to understand how your mind works and how much of the modern world is designed to create addictive behaviors and capitalize on them. In order to successfully work with your mind, you have to first know how your mind works. Once you understand how your mind works, you can begin to work with it. It's that simple. Now you know how your mind forms habits. And with this understanding, you are ready to take the next step: mapping your mind.

Ready for the first reflection?

Anxiety is a bit trickier than most habits. To manage anxiety, you need a bottom-up approach, so let's start with something simple. What are my top three habits and everyday addictions? What bad habits and unwanted behaviors do I keep doing, despite adverse consequences?

CHAPTER 4

Anxiety as a Habit Loop

When I'm teaching seminars or being interviewed about habit loops, I find that few people understand that anxiety can be a habit loop.

To understand why, let's look at our old brain again.

Imagine what it was like for our ancient ancestors out there on the savannah. Their cave-person brains were focused on two things: finding food to eat and not becoming food. Before agrarian cultures emerged, our ancestors had to explore unknown territories to find new food sources. When they moved out of their familiar places into parts unknown, their brains went on high alert. Why? Because they didn't know if it was safe out there. They stayed on edge until they were able to map out the new territory and determine if it was dangerous or not. The more they went into the territory and found no signs of danger, the more certain they could be that it was safe.

They didn't know it, but our ancestors were conducting

modern-day science experiments. The more they gathered "data" that the new territory was safe, the more confident they became that they could turn down the high-alert signals in their brains, let down their guard, and relax in that space. In today's world, we scientists repeat an experiment over and over; the more we receive the same result, the more confident we are that the experiment is valid and our conclusions are solid. We even have a statistical term for this called *confidence intervals.* Confidence intervals signify how confident we are (from a statistical standpoint) that our results will hold up with repetition.

From cave people to scientists, our brains have never liked uncertainty. It feels scary. Uncertainty makes it difficult to predict what is going to happen. Both "Am I going to get eaten by a lion?" and "Is my scientific theory going to hold up?" register in roughly the same way in our brains, leading to a particular feeling: an urgency to act. Depending on how large the threat is, uncertainty can feel like a mental itch, saying to us, "Hey, I need some information. Go get it for me." If the potential danger is big or the threat is imminent, that itch gets really itchy, urging us into immediate action. That ants-in-our-pants restless feeling impels our survival brain to go see what that unfamiliar sound was that just woke us from sleep, so that we can determine if something is coming to eat us.

Remember, the definition of anxiety is "a feeling of worry, nervousness, or unease, typically about an imminent event or something with an uncertain outcome." When uncertainty abounds, we get anxious and start scratching that itch that says, "*Do* something." Stress or anxiety becomes the trigger that urges our cave-person brain out of the cave and into the night, as it tries to figure out what to do (i.e., it enacts a particular behavior), and if our brain happens to come up with something that feels like a solution (e.g., I didn't see anything dangerous), we get the reward of feeling less anxious.

Trigger: Stress or anxiety
Behavior: Go find a solution
Result: Find a solution (sometimes)

It's like playing a slot machine in a casino and winning just enough times to keep us coming back for more.

There's plenty of research showing that anxiety gets perpetuated as a negatively reinforced habit loop. Over the past several decades, T. D. Borkovec, a researcher at Pennsylvania State University, wrote a number of scientific papers showing that anxiety can trigger worry. Back in 1983, Borkovec and his colleagues described worry as "a chain of thoughts and images, negatively affect-laden, and relatively uncontrollable," representing an attempt to engage in mental problem-solving on an issue with an uncertain outcome. When worry gets triggered by a negative emotion (e.g., fear), it can also become reinforced as a way to avoid the unpleasantness of that emotion:

Trigger: Negative emotion (or thought)
Behavior: Worry
Result: Avoidance/distraction

In the dictionary, *worry* is defined as both a noun ("I am free of worry") and as a verb (e.g., "I worry about my children"). Functionally, the act of worrying is a mental behavior that results in a feeling of anxiety (nervousness or unease). On top of this, the feeling of anxiety can trigger the behavior of worrying, which becomes cyclical:

Trigger: Anxiety
Behavior: Worry
Result: Feel more anxious

This mental behavior of worry has to happen only a few times before our brain gets in the habit of trying it every time we're anxious. But how often do we come up with a solution that fixes the problem? And how much does worry itself actually help us think creatively or problem-solve? Worry pushes the panic button that gets us running around trying anything to get the anxiety to go away.

Pulling out a smartphone and checking a news feed or answering a few emails might give some brief anxiety relief, but this just creates a new habit, which is that when you're stressed or anxious, you distract yourself. And when the distraction doesn't work, you're left with having to come up with another solution. This can lead to more worrying, and that worry thinking becomes its own trigger. Not much of a reward, is it? And here's the kicker: even though worrying doesn't work, our old brain keeps trying. Remember, our brain's job is to help us survive, and because at some point it linked problem-solving with worrying, it thinks worrying is the best way to go. Our brain keeps pulling that worry slot machine lever hoping that it will hit the solution jackpot.

The Problem with Problem-Solving

So, you can see that worry can function as a mental behavior that results in distracting yourself from the worse-feeling anxiety and/or

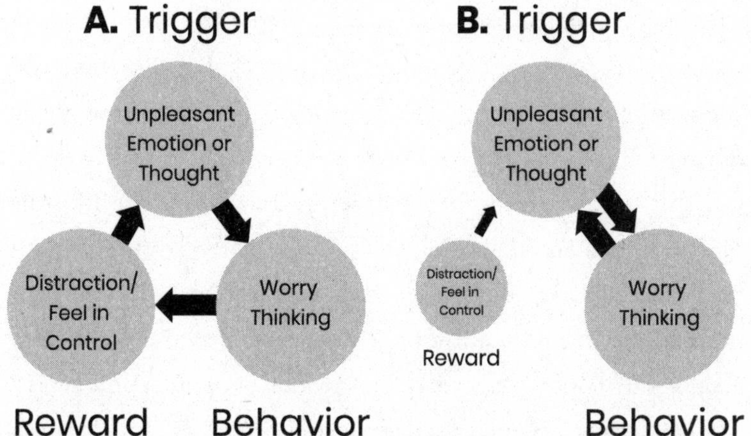

(A) Habit loop that starts the worry cycle: Unpleasant emotion triggers worry as a mental behavior to distract or feel in control; (B) When the "reward" of distraction diminishes, wears off, or fails to outweigh the combined negative qualities of the unpleasant emotion and worry, worry begins to trigger more anxiety (as an unpleasant emotion), which in turn triggers more worry and so on.

feeling like you have some control because you are (in theory) problem-solving. Even if you aren't solving any problems—just spinning out of control by worrying more—that feeling of doing something can be rewarding in itself. Worrying is doing something, after all. Even if you can't observe it as a behavior, it's happening. Mental behaviors still count as behaviors and can have tangible results.

But there are two main downsides to worry. First, if the worrying mind doesn't come up with a solution, worry triggers anxiety, which triggers more worry, and so on. Second, if worry is triggered by anxiety alone, there might not be something specific to worry about. That's often what my patients describe: they simply wake up in the morning, and without any provocation or some specific event that day or in the future to worry about, they're anxious. As one person in our anxiety program put it, "I am particularly troubled by intense anxiety early in the morning. It wakes me up with a jolt." This anxious feeling throws their worrying into hyperdrive, as they try to figure out what they are supposed to worry about. When they can't find anything specific, they start getting in the habit of worrying about just about any old darn thing in the future, whether it warrants worrying or not.

This is the basis for Generalized Anxiety Disorder, which the *Diagnostic and Statistical Manual of Mental Disorders* (the psychiatrist's bible for diagnosing psychiatric "disorders") describes in terms of symptoms that include "the presence of excessive anxiety and worry about a variety of topics, events, or activities"—and I love the subjectivity of this part—"and is clearly excessive." The *DSM* also states that "worry is experienced as very challenging to control," which may seem obvious, as otherwise people wouldn't be coming to see a psychiatrist for help.

Worrying has a Dr. Jekyll and Mr. Hyde quality to it. With its promise of solving your problems, at first it can seem good and helpful. Worry seems to be doing its dutiful best to help you survive by trying to solve whatever problem is at hand. But don't be fooled, because its guts are rotten, and it quickly turns on you when a solution doesn't come. Like someone who has fallen into a raging river, worry calls to you to help from the shore. It frantically grabs on to your hand or leg, causing you to lose balance and get sucked into the rapids with it, or into a never-ending whirlpool of anxiety where you don't know which way is up.

That "anxiety triggering worry triggering anxiety" habit loop can be very hard to break if you don't realize that your worry and anxiety are both pushing your head under water in their attempt to keep themselves from drowning. If you have a tendency to worry, you can probably map these habit loops out in your own life to see how this plays out for you.

But mapping out habit loops is only the first step in working with anxiety. As a psychiatrist, I look to the research and evidence-based interventions to know the best way to help people overcome their anxiety. As a researcher, I am motivated to figure out how to do this so that I can give my psychiatrist self those evidence-based treatments.

The Epidemic of Burnout Culture

Physicians are a subset of a larger group of healthcare providers who are caught in what is being called an epidemic of burnout. Even BC (before COVID-19), facing an increasing number of pressures, physicians have been throwing up their hands (and throwing in the towel) at an alarming rate. Many of these pressures have to do with decreased autonomy as private practices get swallowed up, consolidated, and run by corporations (and the inevitable middle managers), and the rise of electronic medical records, which force us to spend more time looking at computer screens than at our patients' faces during their appointments.

In medical school, we learned to "armor up" when stress and anxiety reared their heads so that we could fight them off, not to let them get in our way of helping others who were *really* suffering. Our life of martyrdom was summed up by one of my surgery professors, who quipped, "See a doughnut, eat a doughnut; sleep when you can; and don't f**k with the pancreas." Basically, this meant that our basic needs took a back seat to patient care (and that the pancreas is really hard to do surgery on). Looking back on my training, I realized that this wasn't a very sustainable (or healthy) way to go about working with our emotions.

No definitive studies have been published about the links between physician anxiety and burnout, but anecdotally the case is clear. The lack of good training in medical school in how to handle our emotions, coupled with decreased autonomy in clinical settings and increased pressure to see more patients to meet our "relative value unit" (RVU) goals (this is a real term that I am measured by in my clinic) seems to have created a perfect storm of increased anxiety and burnout.

So with funding from my hospital, my lab set up a simple study to see if we could use mindfulness training to help physicians become aware of worry habit loops with the goal of reducing their anxiety *and* burnout. (There is more on mindfulness in chapters 6 and 8.)

Because reward-based learning reinforces behaviors in specific contexts (don't forget, it's designed to help us remember where our food sources are), instead of trying to teach people mindfulness in a clinic or research setting, we used our app-based mindfulness training (Unwinding Anxiety) as the intervention that they could use in their everyday lives. We set the app up to deliver mindfulness training via short daily videos (less than ten minutes a day), animations, and in-the-moment exercises that people could use when they were getting anxious. Using the thirty core modules, people would first map out their anxiety habit loops and then learn to work with them (using the same tools that you will learn later in this book). This format is especially important for busy doctors, as they often operate in martyr mode, finding it difficult to do anything that might take time away from helping others to help themselves. (The hero of this study was my research associate, Alexandra Roy, who collected and analyzed all of the data.)

We found that before starting treatment, 60 percent of doctors in the study had moderate to severe anxiety, and over half of them reported feeling burned out from work at least a few times per week. We also found a strong correlation between anxiety and burnout (.71, where 0 is no correlation and 1 is a perfect correlation). After three months of using the app, physicians reported a whopping 57 percent reduction in anxiety scores (measured by the clinically validated Generalized Anxiety Disorder-7 questionnaire). And even though we hadn't incorporated any specific anti-burnout teachings in the training (it was focused solely on helping reduce anxiety), we also found significant reductions in burnout, especially in the areas of cynicism (where people become more and more skeptical of the system), which can easily get perpetuated by anxiety:

Trigger: Get another email about how behind I am on my RVUs
Behavior: Think about how the system sucks and is only getting worse
Result: Get more cynical, become burnt out

This is not to say that an app is going to fix our healthcare system. Our study actually pointed out burnout contributors that were individual as opposed to institutional. For example, we found a 50 percent reduction in cynicism, but only a 20 percent reduction in emotional exhaustion. This makes sense, because cynicism is on us as individual doctors, yet exhaustion has a heck of a lot to do with the system. If we are being forced to sacrifice quality to the bureaucratic gods of quantity in the name of the bottom line, learning to map out habit loops should help more with cynicism than with exhaustion (which is exactly what we found). And my hope is that with mindfulness training, doctors and other healthcare providers can also learn to redirect some of that habitual cynical energy toward seeing the problems in the system and advocating for change.

Emboldened by the data from this study, and with research funding from the National Institutes of Health (NIH), my lab ran a larger, randomized controlled trial (which simply means we measured two groups who were the same in every possible way yet who got different treatments) in which we enrolled people from the general community to see if we could help anxiety more broadly. In this study (led again by Alex), we randomized people who met the criteria for Generalized Anxiety Disorder to either continue with the clinical care they were getting (medications, therapy, etc.) or add in the app-based mindfulness training.

After two months of using the Unwinding Anxiety app, people with Generalized Anxiety Disorder showed a 63 percent reduction in anxiety. And when we did the mathematical modeling to see how the mindfulness training was working, we found that mindfulness was leading to a decrease in worry, which in turn led to a decrease in anxiety. We had confirmed that training people to become aware of and work with their worry habit loops could lead to clinically meaningful results. Levels of anxiety that began at the moderate to severe level were now back to normal.

Our study participants were happy to see their anxiety drop, and 63 percent is a huge drop. But what does a 63 percent reduction look like in the wild? The medical community has developed simple metrics, bullshit detectors of sorts, to gauge whether something is

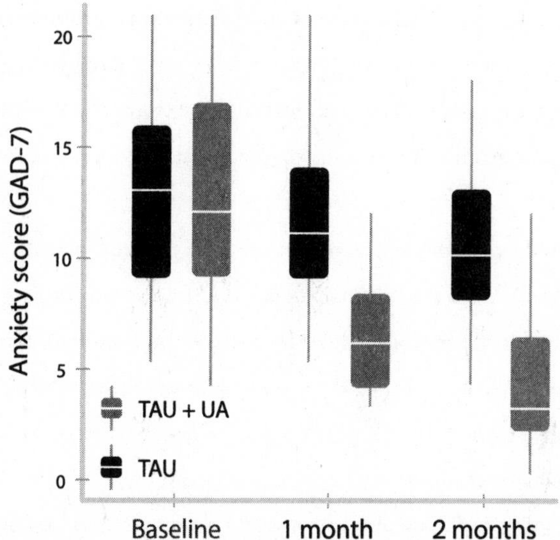

App-based mindfulness training significantly decreases anxiety. There were greater decreases in anxiety scores in individuals with GAD who were randomized to receive Unwinding Anxiety (UA) than in those who received Treatment as Usual (TAU).

clinically significant—basically how big an effect a treatment provides. Of course, because it's the medical community, their BS detector has an acronym: NNT, standing for Number Needed to Treat.

For example, the NNT of a class of gold-standard medications for anxiety (antidepressants, in this case) is 5.15. (That means you have to give just over five people the medication to see an effect in one of them.) It's kind of like playing the lottery: five people take the pill, one person wins (by seeing a significant reduction in symptoms).

The NNT in our study was 1.6.

As a clinician, I was thrilled to see a treatment with such a small NNT. It meant more people would win the lottery with the same number of tickets (for example, an NNT of 1.6 as opposed to 5.15 means that to win, you would need to play only a little under twice as compared to over five times). For me as a scientist, as for anyone who likes to understand how mindfulness training works to change habits, getting right to the mechanism was also very gratifying. And the feedback we got from users was similarly pleasing:

> I started feeling anxious and brought to mind the picture of a feedback loop. I started to retrace my thoughts, and lo and behold, everything I thought had a clear path that ended up in the worst possible scenario at some point in the future. Just this recognition of the feedback loop made my thoughts less personal and less worrisome as I recognized it as a mind habit, or a story.
>
> I'm starting to think that over the years I've tricked myself into believing that anxiety is productive—even a reward. A thought about work arises (trigger), I jump into worrying or distraction (behavior), and I get more anxiety as a result (reward/outcome). During the first few days of this program, I was confused by this loop, and I wondered how anxiety can possibly feel like a reward. A reward? It feels horrible! But I think I'm onto something: for me, feeling anxious, as horrible as it is, has come to seem like the "right" way to feel, the appropriate response to having unfinished tasks ahead of me. After all, it seems logical that this kind of discomfort would lead to productivity.
>
> I understand why I go to food to avoid or cover up or distract from uncomfortable feelings such as anger, sadness, or restlessness. Who wants to feel those things? Trigger: uncomfortable feeling. Behavior: eat something that temporarily diminishes the feeling. Reward: still have to deal with the unpleasant feelings, plus the sugar headache! I can clearly see how I got caught in this habit loop, trying to escape difficult feelings with food, but that ultimately it doesn't work.

Now, anxiety doesn't just magically disappear simply by the realization that it is born and bred through repetition, becoming a self-perpetuating habit. Intellectual understanding is only the first step. I've had many patients come into my office and "get it," only to walk out and struggle with what to do. Over the years I've observed what it actually takes for people to move from concept into wisdom—having the direct experience of unwinding their anxiety. And believe it or not, it can be best explained by a three-step process that has more to do with bicycles than brains.

I grew up riding my bicycle. That's what kept me out of trouble. First it was my BMX bike that had only one gear. Then it was my ten-speed road bike, and finally my mountain bike, with its full set of twenty-one gears. When mountain biking, you never know if you'll be climbing a steep hill, riding a flat section, or zooming downhill. That's why all of those gears are handy: first gear got me up the hills, while twenty-first gear helped me zoom down the mountains I had just climbed. That's also why cars have gears—to move them forward, no matter what the terrain.

The gears analogy came to me after I had developed our program to help people who struggled with stress and overeating (called Eat Right Now). Anyone in the program gets free access to join me on a live weekly video session, in which they can ask questions about the practice and science of mindfulness. I can help make sure they are understanding the concepts and using the practices properly, and if they are struggling, I can give them tips for moving forward. After a year or so of running these groups both online and in person at the Mindfulness Center (first at UMass Medical School, now at Brown University), I noticed a trend in how people were progressing through the program. They seemed to naturally be following a sequence that could be broken down into three simple steps. Of course, the first thing my mind went to was gears because it was a perfect analogy for their experience. I'll use this gears analogy as a pragmatic framework for you to use as you go through the book.

Part 1 (first gear) will help you get started mapping out your own anxiety "habit loops."

Part 2 (second gear) will help you tap into your brain's reward system to systematically work with anxiety (and other habits).

Part 3 (third gear) will help you tap into your own natural neural capacities to step away from anxiety-related habits (e.g., worry, procrastination, self-judgment), and into new ones (e.g., curiosity and kindness), potentially for good.

Generally speaking, I've found that people immediately nail first gear (at least conceptually), yet often have a bit of resistance when it comes to second gear. Even so, most are able to develop skills to shift into third gear pretty quickly, and enjoy honing, crafting, and refining their third-gear skills for years to come. Some spend quite a bit of time riding/driving in first and second gear before they are ready to transition to third. No matter where you fall in this spectrum, all of the gears move you forward, and the next sections will give you both the conceptual understanding and the pragmatic practices that you need to step out of anxiety (and other habit) loops for good.

PART 1

Mapping Your Mind: First Gear

Nobody can go back and start a new beginning, but anyone can start today and make a new ending.

—MARIA ROBINSON

CHAPTER 5

How to Map Your Mind

My outpatient psychiatry clinic specializes in anxiety and addictions. Here's the story of one of my patients.

John (not his real name), a man in his mid-sixties, was referred to me by his primary care physician for help with alcoholism. The facts were stark. John had six to eight drinks per night, virtually every day. When I asked what triggered the drinking, John told me that he was self-employed and had a bad habit of focusing on all of the work piled up on his desk. Looking at what remained to be done made him anxious. He would assuage that anxiety by watching television or a movie instead of doing the actual work that he needed to do. At the end of the day, he would realize that he hadn't gotten anything done, which would then add to his anxiety, and he would then drink to numb those feelings. The next morning, John would wake up with a hangover, feel even more guilty, and tell himself that he would handle things differently that day. But his willpower lasted only an hour or so, and soon he would be right back at it, repeating the same patterns, day after day. (We'll talk more about why willpower fails in the next chapter.)

I pulled out a blank piece of paper, and together we mapped out his primary drinking habit loop:

Trigger: Anxiety in the late afternoon
Behavior: Start drinking
Reward: Numbing, forgetting, feeling intoxicated

This habit loop might seem pretty straightforward on paper, but John, being in the middle of it, couldn't see it for himself. I explained to him that this was how his brain was set up to learn and survive, and that he shouldn't beat himself up for struggling with it. Many people struggle with anxiety and drink alcohol to alleviate those feelings. How many of us were first introduced to drinking alcohol at high school parties and quickly learned that drinking made us feel less self-conscious and more at ease?

After we went through the basics, John and I were able to then map out his related habit loop of procrastination:

Trigger: Anxiety in the morning from seeing how much work he had to do
Behavior: Procrastination
Reward: Avoidance

For John, the adverse consequences of these habit loops were severe enough that his primary care physician had referred him to me.

He was significantly overweight (a shot of whiskey—his drink of choice—has over a hundred calories, so he was kicking back close to a thousand calories in alcohol alone each day) and was showing signs of liver damage. Moreover, his business was failing because he had fallen so far behind on work (this despite the fact that he was actually quite good at his job and liked what he did).

Within just a few minutes of meeting John and helping him map out his habit loops, I saw his demeanor change dramatically. He had come into my office looking anxious and feeling hopeless that he could never change. But after we clearly mapped out his habit loop—anxiety triggering drinking as a way to numb himself—which up to this point he had failed to recognize, he became animated and hopeful.

Many of my patients have been wandering around for a number of years not knowing how their minds work. It's incredibly gratifying when they see and understand their habit loops for the first time. It's as though they had been standing in a dark room, and instead of wandering around bumping into things trying to see what might work to change their habits, suddenly someone switched on the light, illuminating that black box of their mind.

I sent John home with the simple instructions to start mapping out all of his habit loops around anxiety.

A few weeks later, John returned to my office, and before he even sat down, he excitedly started to walk me through what he had learned about his mind. Not only was he able to clearly map out his anxiety habit loops, but he realized that the drinking only made the anxiety and his health problems worse: his hangovers contributed to his anxiety and difficulty in getting motivated each day to get his work done. So he had quit drinking cold turkey.* John realized that his primary issue was *anxiety*, and that the drinking wasn't helping. In fact it was only making the situation worse.

John had also discovered another major habit loop around how he interacted with his wife. John was American and his wife was Chinese, which contributed to a bit of inadvertently triggered anxiety arising from their being raised in different cultural backgrounds. Overall, they had a good relationship, but at times she would raise her voice in a way that was culturally in context for her, but not for him, thus making him anxious. They would be in a casual conversation and she would get excited by something. Her tone would change, and this would be enough to trigger his anxiety.

Trigger: Wife speaks a certain way
Behavior: Worries that there might be conflict
Result: Anxiety

John was really excited to have discovered this, because for years it had caused strife in their relationship. When his wife's tone changed, John got anxious, and he would react by yelling at his wife. She in turn would get confused, wondering why he was yelling, and would react to his reaction, and so on.

* But I must make this point. Any of you who drink heavily and get the idea that you are going to stop cold turkey like John, please consult your physician before doing so. Had I known John was going to do this, I would have recommended that we carefully help him detox, whether at home or in a detox facility, as suddenly stopping can lead to problems with withdrawal, seizures, and even death. John got lucky, being able to detox at home without problems.

Trigger: Anxiety
Behavior: Yells at wife
Result: Marital strife

After mapping this series of habit loops, John was happy to report that his relationship with his wife was much better now. Simply by identifying that habit loop, he had been able to step out of it. But our work was not complete. John then worked on a set of new behaviors informed by his recent insights. So whenever his wife raised her voice excitedly, he would simply remind himself that his overreaction was out of habit, take a deep breath, and respond calmly. That anxiety bubble had burst.

John is a good example of the first gear, where we just describe to ourselves the habit loops that keep us in damaging emotional places. We map out how the pieces fit together and drive one another. Sometimes simply becoming aware of the habit patterns helps us step out of them, with significant results. At other times, we need a little handholding along the way.

How many times have you struggled with trying to force yourself to overcome old habit loops and failed? How can you fix something if you don't know how it works? Mapping out habit loops is an obvious place to start. We'll define this mapping effort as first gear.

First Gear

First gear is all about recognizing our habit loops and seeing the different components clearly: trigger, behavior, and reward. To be clear, *reward* is a brain term, as in it's the result of the behavior that at some point was rewarding, that's why the behavior got reinforced in the first place. The behavior might not seem that rewarding right now, so you can simply think of the habit loop as a trigger, a behavior, and a result.

Mind-Mapping Exercise

If you're ready, try mapping out the TBR (T = trigger, B = behavior, R = result) components of your own anxiety (or other) habit loops over the next few days and see what clarity that brings. Don't worry about changing them yet; learning how your mind works is the first step in this change. Don't rush it. You can download a mind-mapping template from my website, www.drjud.com/mapmyhabit, or—as I did with John—take a blank piece of paper, write out the three components, and start mapping out your habit loops. Begin with the most obvious ones.

A Word of Warning

As you saw with John's example, mapping out habit loops might appear a relatively easy thing to do. And once you begin seeing your habit loops clearly, it's much harder to unsee them. That's important, right? (Yes.)

More often than not, when a new patient comes to my clinic, or someone starts using one of my app-based mindfulness training programs, they are able to map out their habit loops really quickly. Like John, they often see layers upon layers of habit loops. They get excited that they've learned how their mind works, and they then fall into an ironic habit trap: immediately trying to fix it. This is analogous to hearing a funny sound in your car, calling the mechanic, and once she or he explains the problem to you, going back home and tinkering with it, thinking that you can fix it yourself. What happens? You end up taking it back to the mechanic to fix both the original problem and the one you created by messing with it. Don't fall into this trap!

Let's map this extra habit loop out together:

Trigger: Start to see habit loops clearly
Behavior: Try to fix them using tools that you've tried in the past
Result: (Surprise!) It doesn't work

We'll talk about how seemingly unrewarding habit loops get set up later in the book.

On top of this, you might even reinforce other unhelpful habit loops like getting frustrated or judging yourself. (Don't worry. There's also a chapter on how to work with these types of habit loops.)

When you are trying to overcome anxiety and change habits, you must get to know how your mind works and how it establishes those habits, including those habit loops of trying to fix yourself. Knowing things intellectually or conceptually is just the first step. First gear is first gear: intellectually knowing how habits form and play out in your life builds speed and momentum so that later, when you have all of the tools in hand, you can change them.

While I was growing up, my favorite teen crush movie was *The Karate Kid*. I moved around a lot as a child, so I could totally relate to Ralph Macchio as Daniel, the new kid on the block who gets bullied by the cool kids. And what teenage boy wouldn't want to date Ali (Elisabeth Shue), the girlfriend he eventually lands by learning how to be himself? As Daniel endeavors to learn martial arts for self-defense, Mr. Miyagi (Daniel's teacher, played by Pat Morita) doesn't just hand him a book on karate, with the assignment to write a report about it. Daniel had come to him, all excited to learn karate, yet Mr. Miyagi knew about the mental trap of learning something conceptually, getting excited, and going out and trying to do it, without actually knowing *how* to do it. You can't read a book written by Bruce Lee and then walk outside and be Bruce Lee. Concepts don't magically become wisdom with the wave of a wand. You actually have to do the work so the concepts translate into know-how *through your own experience.*

Famously, all of the "wax on, wax off" fence painting and car polishing paid off for Daniel when he realized that Mr. Miyagi was training him to get out of his head and into his body, helping him avoid the trap of thinking he knew karate and then getting stuck trying to act out the martial arts movies he had seen. Mr. Miyagi was teaching Daniel how to put concepts into action.

Can you relate to this habit loop?

Trigger: See a new book about anxiety (or habit change)
Behavior: Devour the book in one sitting
Result: Understand the concepts, but fail to change the habit

With habit change, concepts are important. And as you start to map your habits out, you'll put those concepts into action. Notice how mapping does not automatically equate to fixing or being fixed. Yes, by mapping out an unhelpful habit, like John did, you might quickly and easily stop doing it. In fact, I have gotten a number of thank-you emails from people who have watched my ten-minute TED talk ("A Simple Way to Break a Bad Habit") and have quit smoking, stopped procrastinating in college, and so on. But if it were always this simple, everyone struggling with habit change would have kicked their habit(s) to the curb after watching that short video and then never looked back. TED talks can be inspirational and informative, but often they're just that, and we must be patient with the process to see results.

Most of us have habits that have been around for a long time; mapping these out is only the first step in changing them. You really have to get the mapping both conceptually and experientially before you can move on to changing them. That's why the first third of the book is devoted to mapping. Don't skip over it. Don't go right to the "fix" section, because you will have fallen into the concept trap of trying to think your way into habit change. Do the "wax on, wax off" work. As you will see, it is critical to learn the process from your own experience.

Changing Habits Can Be Hard Work But . . .

For five years, I taught Yale medical students how to help their patients quit smoking.

The lecture was handed down to me by a more senior psychiatrist who had packaged everything he's learned into a 45-minute spiel. Those 45 minutes were the only time in their four years of medical school that these students were going to learn how to help their patients quit smoking. For this to be useful and to have an impact, the students had to be able to memorize, internalize, and actualize it.

The best I could come up with was having the students do an oral drill. This consisted of my stating in all seriousness: "Repeat the following phrase after me."

Not my finest moment, but it was the best I could come up with to keep them awake and learning.

Repeat after me: "As your physician, the most important thing I can tell you today is that quitting smoking is the best thing you can do for your health." This is the best option we have for helping people quit smoking: "In a clear, strong, and personalized manner, urge every tobacco user to quit." The follow-up question is: "Are you willing to make a quit attempt at this time?" Perhaps a bit stunned that their medical school professor was using kindergarten-style teaching, most of the students merely parroted the phrases back to me. To make the lecture more engaging, I would time them to see how quickly they could say it. (Who doesn't like a little competition?) Over a decade has passed between my teaching that class and writing this book, yet the phrases that I just quoted are still the "gold standard" for helping people quit smoking. If you don't believe me, you can look it up.

Repetition is king when it comes to forming habits, so I wanted them to repeat this phrase as many times as I could get them to in our short time together (while of course finishing the rest of the lecture). But there has got to be a better way to help people change habits!

The point is, changing habits *is* hard work, but it doesn't have to be dry, boring, or even painful.

So repeat after me:

"Changing habits is hard work but doesn't have to be painful."

"Changing habits is hard work but doesn't have to be painful."

One more time so it is more likely to stick:

"Changing habits is hard work but doesn't have to be painful."

You've just memorized a very important piece of habit change. The next step is for you to see how you can actually hack into your brain's very own habit-forming machinery, and instead of pushing against it, you can harness its power to do the work for you. That way, your mental muscles don't get sore and it doesn't have to hurt.

Find Your Own Story Line

Good movies and bestselling authors make story lines entertaining by following the arc of the mythic hero's journey, which has been around since the beginning of storytelling, yet codified by the writer Joseph Campbell back in 1949. In the entertainment business, this has become a basic formula of creating a hook (a problem to be solved and intrigue about how it can be done), telling the story in a compelling way (tension, struggle, hardship, etc.), and making sure it ends not necessarily happily, but well (resolution). Perhaps you can even see the reward-based learning elements that get us excited to watch the sequel of the movie that we loved, or read the next book in the Harry Potter series:

Trigger: Tension
Behavior: Hero's journey involving struggle, etc.
Result: Resolution

When a good story is complete, we itch for another.

This same formula is at play in the age of binge-watching Netflix, Amazon, and the like, yet with a twist. What happens when you have a whole series—say, *Game of Thrones*—and you want your audience to return, season after season? Yup, you take out that resolution part, which makes it look like this:

Trigger: Tension
Behavior: Hero's journey involving struggle, etc.
Result: No resolution

That lack of resolution is like sitting down in the woods for a rest during a long hike and suddenly realizing that you're sitting on an anthill. When you start to feel that restless itchy feeling, your brain goes on high alert, screaming, *Fire! Fire! Put out the fire!* Fortunately, Netflix and its co-conspirators put that fire extinguisher at easy reach with the "next episode" option; in fact they assume that you can't wait and even take the liberty of pushing the button for you.

To change your own habits, you have to relate to the hero of the story (that's easy, it's you), the plot (whatever habits you have), the intrigue (why do you have to eat green M&M's before brown ones?), the tension (can you do it?), and the resolution (yes, you can!).

In this book, we're going to stick closely to the story line. That's why you have to carefully and diligently map out your habit loops. Yes, like Daniel-san in *The Karate Kid*, who wasn't particularly fond of waxing floors, painting fences, and washing cars, you might find mapping your own mind to be boring, menial labor. And it *is* hard work. But this mind-mapping business is critical to help you along your own hero's journey, so that you'll have one hell of a (true) story at the end to tell.

CHAPTER 6

Why Your Previous Anti-Anxiety (and Anti-Habit) Strategies Failed

Now that you know some of the essentials of how your brain works, let's get down to solutions. Psychologists and treatment specialists have identified several strategies to breaking harmful habits ranging from anxiety to overeating to procrastination. However, whether these therapies are effective often depend on one's individual genetic makeup. Fortunately, modern science may have revealed how certain ancient practices can bring the old and new brain together to defeat these harmful habits, no matter whether you've won or lost the genetic lottery.

But first, let's return to the brain model we discussed earlier. Remember, our old brain is set up to help us survive. In addition to reward-based learning, it has another trick up its sleeve: it takes what it learns and moves the learning into "muscle" memory as soon as it can. In other words, our brains are set up to form habits so we can free up the brain space to learn new things.

Imagine getting up every morning and having to relearn how to stand, put on your clothes, walk, eat, talk—you'd be exhausted by noon. In "habit mode," we act quickly, without thinking, as though our old brain is telling our new brain: "Don't worry, I've got this. You don't have to spend energy here and can think about other things." This division of labor is partly how the newer parts of our brain, such as the prefrontal cortex, were able to evolve the ability to think and plan ahead.

This is also why old habits often stick around even after you've done a thorough job of mapping them. No one wants to spend a beautiful weekend indoors cleaning a cluttered closet when there's still space to shove in more junk. It's only when the closet is stuffed to the gills that you are forced to clean it. Well, it's the same with your brain, which won't bother with the old stuff until it reaches a critical level. The newer parts of your brain would much rather spend time on "more important" matters such as planning your next vacation, answering emails, learning the latest tricks for staying calm in a frantic world, and researching what the current nutritional trends are.

Besides serving as the location for thinking and planning ahead, the prefrontal cortex is also the part of the brain that you count on for controlling your urges. Your old brain functions in scarcity mode; it's always worried about starvation. If you see a doughnut, your old brain impulsively tries to pounce on it, thinking, *Calories! Survival!* You might remember the odd runs on commodities—toilet paper, flour, pasta—at the grocery store at the beginning of the COVID-19 pandemic. If you're at the store and you see someone's cart piled high, you rush to grab whatever is left, even if you have plenty of it at home. In contrast, your new brain says to your old brain: "Hold off a minute.

You just had lunch. This is not healthy, *and* you're not even hungry!" or "We have plenty of toilet paper. No need to buy more right now." Your new brain is that rational voice that reminds you to eat your vegetables before you have dessert. It's also the part of the brain that helps you keep your New Year's resolutions (and ironically, it's that same inner voice that judges you when you fail—more on this later).

Now let's discuss some strategies that you've been told will help you deal with anxiety or other negative emotions or will enable you to change entrenched bad habits (strategies you might even have tried), and why they might not. This will set a foundation for understanding how these apply to anxiety habit loops such as worrying too much.

Anti-Habit Strategy 1: Willpower

When you tap into your willpower reserve, your new brain is supposed to tell your older brain to take a hike and simply order the salad instead of the hamburger, right? If you're anxious, you should be able to tell yourself to relax, and then be more relaxed. Willpower seems like it should work, but there are two big caveats.

First, recent research is calling into question some of the early ideas on willpower. Some of these studies have shown that willpower is genetically endowed for a lucky subset; still other studies have argued that willpower is itself a myth. Even studies that acknowledge willpower as real tended to find that people who exerted more self-control were not actually more successful in accomplishing their goals—in fact, the more effort they put in, the more depleted they felt. The short answer is that buckling down, gritting your teeth, or forcing yourself to "just do it" might be counterproductive strategies, possibly helping out in the short term (or at least making you feel like you are doing something) but not working in the long term, when it really counts.

Second, while willpower may be fine under normal conditions, when you get stressed (saber-toothed tiger, email from the boss, fight with a spouse, exhaustion, hunger), your old brain takes control and overrides your new brain, basically shutting the latter down until the stress is gone. So exactly when you need your willpower—which resides, remember, in the prefrontal cortex/new brain—it's not there, and your old brain eats cupcakes until you feel better and your new brain comes back online. Think of the PFC this way: as the youngest and least evolutionarily developed part of the brain, it is also the weakest. This means that we're putting all our faith in the puniest part of our noggin to restrain us from being led into temptation. Is it any wonder many of us feel so guilty? For most of us, an absence of willpower may be more of a failure of brain wiring (and evolution) than our own fault.

Applying willpower to anxiety is logical yet a bit misguided for the masses. When my friend Emily (the high-powered lawyer who can think her way out of any mess, real or imagined) had panic attacks, she would tell herself, "You feel like you're going to die, but you won't. This is your brain playing games with you. *You* decide what happens next." She's one in a million, with a highly trained brain at her beck and call. If the rest of us found it easy when anxiety reared its ugly head just to tell ourselves to stop being anxious, I would happily be in another line of work. That's not how our brains work, especially when stress and anxiety are shutting down the very parts that are supposed to be reasoning us through a tough spell. If you don't believe me (or the data), try this: the next time you're anxious, just tell yourself to calm down and see what happens. If you want an extra challenge, say the command in the stern tone of your parent's voice.

Anti-Habit Strategy 2: Substitution

If you have a craving for *X*, do *Y* instead. Like willpower, substitution relies on the new brain. This strategy is backed by a lot of science and is one of the go-to strategies in addiction psychiatry. For example, if you want to quit smoking but crave a cigarette, eat candy instead of lighting up. This works for a subset of folks (and was one of the approaches I was taught in residency training), but as research from my lab and others has shown, it may not uproot the craving itself. The habit loop stays intact, but the behavior is simply changed to something healthier. (Okay, okay, we can argue about how healthy candy is later, but you get the idea.) Since the habit loop is still there, this also makes it more likely that you will fall back into the old habit at some point in the future.

This is also a strategy suggested for use in handling stress and anxiety. When you're anxious, distract yourself by looking at cute pictures of puppies on social media. One of the people using our anxiety app even programmed a bot that would retweet pictures of puppies so he didn't even need to search for them. He could simply open up his Twitter account and an endless supply of puppy pictures was available for him to scroll through. This didn't fix his anxiety (and procrastination), and as you'll see in Part 3, our brains start to tire of these tactics.

Anti-Habit Strategy 3: Prime Your Environment

If you are tempted by ice cream, don't keep cartons of it in the freezer. Again, this strategy involves the pesky new brain. Several labs studying priming an environment have found that people with good self-control tend to structure their lives in such a way that they don't need to make self-control decisions in the first place. Getting into the habit of exercising every morning or buying healthy food at the grocery store makes staying fit and cooking nutritiously a routine, so it's more likely to stick. There are two caveats here: (1) you have to actually get into a habit of doing the healthy thing; and (2) when you slip, because your brain has grooved your old habits much more deeply than your new ones, you're prone to fall back into the old habit pattern and stay there. I see this all the time in my clinic. My patients try this strategy for a while, yet fall back to smoking, drinking, or using drugs (it's surprisingly hard to avoid driving by liquor stores unless you move to an alcohol-free desert island or Utah). This is the reason that gyms often give a membership discount at the beginning of the year. They know that you'll sign up, go for a couple of weeks, skip a few days when it's cold or rainy, stop going altogether, and eventually simply leave their equipment in pristine condition to repeat the ritual in January of the next year when you feel guilty about not being in shape.

How does priming your environment work for anxiety? You can't not keep anxiety in your freezer or avoid the anxiety store so you aren't tempted to pick one of its thirty-one flavors up on your way home from a hard day at work. As nice as an "anxiety-free zone" in your house sounds, even if you build it, the anxiety will come.

Anti-Habit Strategy 4: Mindfulness

Jon Kabat-Zinn is perhaps the most well-known Western mindfulness maven. While he was on a silent meditation retreat in the late 1970s, the idea to develop and test an eight-week mindfulness program that could be taught and researched in medical settings popped into his head. Thus mindfulness-based stress reduction (MBSR) was born. Over the next four decades, MBSR became the most well-known and studied mindfulness course on the planet.

Kabat-Zinn's definition of mindfulness is "the awareness that arises through paying attention in the present moment, on purpose, nonjudgmentally." Basically, Kabat-Zinn is pointing to two aspects of experience: awareness and curiosity.

Let's unpack that a bit. Remember how our old brains react to positive and negative reinforcement to determine what to do, and then are really good at turning that behavior into habits?

If you aren't aware that you're doing something habitually, you will continue to do it habitually. Kabat-Zinn describes this in terms of operating on autopilot. If you've driven the same road a thousand times, your trip becomes pretty habitual. You tend to zone out and think of other things while you're driving—sometimes to the point where you don't even remember how you got home from work. Is this magic? No, it's habit.

Building awareness through mindfulness helps you "pop the hood" on what's going on in your old brain. You can learn to recognize your habit loops while they're happening, rather than "waking up" at the end of them when you've almost crashed the car.

Once you're aware of your habit loops—when you're on autopilot—you can then get curious about what is happening. Why am I doing this? What triggered the behavior? What reward am I really getting from this? Do I want to keep doing this?

It might sound odd at first, yet curiosity is a key attitude that, when paired with awareness, helps you change habits—a connection backed up by research done in my lab and by others. And curiosity can become a powerful reward on its own. Do you remember the last time you were curious about something? That emotion feels pretty good itself—signaling to your old brain that this is better than a quick sugar rush followed by tons of guilt.

Staying out of habit mode frees up the new brain to do what it does best: make rational and logical decisions.

Which conditions make it easier to change a habit, do you think—when you wake up in the middle of an ice cream binge, filled with shame and self-judgment, or when you simply become *aware* of a behavior and then get curious about it and start mapping out what your mind is really doing?

That curiosity is key to being open and receptive to change. Dr. Carol Dweck, a researcher at Stanford University, talked about this years ago when she contrasted *fixed* and *growth mindsets*. When you're stuck in old habit loops (including judging yourself), you're not open to growth. (My lab has even mapped out a part of the brain associated with this.)

While the scientific research into mindfulness is still in its early stages, some consistent findings are coming out of the work. Studies from multiple labs have found that mindfulness specifically targets the key links of reward-based learning. For example, my lab found that mindfulness training was key in helping smokers recognize habit loops and be able to decouple cravings from smoking. In other words, patients could notice a craving, get curious about what it felt like in their bodies (and minds), and ride it out, instead of habitually smoking. Breaking this habit loop led to five times greater quit rates than the current gold-standard treatment.

My lab found some remarkable shifts in habitual behaviors when people learn to understand that habit loop process and apply mindfulness techniques. Learning to pay attention led to behavior change not only with smoking but also with problem eating and even, as you saw from our clinical studies, with anxiety itself.

And I've seen this work powerfully in my own life as well. There's a corollary to the maxim "the less you know, the more you say" that I mentioned in the beginning of this book: "Don't just do something, sit there!" This is a simple and powerful paradox that has had big effects on me both personally and professionally. If a patient of mine is getting anxious or worried while in my office (which can result from simply telling me about something that has happened or discussing an upcoming event), I might catch that social contagion and become anxious or worried ("Oh no, this is serious. Will I be able to help her/him?").

Why? For one, if I start going down the anxiety rabbit hole and my prefrontal cortex has trouble thinking, I might habitually react to *my own* anxiety and jump in to try to "fix" my patient as a way to make *my* anxiety go away. Of course, this usually results in making things worse, as then my patient doesn't feel that I understood him or her, or the solution isn't really a good one because we haven't gotten to the root cause of what was making him or her anxious (because we were inadvertently focusing on me). The adage "don't just do something, sit there" also serves as a powerful reminder that being is the doing. In other words, by being there, deeply listening to my patients, I am often doing the best thing I can do for them in that moment: empathizing, understanding, and connecting. Finally, I like the saying because it reminds me that my willpower instinct, which is to do something, is a habit loop itself (well-meaning but misguided), that I can simply observe: observing is really the only necessary "action," and ironically the most effective one.

Ready for another question to reflect on in your anxiety (and other) habit-mapping? If this isn't your first attempt to change a habit, go back and review all of the different anti-habit strategies that you have tried over the years. Which ones worked? Which ones failed? Did your successes and failures fit with what you now know about how your brain (and specifically reward-based learning) works? If you are new to the game of habit change, you're in a good place because you haven't set up "bad" habits around trying to change bad habits (that is to say, strategies that failed, yet you repeat them over and over). Stay on track and keep mapping out your habit loops. Pay attention to the urge to get in there and fix them (and map that out as a habit loop). Wax on. Wax off.

CHAPTER 7

Dave's Story, Part 1

DAVE (NOT HIS real name), a patient of mine, told me during our first session that he began to get panic attacks on the highway sometime in the past year or two. He'd be idly driving along, not thinking about much of anything, when it would pop into his head how dangerous it was to drive sixty miles an hour in his car. "I'm in a big bullet hurtling down the highway" is how he described the feeling. The panic attacks got so bad that Dave completely stopped driving on the highway.

Unfortunately, his panic attacks weren't limited to driving. One night at a sushi restaurant with his girlfriend, he had a sudden thought that he might be allergic to fish. He became so anxious that they had to immediately leave the restaurant. He knew rationally that this was crazy—he wasn't allergic to fish and wasn't likely to have developed a new allergy that very evening. But his thinking mind had no chance against the voice in his head: "This isn't up for discussion. Danger! We're going *now*."

Dave went on to say that he couldn't think of a time when he hadn't been anxious—even since childhood. He had tried using alcohol in his twenties (which made him feel worse); he had been prescribed medications (but was too afraid to take them); he had seen psychologists, therapists, and even a hypnotist, but as he put it, "None of it worked." Dave then went on to tell me that one of his primary coping mechanisms for anxiety was eating. Anxiety would trigger him to eat something, and the food would temporarily numb him out or distract him from being anxious. This eating habit loop had led him to gain a huge amount of weight. And because of the weight gain, Dave now had high blood pressure, a fatty liver, and severe sleep apnea.

Trigger: Anxiety
Behavior: Eating
Result: A few minutes of distraction from feeling anxious

So here he was, forty years old, and with Generalized Anxiety Disorder, panic disorder, and significant weight gain. His anxiety had gotten so bad that many days Dave had been too terrified to even get out of bed. By the time I met him, he was frantically looking for something, anything, that would help him break through to the light.

During that first clinic visit, I pulled out a blank piece of paper and wrote the words *trigger, behavior,* and *reward* in the pattern of a triangle, with arrows pointing from *trigger* to *behavior* to *reward* and back to *trigger.* I pushed it across the desk and asked Dave, "Is this picture correct? Does a fear thought (trigger)—like 'Oh, I might be allergic to fish'—trigger you to leave or avoid a situation (behavior), leading to you feeling better (reward)?"

"Yes," Dave said.

"Has this created specific habit loops that your brain thinks are keeping you safe, but in fact are driving your anxiety and panic?"

"That's it in a nutshell," he said.

In just a few minutes, Dave and I had mapped out how his brain's survival system had been hijacked to make his life a self-perpetuating and never-ending cycle of anxious worry. Anxiety triggered worry and avoidance, which triggered more anxiety and avoidance. On top of this, his coping mechanism of eating was making him obese and hypertensive.

I sent Dave home with a simple goal: map out your anxiety habit loops. What are your anxiety triggers? What are your behaviors? What are your rewards? I wanted him to see all of them, and then see what he was getting from those behaviors.

This latter part was especially important. Our brains set up habit loops through reward-based learning. In other words, if a behavior is rewarding, we learn to do it again. It was clear to me that Dave had learned to avoid fearful situations (and to stress-eat) because it was rewarding.

And these rewards, even though they were irrational and profoundly unhelpful over the long term, were keeping him stuck in those habit loops. How rewarding a behavior is drives future behaviors, *not* the behavior itself. Another way of putting this is that the behavior itself is less important than the result of the behavior; if it were simply a matter of identifying the behavior and then telling someone to stop doing it, I'd happily be out of work. "Just stop doing it" never made it as a slogan for good reason. After years of research and clinical practice, I'm thoroughly convinced that willpower is more a myth than an actual mental muscle.

The reason I use Dave's story is this: it's a good example of the simplicity and importance of mapping out habit loops. It doesn't take a lot of time or an appointment with a psychiatrist or psychoanalyst. It just takes awareness (which is free).

For example, if you're in a big meeting and your habit loop is to speak out of turn, you can see what happens when you map it out in your mind *before* jumping in:

Trigger: "I have a great idea" thought
Behavior: Interrupt whoever is speaking and blurt it out
Result: Ruin the flow of the meeting

We'll revisit Dave's story as we go through the book so you can get a sense of his progress through mapping and working with his mind in the same way that you are learning to work with your own mind.

Habit loops (anxiety and otherwise) control you until you can see them clearly. The first step to regaining control is simply to pay attention and map them out. Each time you create a map, you are less on autopilot and more in control because you see where you are headed.

But Isn't a Little Bit of Anxiety Helpful?

Our brains are brilliant at making associations. That's how we learn. We associate cake with yummy goodness, and then when we see cake, we automatically eat it. If we get food poisoning at a restaurant, we quickly learn to avoid that establishment. In fact, the association between that restaurant and yuck can be so strong that we may even feel nauseated when we simply pass by the store. Yet this brilliance goes only so far. A restaurant sign isn't poisonous in itself, but we learn to associate it with a DON'T GO THERE sign in our minds. And our minds—being the good associative learning machines that they are—can easily make false associations between anxiety and performance.

My PhD mentor, Dr. Louis Muglia, taught me the phrase "true, true, and unrelated." This was his reminder to me when performing experiments in the lab to check for a chain of causality. In other words, I could be studying behavior or process *X* and seeing *Y* happen, yet had to prove (to myself, my mentor, and the world) that *X* caused *Y*. *X* could be happening (true). *Y* could be happening at the same time or right afterward (true). But that didn't prove that *X* caused *Y* to happen.

Our minds do this all of the time. One of my favorite examples is professional baseball players standing at home plate to bat. They go through various rituals each time they set up for the pitch—digging in with their feet a certain number of times, touching their helmet in a certain spot, and so on. For many players, they have associated these specific behaviors with success: do *X*, *Y*, and *Z*, and you're more likely to hit the ball. But the fact is, they can complete the ritual (true) and hit the ball (true), but there's nothing to prove that the two truths are related.

And of course, many of us link anxiety with success in the same way. When I am teaching a seminar, almost without fail, someone approaches me afterward and says with certainty (ahh, how we love certainty!) that they would never have gotten where they are in the world without anxiety as a driver. I see this in my clinical anxiety program as well. For example, one person described it this way: "For me, I actually started to attribute my success to my anxiety. I performed very well in school and thought that my anxiety incentivized me to do well, so deep down, I was afraid, even hesitant, to let go of my anxiety." Another commented: "I feel the same way. I was fearful that if I let go of my anxiety, I would lose the capacity to push myself as hard as I did."

In these discussions, whether with my patients or workshop students, I could almost hear my mentor in my head. *Is this true, true, and unrelated?* Lou's voice would ask. Then I would start explaining that correlation does not equal causation. I would then dive into an exploration of their experience to help them identify if they were falsely associating the feeling of anxiety with performing well.

One fascinating observation I've made is how attached people are to the notion that anxiety is critical for success. I was discussing this with Caroline Sutton, my book editor, and she made a striking statement that really rang true: people romanticize their anxiety and/or stress. They wear it like a badge of honor, without which they would be a lesser person, or worse, lose a sense of purpose. To many, stress equals success. As she put it, "If you are stressed, you are making a contribution. If you're not stressed, you're a loser."

This notion that we must be at least a little anxious to perform well has also been romanticized in the research literature. Back in 1908, when the field of psychology was in its infancy, two animal behavior researchers at Harvard, Robert Yerkes and John Dodson, published a paper entitled "The Relation of Strength of Stimulus to Rapidity of Habit Formation." In this manuscript, they described an interesting observation: that Japanese dancing mice learned a task more efficiently when they received a moderate shock as a negative reinforcer as compared to a mild or severe shock. They concluded that animals needed some level of arousal, but not too much, to learn best. This paper was referenced only ten times over the next half century, yet in four of the citing articles, these findings were described as a psychological law (now perhaps irrevocably imprinted on the Internet as the Yerkes-Dodson Law or the Yerkes-Dodson Curve).*

In a paper published in 1955, the German-born British psychologist Hans Eysenck suggested that the Yerkes-Dodson "Law" could hold true for anxiety: he speculated that increased arousal *might* improve a subject's task performance. Two years later (1957), one of Eysenck's former graduate students, P. L. Broadhurst, at that point working as a researcher at the University of London, published a paper boldly entitled "Emotionality and the Yerkes-Dodson Law." In it, he reported that holding a rat's head underwater (i.e., air deprivation) for increasing amounts of time—which he described as a measure of "intensity of imposed motivation"—increased the rat's swimming speed up to a point where it then slightly dropped off again. Using the terms *motivation, arousal,* and *anxiety* interchangeably, he boldly concluded, "it is clear from these results that the Yerkes-Dodson Law may be taken as confirmed." (I wonder if he considered whether the rats whose heads had been held under the longest were just trying to catch their breath for a moment before swimming.) From studies involving dancing mice and drowning rats, the anxiety-performance inverted U-shaped curve, or bell curve, was psychologized into existence: a little anxiety is good for performance, a lot of anxiety, not so much.

* The historical shift from obscurity to law is expertly described by Martin Corbett in a paper published in 2015 entitled "From Law to Folklore: Work Stress and the Yerkes-Dodson Law," *Journal of Managerial Psychology* 30, no. 6 (2015): 741–52; doi: 10.1108/JMP-03-2013-0085.

Fast-forward half a century, when a review of the psychological literature pertaining to stress and work performance established that only 4 percent of the papers supported the inverted U-shaped curve, while 46 percent found a negative linear relationship, which basically means that any level of stress inhibits performance. Despite these clear differences (data be damned!), the overgeneralized Yerkes-Dodson "Law" has become folklore, perhaps even reaching mythic status in modern day, evidenced by a seeming exponential growth in the number of citations (fewer than 10 in 1990, fewer than 100 in 2000, and greater than 1,000 a decade later).

Anxiety as a badge of honor, a critical component of job competence, an identity taken on (*Thank goodness for my anxiety. Where would I be without it?*), perhaps combined with the aesthetics of a pseudoscientific explanatory model (bell curves are quite the rage), has led to a resultant reluctance to reevaluate this explanation, not just by therapists (some of whom have written entire books based on this premise), but also by patients and the general public.

If there is a voice in the back of your mind telling you that anxiety is a good thing, now is the time to start exploring whether that cause-and-effect relationship is real. Does anxiety always make you perform well? Have you accomplished things when you weren't anxious? And you might not be ready for this one, but I'll put it out there anyway: Does anxiety sap your energy, make it hard to think, or at times get in the way of good performance? (Gasp!) As a corollary, when Olympians or professional musicians are crushing it, do they look nervous? (Hint: watch old clips of a Michael Jordan 60-point game and look where his tongue is, Chloe Kim's gold-medal-winning snowboard performance on the halfpipe at the 2018 Winter Olympics, or take a gander at the size of Usain Bolt's smile when he is blowing away the competition in the 100-meter.)

As you move forward with changing any habit, anxiety or otherwise, don't worry about finding *all* of the triggers. When mapping out habit loops, you can often get stuck focusing on the triggers and lose sight of what actually helps you change them. This usually occurs when people focus too much on figuring out *why* they started getting into this or that habit loop in the first place. It's as if by going back and psychoanalyzing all of their birthday parties to see exactly when they started liking cake, they will magically fix their "see cake, eat cake" problem. Knowing why something became a habit isn't going to magically fix it in the present moment. In fact, triggers are the *least important* part of the habit loop. Reward-based learning is based on rewards, not the triggers (hence the name). That's where the money is. Don't worry, we'll go there in Part 2. For now, keep mapping out your habit loops.

CHAPTER 8

A Brief Word on Mindfulness

HERE AGAIN IS Jon Kabat-Zinn's definition of mindfulness:

> [Mindfulness is] the awareness that arises through paying attention in the present moment, on purpose, nonjudgmentally.

If you recall, our old brain reacts to positive and negative reinforcement to determine what to do, and then is good at turning that behavior into habits. Most of this happens subconsciously. If we aren't aware that we're doing something habitually, we will continue to do it habitually. (That's the autopilot part that we talked about in chapter 6.)

But we *can* become more aware of these habit patterns in action. That's what mindfulness helps us do: build awareness so that we can observe our cave person brains in action.

People often get confused about how mindfulness relates to med-

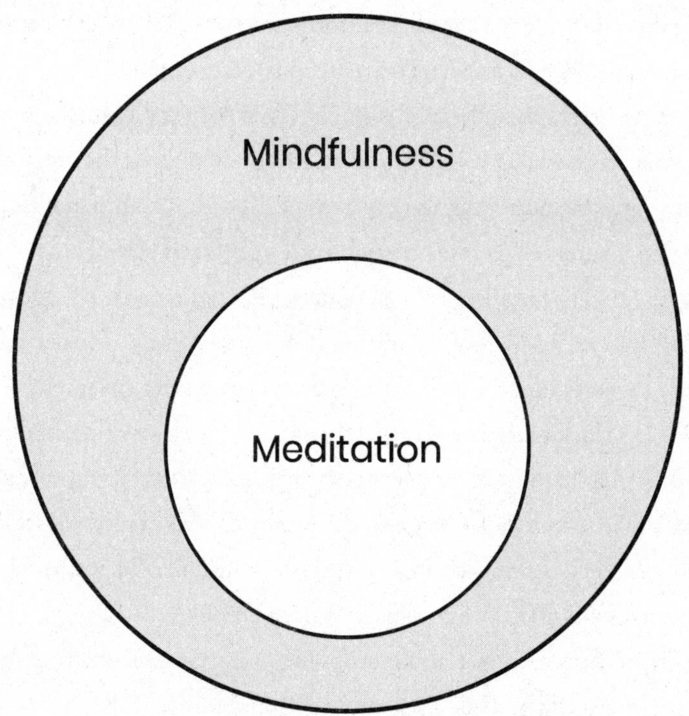

itation, whether they are the same or different. A simple way to visualize this is by employing a Venn diagram in which mindfulness is a big circle and meditation is the smaller circle within it.

In other words, meditation falls within the category of ways to train mindfulness. You don't need to meditate to be mindful, yet meditation helps you become more and more aware of what's happening right now. Meditation is like a gym for your brain, allowing you to build and strengthen your mindfulness muscles.

Awareness also helps you pay attention to triggers and automatic reactions. This goes for much more than anxiety and worry habit loops; in fact, it applies to anything that we're reacting to. But a word of warning: there is a lot of misinformation out there which argues that mindfulness is a special (non-anxious) state of mind, or merely a relaxation technique. I see this in my clinic patients a lot: the more they try to clear their mind of anxious thoughts or think their way out of anxiety, the more anxious they become. The most common misperception is summed up by a question I often get asked when I am teaching at retreats or when I'm introducing my patients to the idea of mindfulness: "How do I rid my mind of my thoughts?" This erroneously suggests that the goal of meditation is to "empty the mind."

Good luck with that—I tried that for ten years, sweating through T-shirts in the middle of winter on long silent meditation retreats, and it didn't work. Besides, I also spent the majority of medical school and residency training trying to stuff my brain full of as much information as possible. Why would I want to empty it?

Mindfulness is *not* about stopping, emptying, or ridding ourselves of anything. Thoughts, emotions, and physical sensations are what make us human. And thinking and planning are both crucial things to master. If I wasn't able to use my thinking brain to take a clear clinical history and make a solid diagnosis, I would have one heck of a time providing good care for my patients.

So rather than changing or not having the thoughts and feelings that make up our experience, mindfulness is about changing *our relationship* to those thoughts and emotions.

But this isn't an easy thing to do. In fact, a 2010 Harvard study showed that we get caught up in thinking (mind-wandering, to be exact) for about 50 percent of our waking lives. That's a lot of time running on autopilot.

Because this state of mind is so common, it can be measured in the brain. There is even a network of regions called the default mode

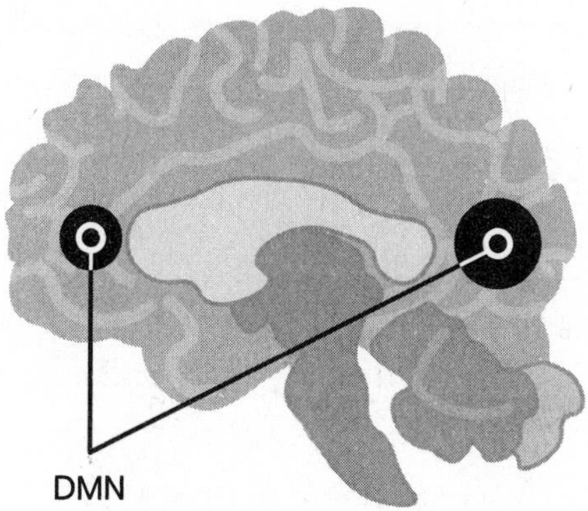

network (DMN). The DMN was discovered by Marcus Raichle and his crew at Washington University in St. Louis. It was called the default mode network because this is what our minds go to whenever they are not engaged in a specific task.

The DMN gets activated when our mind is wandering, thinking about things in the past or future, caught in repetitive thought patterns such as rumination, anxiety, or in other strong emotional states, and when we're craving various substances. And for better or worse, we default to thoughts and memories about things that are related to us. We regret things that we've done in the past, worry about events coming up in the future, and so on.

A hub of the DMN called the posterior cingulate cortex (PCC) connects a bunch of other brain regions together. The PCC is interesting because it gets activated when people are shown pictures that are reminders of or triggers for their addictions. For example, the PCC lights up with cocaine cues (e.g., a picture of a few lines of cocaine on a mirror) in cocaine-addicted individuals, with smoking cues (e.g., a picture of someone smoking) in nicotine-addicted individuals, and with gambling cues (e.g., a picture of someone playing roulette) in individuals addicted to gambling. Basically, the PCC gets all fired up when we get caught up in craving and other types of perseverative thinking habit loops like rumination (focusing on one's distress and repeatedly thinking about it over and over), which is a hallmark of depression and anxious worry. Perseveration simply means thinking the same thing over and over; worry is the poster child for this. To make sure this concept is clear, I'll give you some examples:

Craving Habit Loop

Trigger: See cake
Behavior: Eat cake
Result: Feel good

Rumination Habit Loop

Trigger: Feel low in energy
Behavior: Think about how down you feel, how you will never get anything done, etc.
Result: Feel (more) depressed

Anxious Worry Habit Loop

Trigger: Look at unfinished to-do list
Behavior: Worry about not getting it done
Result: Feel anxious

As a side note, depressed individuals seem to be so good at perseverative thinking habit loops that two-thirds of them also meet the psychiatric diagnostic criteria for anxiety disorders. This commonality between depression and anxiety is an example of perseverative thinking habit loops that are basically out of control—they feed on themselves. Why is that? Well, a research study by Yael Millgram and her colleagues at the Hebrew University suggested that the familiarity of a mood state contributes to our staying in it. When we are sad or anxious all the time, that sadness or anxiety becomes familiar, a place that we gravitate toward, something like a morning routine or a regular route to work. Any deviation feels unfamiliar, perhaps scary or even anxiety-provoking. From a survival standpoint, this makes sense: if we are traveling in unknown territory, we have to be on guard because we don't know yet if it is safe or not. Don't forget, not all habits are bad. They become bad only when they are tripping us up or slowing us down instead of helping us move forward.

We can become so identified with mental habit loops that they become our identity, who we think we are. In fact, an early pilot tester of my Unwinding Anxiety program wrote me the following email:

> Is there any difference between how one would approach unwinding "I am having an anxious thought" vs "I am anxious?" . . . I am learning to use the techniques well enough to work with reflexive type episodes—anxiety arising from a busy day, stress of a missed deadline, an upcoming event . . . what I'm struggling with is the kind of anxiety that comes from who I perceive myself to be and the seemingly impermeable blanket of not-good-enough-ness that it is wrapped in. Deep etched in the bones anxiety.

Anxiety felt like it was part of her; it was carved in her bones to the point where she couldn't differentiate it from herself.

If researchers and clinicians can find and understand links between how people behave and what's going on in the brain, we can find ways to accurately and precisely target the underlying mechanisms and have a better shot at helping people achieve real and lasting change. As a clinician, I see perseverative thinking as possibly *the* top issue tripping up my patients. And more often than not, this type of thinking has grooved a deep pattern in their brains to the point that they have identified with their habits: "I am a smoker." "I am anxious." Because perseverative thinking habit loops seem to be a clear and present danger for my patients and mindfulness might help, as a researcher, I was motivated to science the shit out of it.

In theory, mindfulness and meditation help us become aware of perseverative thinking. Instead of getting stuck in a groove of repeating the thought pattern, we can see that we are stuck and pull ourselves out of it, creating new and more positive habits along the way. (I'll go into some depth about the specifics of how you can do this in subsequent chapters.)

The DMN activates when we get caught up in perseverative thinking (and cravings). Because mindfulness is theoretically supposed to help people not get caught up in these loops and enable them to be less identified with their thoughts, our hypothesis was that mindfulness might have a positive effect on this brain network.

In our first study, we used an MRI scanner to compare the brain activity of people who had never meditated to that of experienced meditators. We instructed the novices as to how to meditate, then asked both groups to meditate while they were in the scanner. Lo and behold, only four brain regions showed different activity between the meditators and the non-meditators—two of those being the main hubs of the DMN. And yes, the DMN was much quieter in experienced meditators.

This was a new finding in the field, so we repeated the experiment to make sure our results were solid, and they were. We even did several real-time neurofeedback experiments to make sure the deactivation in the DMN that we were seeing was lining up with the participants' subjective experience of observing thoughts, emotions, and cravings, instead of being caught up in them.

But actual proof that we are identifying and targeting specific neural networks comes only when we can line them up with real-world behavior change. My lab looked to see if we could use app-based mindfulness training to help people quit smoking and if it would change brain activity in the DMN (we specifically focused on the PCC in this study). We got a grant from the National Institutes of Health to do a study in which we compared our app (Craving to Quit) to the National Cancer Institute's app (QuitGuide), which uses other strategies that don't involve mindfulness, such as health information. We scanned participants' brains before they got treatment and then again a month later to see if changes in brain activity in the PCC could predict how well they were able to cut down on smoking. We found a strong correlation between reductions in PCC activity in the group that used our app, but not the group that used the National Cancer Institute's app.

We found that our theory—that mindfulness would change brain activity and correlate with clinical outcomes—was true. This is a great example of the type of translational research that researchers and clinicians call *bench to bedside*. The idea is to translate ideas and concepts and fundamental basic research questions into treatments that can effect behavior change in real-world settings. More work needs to be done here; in particular, large-scale studies looking at long-term outcomes will be necessary. But we can do these types of studies now that we have a better mechanistic understanding of how mindfulness works. Already this understanding might explain why mindfulness training works best with depression and anxiety: it targets that shared element of perseverative thinking. People who are depressed perseverate about the past. People who are anxious perseverate about the future. Regardless of content (past/future), mindfulness jumps in and helps to dismantle the *process* of perseveration—so much so that the National Health Service in the United Kingdom has adopted one type of mindfulness training (mindfulness-based cognitive therapy) as a first-line treatment for depression.

Hopefully, this chapter has helped you to get a better understanding of what mindfulness is and how it can specifically target habit loops in your brain. More important, you can use this information to take action. Once you've mapped out your main habit loops, see how much you can zoom in throughout the day and count the number of times that they make it to the top of your brain's "playlist." Are there specific perseverative loops that you can map out? Can you count how many times they get played? Which ones make it to the top of the charts?

CHAPTER 9

What Is Your Mindfulness Personality Type?

SINGLE-CELLED ORGANISMS LIKE protozoa have simple binary mechanisms for survival: they move toward nutrients and away from toxins. The sea slug has a slightly more complicated nervous system, yet learns basically the same way.

Could it be that much of human behavior can be attributed to a similar "approach and avoid" survival strategy? In the face of danger or threat, for example, you might turn toward the danger and fight, turn from it and run, or freeze in your tracks, with the hope that whatever threatens you doesn't see (or smell) you. That is your fight/flight/freeze reaction, the automatic response that we all have in the face of danger. Think back to the last time someone yelled, "Look out!" or you heard a loud bang. Perhaps you might have surprised yourself at how quickly you moved out of the way of an oncoming car, ducked when you heard a loud noise, or froze when the lights suddenly went out—all without needing or having time to think. In the name of safety, the primitive parts of your brain and nervous system take care of everything for you (thankfully!). Just as trying to think your way out of bad habits doesn't work, thinking your way out of danger is risky if you have to act fast. Thinking is way too slow a process when danger is near—your response has to be at the reflex level. Could these instincts explain some habitual elements of our personalities?

A couple of years ago our research team found that a fifth-century "meditation manual," titled *The Path of Purification,* describes how many of our tendencies, habitual behaviors, and mental personality traits fall into one of these three fight, flight, or freeze buckets. Why did the writer of this manual bother spelling this out? So he could give personalized recommendations for people who were learning to meditate and to change habitual behavior patterns. This may be one of the first descriptions of what we now think of as personalized medicine—matching a treatment to an individual's phenotype.

What's more, the manual's author didn't have access to modern equipment like heart rate and blood pressure monitors, or functional MRI and EEG machines to measure physiology and brain activity. He relied on what he could see, such as the type of food one eats, how one walks or dresses, and so forth. Here's how he described the method in *The Path of Purification*:

By the posture, by the action,
By eating, seeing, and so on,
By the kind of states occurring,
May temperament be recognized.

His observations broke behavioral tendencies into three general categories or buckets that line up surprisingly well with modern-day science:

Bucket 1: Approach/fight
Bucket 2: Avoid/flight
Bucket 3: Neither approach nor avoid (freeze)

Let's break this down a bit.

Imagine you're walking into a party. If you're in bucket 1 (approach), you might marvel at the wonderful food that is being served and excitedly start mingling with friends. In contrast, if you're in bucket 2 (avoid), you might make a judgment about the food or the people who were invited, and later in the night be found arguing with someone over the details or accuracy of a topic under discussion. If you fall into bucket 3 (neither approach nor avoid), you would be more likely to go with the flow and follow the lead of others.

Our research group recently took this one step further. We found that the behavioral tendencies described in the manual line up pretty well with modern-day mechanisms of reward-based learning—approach/fight, avoid/flight, freeze. People who are in the approach bucket (1) may have a tendency to be more motivated by behaviors that are *positively* reinforcing. People who are in the avoid bucket (2) may have a tendency to be more motivated by behaviors that are *negatively* reinforcing. People who are in neither bucket (3) may be more in the middle—not pulled or pushed into a positively or negatively reinforcing pathway/tendency by pleasant and unpleasant situations as much as the others.

These buckets lined up so well with current science that we made a modern-day measure and used psychometric research methods to validate our behavioral tendencies questionnaire (BTQ) that anyone can take (it's only thirteen questions).

BEHAVIORAL TENDENCIES QUIZ

Please rank the following in the order that is most consistent with how you *generally* behave (not how you think you *should* behave or how you *might* behave in a very specific situation). You should give your first and initial response without thinking about the question too much. Place a 1 by the answer that best fits you, followed by a 2 for your second choice, and a 3 for the answer that least fits you.

1. If I were to plan a party, . . .
   - ❑ I would want it to be high-energy, with lots of people.
   - ❑ I would want only certain people there.
   - ❑ it would be last-minute and free-form.
2. When it comes to cleaning my room, I . . .
   - ❑ take pride in making things look great.
   - ❑ quickly notice problems, imperfections, or untidiness.
   - ❑ don't tend to notice or get bothered by clutter.
3. I prefer to make my living space . . .
   - ❑ beautiful.
   - ❑ organized.
   - ❑ creatively chaotic.
4. When doing my job, I like to . . .
   - ❑ be passionate and energetic.
   - ❑ make sure everything is accurate.

- ❑ consider future possibilities/wonder about the best way forward.

5. When talking to people, I might come across as . . .
   - ❑ affectionate.
   - ❑ realistic.
   - ❑ philosophical.
6. The disadvantage of my clothing style is that it may be . . .
   - ❑ decadent.
   - ❑ unimaginative.
   - ❑ mismatched or uncoordinated.
7. In general, I carry myself . . .
   - ❑ buoyantly.
   - ❑ briskly.
   - ❑ aimlessly.
8. My room is . . .
   - ❑ richly decorated.
   - ❑ neatly arranged.
   - ❑ messy.
9. Generally, I tend to . . .
   - ❑ have a strong desire for things.
   - ❑ be critical but clear-thinking.
   - ❑ be in my own world.
10. At school, I was known for . . .
    - ❑ having lots of friends.
    - ❑ being intellectual.
    - ❑ daydreaming.
11. I usually wear clothes in a way that is . . .
    - ❑ fashionable and attractive.

- ❑ neat and orderly.
- ❑ carefree.

12. I come across as . . .
    - ❑ affectionate.
    - ❑ thoughtful.
    - ❑ absent-minded.
13. When other people are enthusiastic about something, I . . .
    - ❑ jump on board and want to get involved.
    - ❑ tend to be skeptical of it.
    - ❑ go off on tangents.

Now add up the numbers to get a crude score for each of the top options, middle options, and bottom options. The option with the lowest score equals the greatest tendency.

Top = approach type; Middle = avoid type; Bottom = go-with-the-flow type. For example, if you scored an 18 for the top option, a 25 for the middle option, and a 35 for the bottom option, you have a much higher tendency for the approach type.

You can think of the BTQ as a mindfulness personality quiz. And the hope is that it can be helpful in your ordinary life. By more clearly seeing and understanding your everyday behavioral tendencies, you can learn about yourself and your habitual responses to your internal and external world. You can also learn the personality types of family members, friends, and coworkers, such that you can learn to live and work more harmoniously with them.

Being more in tune with the kind of person you are will also help you build on the strengths of your habitual tendencies. For example, a person displaying a predominantly approach type might do well at marketing or sales. One might give an avoid type an assignment requiring a high level of precision and attention to detail because such a person loves to focus in on figuring things out and thrives in those situations. And a go-with-the-flow type might be the best at coming up with creative ideas during a brainstorming session or the start of a large project.

Understanding your habitual tendencies will also help you grow as a person and avoid unnecessary heartaches. For example, if you are the approach type, you can map out all of the habits in your life where you tend to go overboard, where wanting too much of a good thing actually makes things worse (e.g., overeating, getting jealous in friendships, etc.). If you are the avoid type, you can pay attention to related behaviors such as being overly judgmental (of yourself and others) or overly focusing on accuracy to the detriment of the bigger picture. And if you are the go-with-the-flow type, you can focus on becoming aware of situations where you might step back from making decisions and agree with others for the sake of not causing friction.

Below are general summaries for each personality type. Remember, these are tendencies and not labels. More often than not, people have a predominant tendency, and depending on the situation, may lean more heavily into one tendency or another. For example, my wife and I both fall heavily into the avoid bucket. This may explain why we are both academics: we love to spend our time questioning premises and theories, researching and figuring things out. As a second tendency, we both fall more into the approach than the go-with-the-flow bucket. So if one of us is struggling or having a bad day, the other, instead of fueling the fire of judgment, tends to lean in and be optimistic and supportive.

In fact, knowing our behavioral tendencies has helped my wife and me see our habit patterns more clearly. If my wife happens to tell me about something that happened at work with a colleague, and I tend to judge that person, she can gently point out my judgment habit loop so that I can step back to see the situation more clearly.

Approach: You tend to be optimistic and affectionate and might even be popular. You are composed and quick thinking in everyday tasks. You're more likely to be attracted to pleasant things. You put faith into what you believe, and your passionate nature makes you popular with other people. You have a confident posture (that is to say, you walk proudly). At times you might have the tendency to become a little greedy for success. You crave pleasant experiences and good company.

Avoid: You tend to be clear-thinking and discerning. Your intellect allows you to see things logically and identify flaws in things. You are quick to understand concepts and tend to keep things organized and tidy while getting things done quickly. You pay attention to detail. You might even have a stiff posture (that is to say, you walk stiffly and hurriedly). At times you might notice that you are overly judgmental and critical. You may come across as a perfectionist.

Go with the flow: You tend to be easygoing and tolerant. You are able to think about the future and speculate on what might happen. You think about things deeply and philosophically. At times you get caught up in your own thoughts or fantasies. As you daydream, sometimes you might become doubtful and worried about things. At times you might notice that you find yourself going along with what others suggest, perhaps becoming too easily persuaded. You might notice that you are less organized than others and can come across as dreamy.

The more you understand how your mind works, the more you will be able to work with it. The more you explore your own behavioral tendencies, the more you will be able to capitalize on your own strengths and grow and learn from the moments when your tendencies trip you up.

You can think of these tendencies as helping you see the habitual grooves you might be more likely to fall into. Being aware of this can be really helpful when you are going through the process of changing habits, because if you don't see these basic tendencies, you can't change them (both letting go of unhelpful tendencies and leaning into their strengths). One of my clinic patients put it nicely: when she was stuck in a habit loop of self-judgment (e.g., "That was stupid. Why did I do that?"), she would simply say to herself, *Oh, that's just my brain,* which helped her not take things so personally.

So keep your behavioral tendency (or tendencies) in mind as you read the rest of this book, and see if you can tap into your strengths to help you work with anxiety and with changing habits in general. Perhaps you can even step out of some of your habitual behavioral tendencies when they start to trip you up. Okay, do you feel like you're pretty good at mapping your mind at this point and are ready to take the next step? Let's move on to Part 2.

PART 2

Updating Your Brain's Reward Value: Second Gear

1. *You must let the pain visit.*
2. *You must allow it to teach you.*
3. *You must not allow it overstay.*

—IJEOMA UMEBINYUO

CHAPTER 10

How Your Brain Makes Decisions (Why We Prefer Cake to Broccoli)

PERHAPS ONE OF the most frustrating anxiety habit loops that people struggle with is procrastination. Why do anxiety habit loops like worry or procrastination stick around so long? One of the worries that often drives procrastination is a fear of failure or inadequacy. One person in my anxiety program put it this way:

> I struggle significantly with the "worry loop" in that my anxiety feeds on a tasty combo meal that includes worried thoughts and self-criticism. One of the biggest consequences for me of this vicious cycle is PROCRASTINATION. I am procrastinating right now . . .

Another described her habit loop thus:

> I've spent all morning trapped again in the avoidance loop. Open project, flip to social media, lose half an hour. Flip back to project, pick up

> phone for "just one round" of a mobile game, lose an hour. The "reward" of the avoidance is that I don't have to face the icky feelings of being behind, of knowing that I have too much to do. The game or the social media numbs me for a while, lets me hide from it.

Trigger: Working on project
Behavior: Play a game on her phone (i.e., procrastinate)
Result: Avoidance, lose an hour of work time

The irony here that we all can see is that the temporary avoidance of the "icky feelings of being behind" actually puts her more behind. She continued:

> I've spent the last 15 years experimenting with various tools and techniques, I have five different apps and subscriptions services I use daily that help me track my time and block various sites and apps during certain hours, I keep my phone on Do Not Disturb almost 24/7, etc. What I'm looking for is guidance on how to engage with the emotional response around this. Because at the core, no matter what tools and tactics I employ—if I really want to procrastinate, I will. I will always find a way around it.
>
> What I am trying to investigate here is how to interact with the underlying desire—or more accurately, the underlying fears. The cause for the anxiety. I have done years and years of work, both on my own and with my regular therapist, on making sure that the activities I'm doing are the ones I want to be doing. The problem is that I still have terrible, deep, decades-long fears of not being good enough, of being rejected, etc.—all of which unfortunately are supported by a ton of

> events where these things actually happened—that no matter how badly I want to do something, the fear overwhelms me and I fall into my avoidance loop for the short-term relief instead. If tactics and tools were the answer, I'd already have conquered this, because I've tried them all . . . I can't even tell you how many people in my life over the years have been like "Well, you just have to dig down into your willpower and do it!" Which makes me want to ask them if they think I just haven't thought of that, or that I have thought of it and simply don't possess the strength of character. Neither is an attractive thought.

Not only would she not be admitted to the very, very exclusive willpower club—which my friend Emily and *Star Trek*'s Mr. Spock are probably two of only a handful of members—but over the past few decades nobody taught her what the key to behavior change is (reward value) and how it works in her brain.

Why does your brain prefer cake to broccoli?

It's not as simple as "cake tastes better." The real answer gives us insights into *why* we act certain ways and how we can break a wide range of bad habits from stress-eating to procrastination.

Let's start with why and how our brains form habits. This will involve a little repetition from chapter 3, but bear with me. The why is simple: habits free up our brain to learn new things. But not every action becomes a habit. Your brain has to choose what to lay down as habit and what not to do again. Remember, you learn a habit based on *how rewarding* the behavior is. The more rewarding a behavior is, the stronger the habit.

This is important, so I'm going to repeat it: *The more rewarding a behavior is, the stronger the habit.*

In fact, our brains set up a hierarchy of behaviors based on their reward value. The behavior with the bigger reward is the one our brains choose and the one we act out. From a neurobiological perspective, this probably has to do with the amount of dopamine that fires up our brain's reward centers when we first learn the behavior. This goes all the way back to our cave person brains, which are set up to help us get the most calories we can so we can survive. For example, sugar and fat have a lot of calories, so when we eat cake, part of our brain thinks, *Calories—survival!* Hence we start to prefer cake over broccoli. A study from the Max Planck Institute recently found that our brains get two dopamine hits: the first comes when tasting food, and the second when the food hits our stomach. Depending on the caloric promise, our brains remember which foods are more rewarding (more calories = more reward), which is why our parents never served dessert at the same time as dinner. Given a choice, we'd fill up on cake before we ate our vegetables.

But it's not just calories that count. Our brains also learn the reward value of people, places, and things. Think back to all of the birthday parties you went to as a kid. Your brain combines all of that information—the taste of the cake, as well as the fun you had with your friends—into a single composite reward value.

Reward value has been mapped to a certain part of the brain called the orbitofrontal cortex (OFC). The OFC is a crossroads in the brain where emotional, sensory, and previous behavioral information gets integrated. The OFC takes all of this information, groups it together, and uses it to set that composite reward value of a behavior, so we can quickly retrieve it in the future as a "chunked" bit of information.

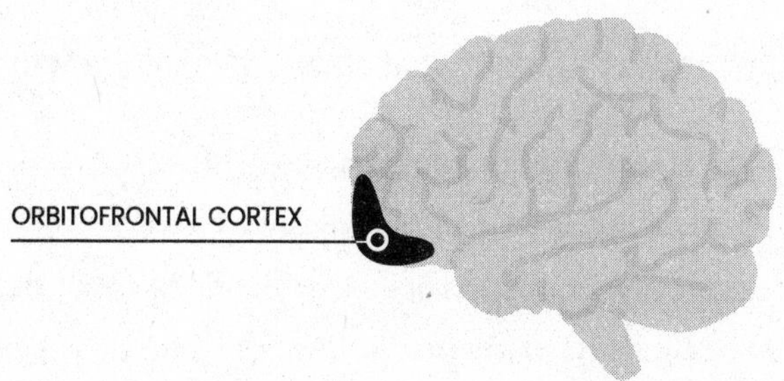

Once you're an adult and see a piece of cake, you don't have to relearn what it tastes like or remember any of the fun from the times you ate it; instead, that association you learned as a kid kicks in. Eating cake makes you feel good and triggers an automatic and habitual response. Think of learning a habit as a kind of "set and forget"—set the reward value and forget about the details.

This is also why it is so hard to break habits.

If you are trying to cut down on automatically eating every piece of cake you see, someone will probably tell you to use your willpower and just not eat it. But can you really think your way out of eating? This way of proceeding might work sometimes, but more often than not, in the long run, it fails. And that's because it's not how your brain works.

To change a behavior, you can't just focus on the behavior itself. Instead, you have to address *the felt experience of the rewards* of that behavior. If all we needed to do was to think our way out of a behavior, we'd just tell ourselves to stop smoking, stop eating cake, stop yelling at our kids when we are stressed, stop being anxious in general, and snap! it would work. But it doesn't. The only sustainable way to change a habit is to update its reward value. That's why it's called reward-based learning.

Awareness: Update Your Reward Value System

So how do we update reward values and break worry, procrastination, and other bad habits? One simple thing: awareness.

We need to give our brains new information to establish that the value they had learned in the past is now outdated. By paying attention to the results of behavior in the present moment, you can jolt your brain out of habit autopilot and see and feel exactly how rewarding (or unrewarding) the habit is for you right now. This new information resets the reward value on the old habit and moves better behaviors up in the hierarchy of reward value, and, eventually, into automatic mode (more on that in Part 3 of the habit loop trilogy).

Here's an example. I don't have to tell my patients that they should force themselves to stop smoking or that smoking is bad for them—they know this already from watching their beloved Marlboro man get emphysema (in fact, no fewer than four Marlboro men have died from COPD). No patient of mine has ever marched into my office and asked me how to help them smoke *more*. Instead, I go to where the money is: direct experience. I teach people to pay attention when they smoke.

Most people start smoking when they are teenagers, so they've laid down a strong reward value for cigarettes: being young and cool at school, rebelling against their parents, all of that. I have them pay attention when they smoke so they can see how rewarding smoking is to them *right then and there*. One woman who was doing the noticing reported that smoking "smells like stinky cheese and tastes like chemicals, YUCK."

Did you notice how she paid attention? She wasn't thinking,

Smoking is bad for me. Instead, she brought a curiosity and an awareness to her experience of smoking *as* she was smoking—noticing the smell and tasting the chemicals in cigarettes. Smoking tastes like crap when you actually pay attention. Anxiety is pretty straightforward on this front: patients never come into my office telling me that they're not anxious enough or asking for a pill to make them more anxious. Anxiety sucks.

This kind of awareness is critical for resetting that reward value in your brain, which in turn helps you break that habit.

This is the essence of second gear.

Tell me if you can relate to this:

You come home from a long day at school or work. Maybe it's been a tough day, you're carrying a bit of stress, or you're just plain tired. It's not quite dinnertime, but you head into the kitchen for a snack. You grab a bag of potato chips or a candy bar and start mindlessly eating while you sit down to watch TV, check your email, or talk on the phone.

Before you know it, half the bag of chips is gone and you might well feel stuffed and slightly ill.

Let's map this out.

Trigger: Time of day, stress, hunger, etc.
Behavior: Mindlessly eat a snack
Result: Hmmm, how did those chips taste? I wasn't really paying attention.

Yes, exactly. That's why those old pesky habits are so hard to break. Remember that "set and forget" from earlier? Your brain has lumped together all of the times that you relaxed and ate chips while watching TV and combined them into a single reward value of chips + TV = relaxation. Your zombie-like behavior of mindless eating gets triggered the moment you walk in the door. That de-stress reward value doesn't get updated until you start paying attention *right in that moment*. So of course you keep repeating this behavior over and over, wondering why you can't just tell yourself to stop.

As we've seen, reward-based learning is based on rewards (hence the name). Behavior leads to a result, and that result drives future behavior. If the behavior is rewarding, you do it again; if it isn't, you stop doing it. Buddhists describe this as cause and effect; animal behaviorists call it positive and negative reinforcement (or reinforcement learning or operant conditioning).

No matter what you name it, if you want to change it, you have to rub your brain's little orbitofrontal cortex nose in its own poop so that it clearly smells how stinky it is. That's how your brain learns. Behavior doesn't change if the reward value of that behavior stays the same. And the reward value can change only when you bring awareness to bear and see *the actual* reward value. This is NOT the reward value that got set when you were five years old, or thirteen, and could eat a whole bag of chips in one sitting and then go swimming without getting cramps. I'm talking about the reward value right now in your life. Only then can you hit that big red reward reset button.

Something magical happens when you rub your brain's proverbial little nose in whatever your proverbial little habit might be: you start to become disenchanted with the behavior. I don't want you to gloss over this, so I'm going to repeat it in a slightly different form this time, and italicize it for you. *If you really pay careful and close attention—*

without making any assumptions or relying on past experience to guide you—and you see that a behavior is not rewarding right now, I promise you that you will start to get less excited about doing it again.

That's because your brain updates reward values based on the latest information you give it (in this case, by paying attention to how it feels). When the value changes, your OFC reshuffles its reward hierarchy and moves the less rewarding behavior lower on the "if triggered, you must" list. You clearly see (and feel) that it isn't as rewarding as you remembered, so you are less excited to do it in the future.

Disenchantment, Santa-Style

Just like a kid who yanks on Santa Claus's beard and realizes for the first time that Santa was just some guy in a red suit with a fake beard—definitely *not* the real deal—when you pay attention to the results of your behaviors carefully enough that the reward value gets updated in your OFC, *you can't go back and pretend you didn't see the change*. Once you know the truth, you can no longer go back and convince yourself that there is a Santa Claus.

Once you're fully aware that procrastinating puts the project even more behind schedule or inhaling a bag of your favorite chips will make your stomach feel bloated and will lead to a crappy emotional state, you can't have a do-over and pretend you don't feel what you feel.

Every time you pay attention to your actions, you become more aware of what you actually get from them. If you notice that potato chips make you feel crappy when you eat too many, you get less excited about eating the whole bag next time. Not because you have to force yourself to not eat them, but simply because you remember what happened last time (and the time before that, and the time before that, and the time before that). This also holds true for worry, procrastination, or any other anxiety habit loop that you've learned over the years.

This is a pretty neat hack of your brain's reward-based learning system—and it has nothing to do with willpower. You now know how your brain functions, so you can work it rather than it working you.

Second Gear Defined: The Gift of Disenchantment

Second gear is paying attention to the results of your actions.

It's reward-based learning, or good old cause and effect.

When you have identified and mapped out your habit loops (first gear) and are ready to practice driving in second gear, ask yourself this simple question: *What do I get from this behavior?*

Answering this question will require you to pay careful attention to the actual, visceral, embodied sensations, emotions, and thoughts that come as a result of the behavior in question.

WARNING: This is *not* an intellectual training. Don't fall into the trap of understanding how reward valuation works in the brain and then go trying to think your way out of your bad habits and into good ones. If you've ever tried to change your snacking habits, you can probably relate to this:

Trigger: Time of day, anxiety, stress, hunger, etc.

Behavior: Tell yourself you shouldn't eat a snack. Five minutes later you get distracted or your willpower breaks down, and you mindlessly eat the snack anyway.

Result: Feel bad. Tell yourself you shouldn't have done that.

While thinking is helpful for decision-making and planning, we often give the thinking part of our brain too much credit. Remember, it's the weakest part of your brain, so you can't trust it to do the heavy lifting. Let it do the fun, creative thinking. When it comes to actually changing behavior, leave that part to the heavyweights (the OFC and other reward-based learning parts of your brain). How do you get the big muscular guy to do your bidding? You hire someone to become the heavyweight's coach or trainer. The coach helps the heavyweight see that doing the lifting is going to help him become stronger, so he naturally wants to do it for you. Think of awareness as your brain coach.

So if your mind starts turning this into an intellectual exercise of thinking—trying to think your way out of worry, overeating, or another bad habit—simply notice and perhaps map that out as a habit loop (like the example above). Then ask yourself, *What do I get from this?* Don't ask it in an intellectual way.

When you ask this question, put your thinking mind on hold for a few moments and then drop your awareness into observation mode and notice what is happening in your body. At this point it is pretty straightforward for awareness to coach your brain. Obviously, eating a whole bag of potato chips isn't going to help you train for that marathon or lower your blood pressure. If you procrastinate, you aren't going to get the project done—in fact quite the opposite, especially when it adds to the time pressure of a deadline. Awareness. That's where the disenchantment presents are, waiting under the tree to be opened. You must be present to open them.

Ready to roll into disenchantment land? Let's get moving.

Now that you've learned the key idea of how to train your brain, try it out and see if you can get the hang of it. See if you can start driving in second gear now: map out a habit loop (anxiety or otherwise) to get you moving, then shift into second by focusing on the results of the behavior. Bring your awareness into your embodied experience and focus on the question *What do I get from this?* What does the result of that behavior feel like when you simply bring the behavior to mind?

CHAPTER 11

Stop Thinking: Dave's Story, Part 2

When we last saw Dave, I had given him instructions to start mapping out his habit loops around anxiety and had also sent him home with our Unwinding Anxiety mindfulness app to help him with this. Specifically, that mapping homework was to focus on the cause-and-effect relationship between behavior and reward. He needed to see for himself just how actually unrewarding his habitual behaviors were. This was how he would be able to make significant progress. In effect, at that first clinic visit, I was giving him guidelines on how to drive in both first and second gears.

The reward-based learning theory has been demonstrated to be the strongest learning mechanism known in science. So why isn't it easier to harness its power to unlearn old habits in the same way that you learn them? Why not focus on how rewarding a behavior is, and if it is rewarding, do it again? If it is no longer rewarding, stop doing it, right? The theory sounds—and is—simple. Yet this can easily fall into the thinking trap that I mentioned in the last chapter: you can know that something is bad for you, but thinking doesn't change behaviors on its own. It isn't strong enough. Changing a reward value is what gets the heavy lifters on board to do the lifting for you. And the reward value doesn't change without its coach (awareness) helping it see clearly what isn't worth picking up and what is. Old habits can change pretty quickly with the proper brain training, but they don't change instantaneously (more on this later).

Dave came back a few weeks later, visibly different. Before he'd even sat down, he was excitedly telling me about the changes the process had brought about.

"I mapped out my anxiety habit loops," he said, "and I feel much better just knowing how my anxiety drives itself. The app is helping me learn to work with my anxiety."

Oh, good, I thought. *He's driving confidently in first gear.*

Then he smiled and said, "Oh, and I lost fourteen pounds."

"What?" I said.

"I saw pretty clearly that eating to cope with my anxiety didn't relieve the anxiety. It actually made me feel worse, because I felt crappy about my weight," Dave said. "Once I saw that [eating didn't fix the anxiety], it was pretty easy to stop those old eating habits."

This was a great example of putting scientific theory into action. Dave was learning how to bring awareness online to help him not only map out his old habit loops, but more important, see and feel, from his own experience, how unrewarding his habit of eating to cope with anxiety was. His OFC had been telling him that eating had a high reward value (relative to anxiety), but when he looked at the "reward" carefully, he could clearly see that it wasn't rewarding at all. With that awareness, his OFC was not only getting updated information but was acting on it. He was driving in second gear! Awareness was coaching him (and his OFC) in the right direction.

Over the next few months, I saw Dave every couple of weeks to check in on his progress and give him tips for areas to focus on as he worked with his anxiety. As of my writing (about six months into the treatment), he has lost ninety-seven pounds (and is still going strong), his liver is no longer pâté, his sleep apnea has resolved, and his blood pressure has returned to normal.

IT GETS BETTER.

One day recently, I was leaving Brown University's School of Public Health, where I had just finished teaching a class on habit change (my favorite class to teach). The building is situated on South Main Street in Providence, Rhode Island. I was walking along the sidewalk when suddenly a car slowed down and pulled up next to me. The driver rolled down the window.

"Hey, Dr. Jud!" Dave shouted, a big smile on his face.

I'm sure I looked surprised—Dave driving, on a major street? This is the guy who hates freeways.

"Oh yeah, I work as an Uber driver now," he said. "I'm on my way to the airport." And with that he happily drove away.

Just by understanding his mind and observing habit loops in a systematic way (first gear), Dave had managed to create an amazing transformation for himself, but that's only part of the story. He had also managed to hack his reward-based learning and was using the hack to help him literally get back in the driver's seat (second gear).

Dave has an incredible story. But second gear isn't always easy. In fact, much of the time, paying such close attention to the results of our old habits is downright painful. We can become disenchanted with the disenchantment process itself (practicing second gear) and shift from second gear into reverse, moving backward. Why?

Our brains have evolved to try to minimize the amount of pain we have to endure. This makes sense from a survival perspective. If you touch a hot stove, you will sense the heat and reflexively pull your hand away, which in turn keeps you from getting burned.

The world is filled with panaceas sold to you to make you avoid pain and feel good. Clothes, cars, pills, experiences—all are packaged and tied with neat little bows of "this will relieve your aches and pains," "this will make you feel good," or "this will help you forget your worries." But if you stay in your comfort zone, you will never grow. Life is going to throw all sorts of stuff at you, and either you get sucked into creating habits of indulgence, distraction, and numbness through clothes and pills, or you can learn to roll with the punches, even leaning into them as a way to grow (more on this in the next chapter).

Also, second gear can feel like it takes forever. You see the old habit clearly and quickly realize that you aren't getting anything from it. Then you wonder why, now that you see all of this so clearly, nothing is changing. I see this all the time in my clinic and habit change programs, especially with people working with anxious worry (that habit loop is clearly not rewarding). They map out their habit loop and report back to me that worry doesn't get them anything but more anxiety. Then they ask why they haven't stopped worrying yet. Clearly they have seen that what they are doing isn't rewarding and are wondering why the switch hasn't flipped. At moments like this, I ask them how long they've had the worry habit loop (or stress-eating or whatever their habit loop is). Most of them reply, "All of my life." Then I ask how long they've been in the program. The usual response is "two weeks" or "three weeks." (Hearing themselves say that is usually enough to help them gain perspective.)

In a world of instant gratification, it is pretty easy to get trained into an impatience habit loop:

Trigger: See solution (to anxiety, habit, problem)
Behavior: Want problem to change immediately
Result: Frustration that it isn't gone

Simply mapping out habit loops and seeing their lack of value doesn't magically unwind years and years of entrenchment. This is where patience comes in. Some habits unwind faster than others (and even Dave took three months to make serious gains with his anxiety). For the deeply entrenched habits, your brain needs to see the lack of reward over and over before the new habit of not doing the old behavior takes hold. In other words, you need to groove that new neural pathway that signals "not rewarding" often enough and over enough time that *it* becomes the new automatic behavior.

This is like any scientific experiment. A single data point that is different from a thousand other data points that all are pretty much the same is an anomaly until you collect more data to see that, in fact, the seeming outlier is the accurate one. Awareness helps you get up-to-date and accurate information so that you can trust the new data that are coming in, rather than dismissing them as erroneous.

You can probably see the irony here—old habitual behaviors are based on outdated data, yet because they are old, they are familiar; and because they are familiar, we trust them (change is scary). Think of reward value as having a shelf life—it's good for only a certain amount of time before that value becomes outdated. It's important to check with your old habits to see if they are still serving you. That's what second gear is all about.

Like Dave, people step out of habit loops by becoming disenchanted with them, but they have to be aware of the cycle (first gear) and the current reward value of the behavior (second gear) to do this. And the more often they bring awareness online and feel disenchanted, the more they groove the disenchantment pathway in their brain. Repetition works when you are lifting weights and building your biceps; it also works when you are strengthening your mental muscles. If you were training for a marathon, your coach wouldn't send you out to run fifteen miles on your first day. Likewise, try to evenly distribute your mental training through your day. In fact, the best way to train your brain for behavior change is to make your life your mental gym. In other words, use the steps/gears that you are learning in this book throughout your day so that you can unlearn old habits and learn new ones in context—in the very places and spaces that you live. Remember: this whole reward-based learning is about laying down context-dependent memory.

Short Moments, Many Times

Making your everyday life your mental gym also has the advantage of upending the popular "I don't have time to work out" excuse. When the habit comes up, you have to deal with it anyway, so you might as well take a few seconds to map it out and then bring awareness to the results of the habitual behavior. If it happens a lot throughout the day, you get more opportunities to do your mental weightlifting, so that you get stronger (and more disenchanted with old habits) with each awareness repetition. I think of this as "short moments, many times." If you bring awareness to your old habits for short moments, many times throughout the day, you will more quickly and efficiently unlearn the old and move into the new. This is why Mr. Miyagi made Daniel-san wax and paint until he was exhausted. He had to be sure Daniel had grooved those pathways to the point where they were motor memory. Only then was Daniel ready to fight.

If you are feeling disenchanted with driving in second gear, perhaps Dave's story can inspire you and help you realize that while these practices may not be easy, they are simple.

Keep going with the habit loop practice. Map out a habit loop (first gear); ask yourself, *What do I get from this?*; and pay attention to the body sensations, thoughts, and emotions that come as a result of the behavior (second gear). Repeat.

CHAPTER 12

Learning (and Growing) from the Past

How is your habit loop dismantling going? Are you able to drive a bit more in second gear, asking yourself, *What am I getting from this?* and seeing the results of those old behaviors more clearly? Is your OFC getting fresh, updated information to reset those reward values in your brain?

Review the following examples of what other folks went through so you can see if you are on track. I'll start with a few from our Eat Right Now and Unwinding Anxiety programs. Let's explore the elements of first and/or second gear in their community journal writing.

Here's the first one:

> I went to put a teaspoon of honey into my tea and I just put a whole teaspoon of it in my mouth first—"I'm just so tired" was the thought as I did that—but as soon as it was in my mouth, I thought, *Oh, this isn't going to help me at all.* It really didn't even taste good. So I was actually

> grateful that happened. It felt really good to see that the sugar hit didn't actually help me feel better or even taste good.

Trigger: Sugar
Behavior: Hijacked motor neurons that delivered the sugar right into her mouth instead of her tea
Result: It didn't taste good and didn't make her feel better

What do you think about the moment she says to herself, *Oh, this isn't going to help*? Second gear? Or is it? Remember that *warning* I gave you in chapter 10—avoid getting caught up in thinking. If she'd followed that thought alone, she might have simply tried to tell herself not to do it, and in the process gotten stuck in trying to think her way out of the behavior. This thinking pattern had misfired for her in the past.

Not to worry—she moved past thinking alone and drove in second gear. She saw cause and effect pretty darn clearly (the sugar didn't taste good or make her feel better).

But there's more. She also wrote that she was grateful for what happened. This is a super-solid sign of learning, which feels good. We are grateful that we have learned something useful, because with that knowledge, we are less likely to repeat a bad behavior in the future. Learning and making progress are rewarding unto themselves.

Another correspondent wrote this:

> I woke up with a bit of anxiety over what had happened the night before, but instead of giving in to it, I got curious about how that felt. This alone seemed to bring the anxiety level down a notch.

Trigger: Anxiety over the night before
(New) Behavior: Getting curious about body sensations
Result: Less anxiety

I added *new* in front of behavior here, because not only is it a new behavior for this person that lessened his anxiety, but it also highlights the ability to step out of these habit loops, using curiosity. (Yes, that's a bit of third-gear goodness. We'll explore this more in Part 3.) Now back to the example. He continued:

> So then I asked myself the disenchantment question on both sides of the coin:
>
> "What did I get out of being anxious over those body sensations?"
>
> [Answer] Nothing but more anxious.
>
> "What did I get out of being curious about my sensations and the anxiety I was feeling?"
>
> A lessened state of anxiety, which allowed me to comfortably drift off to sleep.

Trigger: Anxiety over the night before.
(Old) Behavior: Getting anxious about body sensations
Result: Seeing how getting anxious leads to more anxiety

This is a great example of a twist on second gear. Notice his active self-reflection on what he gets from giving into anxiety and worry. Notice how he didn't actually go through with it and get sucked in. Instead he simply mapped out the loop and what he had gotten from it *previously*. That was enough to shift into third gear, where he brought in curiosity as a different behavior.

I call this *retrospective second gear.* Retrospectively "driving" in second gear is a way of asking the *What do I get from this?* question after something has happened. This is important. I'm highlighting this because this shows that second gear still works *even after the fact.* You can learn from the situation while it is happening. And you can learn from it afterward, while you are looking in the rearview mirror. Our anxious sleeper was able to reflect on his previous experiences of going down the anxiety rabbit hole, which, when seeing how unhelpful it was for sleep, helped him avoid going down the hole yet again. Sometimes reflecting with hindsight is actually a better time for learning because you are less emotionally affected. Let the dust settle, survey the damage, make notes, and then learn. And you can do this over and over, as many times as you like, as long as the juiciness of the felt experience is still accessible.

By juiciness, I mean being able to recall how rewarding (or unrewarding) the physical sensations, emotions, and thoughts that resulted from the behavior were. This is not intellectually figuring something out or mental finger-wagging at yourself. It's not about *should.* Retrospective second gear is retrospectively recalling the facts: just noting what happened and how rewarding it was, without editorializing. That editorial mental chatter just gets in the way and distracts you from accurately recalling the scenario, making it harder for you to engage with the embodied experience that emerges from that recollection. The embodied, felt experience is that juice that signals to you how rewarding your brain determined the experience to be. If it still has juice when you recall it, you can keep learning from it.

Here's an example to make sure you understand how retrospective second gear works. I've worked with a lot of people who struggle with binge-eating. They come into my office, break down because they had a binge, and then start "shoulding": I *should* have done this, I *should not* have done that. As the joke goes, they "should all over themselves."

To break this unhelpful obsession with what might have been, I ask my patients to recall the most recent binge, one that's still fresh in their memory. This is the essence of retrospective second gear: looking back and mapping out the results of previously performed habit loops. I ask them to do this without judging themselves—that is, to simply describe what happened (behavior) and what happened next (result).

Once they've described the scene of the binge—perhaps how they were out of control or on autopilot—they will often describe how they woke up the next morning feeling bloated, hungover, or mentally and physically exhausted. And that's what we focus on: the result of the binge, the *morning-after part*. What did your body feel like? *Awful*. What was your emotional state? *Awful*. What was your mental state? *Awful*. Then I ask, "Looking back on this now, what did you learn?" Here's an example:

Trigger: Getting into an argument with a family member
Behavior: Bingeing
Result: Feeling physically, emotionally, and mentally awful (with no improvement in family relations)

After this little first and (retrospective) second gear exercise is over, often there is a realization:

"So that binge wasn't a total failure."

"Not if you can learn from it," I say.

That's retrospective second gear in a nutshell. As long as that replay of the loop is fresh enough in the memory, it can help build disenchantment.

Mindset Matters

There's a trick to being able to utilize retrospective second gear effectively, squeezing all of the juice out of that past experience so that you can maximize your learning. You might remember that I mentioned Carol Dweck back in chapter 6. She's the Stanford researcher who coined the terms *fixed mindset* and *growth mindset.* Dr. Dweck defines fixed mindset as when you believe your basic intelligence and abilities are immutable: you've got what you've got and have to utilize them the best you can. Growth mindset, on the other hand, is a belief that your abilities can be developed and improved over time.

Dr. Dweck has been studying mindset for decades. According to one definition, a mindset is a set of assumptions, methods, or notations held by one or more people or groups of people. Or simply put, it is a person's world view. Our mindset or world view can be so habitual that it colors how we interpret events, influencing what choices we make and how we learn. It can even contribute to what is called mental inertia or groupthink when individuals with similar world views come together and start feeding off of one another. Think mob mentality here. In other words, mindset is a big deal.

How do we develop a particular mindset? Here's a hint: it has to do with reward-based learning. Let's use a simple example, say, chocolate. If you get stressed (trigger) and you eat chocolate (behavior) and you feel a little better (reward), your brain learns something: if you are stressed, you should eat chocolate to feel better.

I think of this as learning to see the world a certain way: we put on chocolate-colored glasses, and the next time we are stressed our brains say, *Hey, eat some chocolate, you'll feel better.* That's where sayings like "she wears rose-colored glasses" and "he wears dark-colored glasses" come from. These are euphemisms for people who always see the world a certain way: rosy suggests that we're always seeing the world from a glass is half full, and dark is the glass is half empty world view or mindset. And yes, you can learn to wear the chocolate, or worry, or any other type of mindset glasses. The more you wear them, the more you forget that they are on your face—they become a part of your identity.

The concept is pretty simple: you learn to see the world in a certain way based on your previous experiences. Each time you do something that reinforces your learning, the lenses of your world-view glasses get a bit thicker, and the fit also gets more comfortable.

Dweck has mostly studied mindset in education and school settings, but her work is pretty relevant for, well, just about everything we do, because mindset colors how we see the world. She is famous for describing the two types of opposing mindsets that I've mentioned above: fixed and growth.

According to Dweck, individuals can be placed on a continuum according to their implicit views of where ability comes from. If you believe your success is based only on innate ability, basically what you were born with, you would fit into the category of a fixed mindset. On the other hand, if you believe that progress is based on hard work, learning, and training, you are said to have a growth mindset. What mindset do you identify with most?

You might not even be aware of your habitual mindset, whether you are more on the fixed or growth end of the spectrum, but you need only look as far as your behavior to get a sense of what it might be. This often becomes very clear when you look at your reaction to failure, for example. Fixed-mindset individuals dread failure because it is a negative statement about their basic abilities and a reminder of their inherent limitations. On the other hand, growth-mindset individuals don't mind or fear failure as much because they realize their performance can be improved; indeed, learning comes from failure.

This makes sense because if you believe that you were born with your particular intellectual capacities, for example, every time you fail, it's a reminder of how limited you are. "Oh, I can't do any better, this is as good as it gets for me." On the other hand, if you have a growth mindset, you can see failure as a learning opportunity instead of as a failure.

Let's use an example of walking down the sidewalk. If you have a fixed mindset and trip on something, you might beat yourself up for being a clumsy person. In the same situation, if you have a growth mindset, you might say to yourself, *Hmm, I tripped. What can I learn from this?* In a growth mindset, you can even question the notion of failure itself a bit. What does it mean to fail? If you learn, does what happened count as a failure?

Dweck even argues that the growth mindset will allow a person to live a less stressful and more successful life. This also makes sense, because in a growth mindset, you're always learning and gaining from your experiences. In her book, *Mindset: The New Psychology of Success,* Dweck advises, "If parents want to give their children a gift, the best thing they can do is to teach their children to love challenges, be intrigued by mistakes, seek new strategies, enjoy effort, and keep on learning. That way, their children don't have to be slaves of praise. They will have a lifelong way to build and repair their own confidence."

I love her phrase *enjoy effort*. It's kind of hard to enjoy what is happening when we are clenching our teeth together as we try to force something to change, as we beat our heads against the wall. But what happens when we start getting curious about our experience, loving the challenge, getting intrigued by the mistakes?

I find it helpful to extend these concepts to your direct experience so that you can use awareness to help you move into a growth mindset instead of getting stuck in a fixed mindset while you are driving in second gear.

To get a sense of how to do this, explore the following: What does your body feel like when you have a fixed view—that is to say, are closed to someone else's ideas or feedback about your own ideas?

You might have noticed that your body feels closed down or contracted, as if you are blocking yourself from allowing different information to get in and thereby contaminating your world view. Interestingly, this may have evolutionary parallels. When you are, say, being chased down and cornered by the proverbial saber-toothed tiger, your job is to fold up into a little ball, as small a target as possible, so that you can protect your vital organs.

What does it feel like when you are in a growth mindset? You are open in all ways to new ideas. Can you feel that in your own experience? Only in a growth mindset are you open to learning.

What mindset are you usually (or habitually) in when you fall into an old habit loop that you've desperately been trying to change? When you judge or beat yourself up, of course you are closed down because you are being attacked (even if you are attacking yourself). Here's an example.

One of my patients had the not-so-healthy habit of drinking a pint of vodka every night (the equivalent of eight shots of hard liquor). She would come home from a stressful day at work and start drinking as a way to wind down as she started cooking dinner. She had come to me for help when after several years of this behavior, she realized it was really harming her health, both physically and mentally. I gave her some basic instructions on how to use first gear to map out her habit loop (that part was easy for her), and then to zoom in on the results of her drinking in second gear. Over the course of a month or so of seeing pretty clearly that alcohol wasn't her friend, she was able to cut down to only four drinks a night. A month later, she pieced days of sobriety together, stretching these such that she could go nearly a week without a single drink. When she told me about her progress at her next clinic visit, she wasn't happy about it: she saw this as a failure. Why couldn't she stop drinking altogether? On top of this, she was beating herself up over "failing."

How could she move from a fixed mindset—of herself as a failure and unsure that she could quit—to a growth mindset?

When my students or patients are suffering under the weight of never-ending anxiety, a stubborn habit, or out-of-control addiction, I encourage them to see if they can envision these experiences as teachers. Teachers help us learn. When we learn something, we feel good (it is rewarding). Our best teachers do their magic and help open us to seeing the learning in hardship, even when we are struggling and reflexively close down or turn away from the pain. At these times, I ask my patients and students to see if they can bow to these moments of hardship as teachers, which helps them open up so that they can learn from them, instead of habitually closing down with the first hint of struggle.

When my patient described how she had failed at staying sober for longer than six days at a time, she added, "Well, I guess it's two steps forward, one step back."

I asked her what it felt like over the past several months to have learned so much about how her mind worked and to have gone from drinking a pint of hard liquor a day to enjoying stretches of sobriety.

"It feels good," she said. (In that moment, she was opening and moving into a growth mindset.)

Then I asked her about those "steps back." Was she was able to learn something about her habits and herself, something that she might not have learned otherwise? (Especially if she was stuck in a habit loop of self-judgment and in a fixed mindset.)

I asked, "If you learned something, does that count as moving backward?"

"No, I guess not," she said, realizing that learning actually counted as (and felt like) moving forward.

We talked a bit more about all the progress she had already made in a short period of time, and we discussed how she could acknowledge each "slipup" as a form of instruction, opening to it as a learning experience that could help move her forward. She left my office with a skip in her step, seeing how she could learn from her experiences and at the same time step out of the habit loop of beating herself up. She was almost looking forward to the challenges that lay ahead.

I love the saying: "Running away from any problem only increases the distance from the solution." *Two steps forward, one step back* becomes obsolete when we stop getting in our own way. All experiences move us forward if we are aware and open to learning from them.

TAKE A MOMENT now to see if you can recall a recent habit loop. Map it out in your mind (first gear). Ask yourself, *What did I get from this?* Check to see if you are closing down or judging yourself (fixed mindset), and instead imagine it as a teacher (growth mindset). Ask yourself, *What can I learn from this?* and feel into those results (retrospective second gear). Repeat.

CHAPTER 13

Fixing the Fix: Dana Small's Chocolate Experiment

ONE OF MY favorite neuroscience experiments was performed by a friend of mine, Dr. Dana Small, a neuroscientist and food researcher at Yale. In her job, she gets to design experiments to test how different types of food and sources of calories affect the brain. And to do so, she has created all sorts of crazy contraptions to deliver everything—from milk shakes to different smells—to people in a brain scanner. (Imagine having a research participant lying down in an fMRI scanner and you're in a control room twenty feet away trying to pump different types of milk shakes into their mouth while they are keeping their head still. Not an easy thing to do!)

Dr. Small started her food research as an intrepid young PhD student at Northwestern University, where she was trying to measure brain activity when people ate chocolate. Back then, she used a positron-emission tomography scanner—PET scanner, for short—to measure brain activity, because it is a little more forgiving than an fMRI. (In the PET scanner, her subjects were able to eat while their brain was being scanned, rather than having to keep their head completely still, as they would in an fMRI scanner.)

Dr. Small had participants in her study choose their favorite chocolate bar, and then she'd feed them bites of it while their brains were being scanned. As they were fed, they were asked to rate, on a scale of –10 to +10, how much they would like another piece: –10 was scored as "Awful—eating more would make me sick," and +10 was scored as "I really want another piece." Given that it was the subject's favorite bar, they naturally tended to start the study by rating it as +10.

Over time, though, the ratings started dropping down to something like a +5—"Pleasant. Another piece would be nice." Then the ratings dropped down to a neutral spot, while Dr. Small kept feeding them.

No surprise, their ratings kept going down, right through –5 —"Unpleasant. I don't want to eat any more"—and all the way to a –10: "Awful. Eating more would make me sick."

Over a short period of time, people went from really wanting more to feeling disgusted.

While all of this was happening, Dr. Small was measuring their brain activity; she found something fascinating. The posterior cingulate cortex—the brain region that is activated when we get caught up in experience, but which also quietens down when we meditate, are mindful, or otherwise let go—was the only brain region that was activated during *both* delight and disgust. This means that the activation of that cortex happened during craving *and* aversion. "I really want more" and "I really want this to end" activated both times.

Dr. Small's study showed that wanting more activates the same brain region as wanting less. The common denominator here is craving or wanting, or more precisely, getting caught up in wanting more or getting caught up in wanting less. Notice the push-and-pull element here: a pulling of the pleasant things toward us (or holding on to a thing we like when we have it) and a pushing away of an unpleasant thing, or an effort of distracting ourselves when we are experiencing something unpleasant.

Now, why is this important for changing habits? Let's start with overeating habit loops as an example. If you really like chocolate—substitute your favorite food or activity here—you see some chocolate and want to eat it. After eating it, you feel good at least for the moment, so your brain says, *That's good, do that again.* If you do this activity too much, what happens? Well, it depends on whether you are paying attention or not.

If you are like the people in Dana's chocolate experiment, you pay attention because you're asked to do so. Having to rate how much you want more helps you see more clearly when you've had enough. But in the real world, we are more often mindlessly eating (or mindlessly performing whatever the behavior is), so we tend not to notice when we've reached the tipping point from pleasure to displeasure.

If you train yourself to be aware, though, it's a different story. My lab has even mapped out this disenchantment process using focus groups made up of people from our mindful eating program. Simply by bringing their awareness to the results of eating, individuals in our program learn to enjoy some chocolate, for example, but because they are now paying close attention, they are more able to change their eating patterns and avoid overindulging or overeating. In one pilot study, we found an average of eight pounds of weight loss after two months of participants using our Eat Right Now program, without any specific dieting instructions. We simply emphasized paying attention when eating and stopping when full. This study was proof that mindfulness may be a different and really effective way to approach weight loss without relying on the traditional willpower-based approaches.

Bringing awareness to the results of your behaviors as a way to facilitate habit change goes beyond eating; it may also work with habits like worrying. One example would be planning for the future. Planning is like chocolate—a little tastes good, but too much of it can be counterproductive, as it can induce anxiety about what can go wrong.

So if you are struggling with habit loops involving overindulgence, such as overeating, overplanning, or overthinking, see if you can do your own version of Dana's experiment the next time you start to get caught up in the loop: pay attention as you over-*whatever.* Ask yourself, *What do I get from this?* (second gear), and see if you can identify exactly when the scale starts tipping from delicious to neutral to unpleasant. Does this help you stop at that tipping point (or at least slow down)?

Attitude Is Everything

Taking out the garbage is seldom seen as one of the highlights of our day. But let's think about the role attitude plays in an action such as taking out the trash. If it is time to take out the garbage and you do so with a bad attitude, guess what? You're learning to pair taking out the garbage with something that is bad or unpleasant. On the other hand, if you realize that you have to take the garbage out anyway and don't see it as a big deal, you'll learn that taking the garbage out isn't a big deal. And it will be easier to do the next time and the next and so forth, even when it's the middle of the winter or pouring rain. Changing your attitude toward even the simplest tasks can have a huge effect on your life.

Here's a quote that has been attributed to several sources that sums this up nicely:

> Watch your thoughts. They become words. Watch your words. They become actions. Watch your actions. They become habits. Watch your habits. They become character. Watch your character. It becomes your destiny.

That's true not just for taking out the garbage, but for everything you do in life. If every time you start struggling with a habit loop, you think the equivalent of "not this again" or "I'm not going to be able to deal with this—this is never going to work," then you'll likely add a second unhelpful habit on top of it:

Trigger: Start to struggle
Behavior: Think it will suck (fixed mindset)
Result: Increased likelihood of its sucking

Also, you'll have to deal with the original habit loop for a lot longer because you'll keep reinforcing both habit loops: the one you are struggling with *and* the "bad attitude" habit loop.

On the other hand, if you can start to practice bringing a playful curiosity to your experience as you drive in first and second gears, you get a three-fer: (1) the habit that you are struggling with gets easier to work with; (2) you learn to let go of unhelpful attitudes (seeing that they aren't rewarding); and, (3) you develop the helpful habit of being curious (you'll learn just how rewarding this is in Part 3). See if you can check in with your attitude more regularly.

When something is really ridiculous or absurd, it becomes hard to take it seriously anymore, so it no longer has such a hold on you. Thus, mindfulness can help you pay much closer attention to what your mind is caught up in and allow you to see how absurd it is that something sucks merely because you convinced yourself that it was going to suck. This realization can also enable you to forgive yourself for having set up that harmful habit in the first place. Remember how one of my patients would catch herself when starting to get stuck in a self-judgmental anxiety habit loop? She'd simply say to herself (with a little chuckle), *Oh, that's just my brain.* It's important to always be kind to ourselves, rather than beating ourselves up for the way our brains are set up.

You can bring that same playful attitude to any thoughts and emotions that come up. Instead of fighting against them or pushing them away, you can simply *and playfully* recognize them as thoughts and emotions. That's what the attitude of curiosity is all about. You can get really curious about those feelings and begin to track your habitual responses to them; in this way you can see how much they are driving your life. When you bring in this curious attitude, they are much less likely to have the power they once had over you. It becomes obvious that they are just thoughts and sensations in your body. Yes, they may be driving your life for the moment, but they do not constitute who you are.

You can even turn those thoughts and emotions into your teachers. Instead of getting frustrated that you're struggling or failing to make faster progress, get curious. Since the thought or emotion is already there, you can use it as a way to explore all the different ways that you react to it. Here's an example. You notice that you are getting frustrated.

Trigger: Start to feel frustrated
Behavior: Notice the habitual reaction and ask, "What do I get from this?"
Result: See how unrewarding the old habit is; get disenchanted with feeding the frustration (second gear)

See if you can bring a kind, playfully curious attitude to your habit change process. If you notice you are getting afraid while you are working with a fear-based habit loop, or if mapping out an anxiety habit loop makes you anxious, see if you can distance yourself a little from the feeling. Take a deep breath and remind yourself that this is your brain trying to be helpful and that it's getting a little off track. If frustration or some other bad attitude arises, do you close down or get stuck in some fixed mindset habit loop? If so, take a moment to map that out and see what you get from it. The idea is to realize just how unrewarding that attitude is and to start the process of unlearning it. As you become disenchanted with it, over time, when the attitude pops up again, just notice it and remember that this is some crazy habit you've set up. That simple act of being aware will help pop the old habit bubble and support a new attitude of openness and curiosity.

CHAPTER 14

How Long Does It Take to Change a Habit?

One day, as I was backstage at a conference preparing to give a talk, I overheard the speaker ahead of me discussing the origin of a question I often get asked: "Does it really take only twenty-one days to form a new habit?"

To illustrate her question, the speaker went on to quote a cosmetic surgeon named Maxwell Maltz, who observed that it took about twenty-one days for any patient of his to get used to their new, different-looking face when they got a nose job. Problem is, I have been unable to find any peer-reviewed studies that back up his claim. So while twenty-one is a generally accepted number (as in, it has been plastered all over the Internet enough times and places that it may outlive anyone reading this book), there's no real evidence that it's true.

Habit loops are formed simply and easily: do something, and if it's rewarding, given a chance (and a trigger), you'll likely do it again.

On the other hand, if you are trying to make a new habit stick—one that doesn't have an immediate and clear reward—actually, all bets are off, because you have to take into account everything from genetics to your motivational state to the situation you're in to the behavior itself. Habit formation is a bit more complicated than that figure of twenty-one days would lead us to believe.

This is borne out in the studies, of which there haven't been many. For example, in 2009, Phillippa Lally and her colleagues at the University College London published a study entitled "How Habits Are Formed: Modelling Habit Formation in the Real World." They found a range of 18 to 254 days for behaviors to reach "automaticity." Not only was this range rather large, but since the study lasted only 12 weeks, it was also completely reliant on mathematical modeling. To boot, only 39 of the 62 study participants showed a "good fit" to the model (good fit means that the data points were close to the theoretical graph curve). I'm not knocking this paper—it's very hard to do this work with so many variables at play.

But we can reduce those variables—and by doing so, perhaps come up with a realistic time frame in which new habits can be formed—by doing a couple of things: we can pick a specific behavior to study, and we can measure the changes in its reward value.

And that's exactly what my lab did.

In fact, there's a decades-old literature that goes way beyond aspirational, and very much into the not-just-Internet-based believable but *believable* believable because it has been studied and replicated in multiple experimental paradigms (mice, monkeys, men). In the 1970s, two researchers, Robert A. Rescorla and Allan R. Wagner, put forward a now-famous mathematical model that bears their name. You math geeks out there, take a look at the formula below. (The rest of you can just skip the next three paragraphs; I promise not to quiz you on it later.)

The Rescorla-Wagner reinforcement learning model* looks like this:

$$V_{t+1} = V_t + \alpha\delta t$$

The model posits that the current reward value (V_{t+1}) of a given behavior is dependent upon its previous reward value (V_t) + a learning signal ($\alpha\delta t$). The learning signal is dependent upon what's called a prediction error (δt), which is a discrepancy between an actual outcome of the behavior and what is expected. That learning signal maps onto brain regions such as the OFC (among others). Don't worry so much about α; it's a static subject-level parameter (a constant).

Let me repeat that in non-math speak. Basically, when you perform a behavior (e.g., eat a piece of cake), your brain first lays down a memory of how rewarding that behavior is (e.g., cake is yummy!). Remember, this value is determined based on all sorts of factors, including context, emotional state, and so on (e.g., people, places, and things associated with the behavior), which get chunked together as a single composite value. Once that reward value is learned, your brain expects the behavior to give you the same amount of reward the next time you do it, based on how rewarding it was in the past. The problem is that your brain expects the value to be the same as in the past (eating cake = eating cake) even if the context is different (eating cake when hungry = eating cake when full). If you drink milk that is past its expiration date, as soon as you become aware that it has gone sour, you stop drinking it, because your brain signals that there is a discrepancy in what it predicted/expected to get and what it

* Boll et al., *European Journal of Neuroscience*, vol. 37 (2013): 758–67.

actually got (that's the prediction error for you math lovers who didn't skip). If you habitually eat cake without paying attention to the actual outcome—as in, how rewarding is it right now?—your brain won't signal that anything is amiss or wrong (no prediction error because cake = cake). But if you *do* pay attention to the actual outcome, and eating two pieces of cake isn't as rewarding as it was when you were five years old and could eat cake for breakfast, lunch, and dinner without gaining weight, this prediction error signals to your brain that it is time to update the reward value.

And this is the mathematical basis for second gear. This is how you learn. This is how you change habits.

Understanding this can have real-life consequences, including how quickly you let go of "bad" habits and learn "good" habits (don't worry about the math).

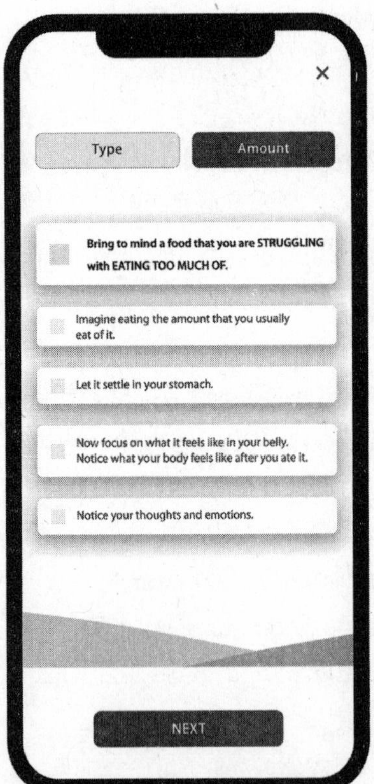

To study just how much and how fast reward value drops for overeating and smoking by using second gear, we built a "craving tool" right into the middle of the Eat Right Now and Craving to Quit apps. We have participants use this tool whenever a craving comes upon them. Step 1 of the tool looks like the image at left.

Then we ask them to rate how strong their craving is now.

Step 1 helps people (and our research team) get an accurate estimate of how rewarding the behavior is for them *right now*. For example, say they have a craving to eat cake, and then go through the craving tool exercise of imagining eating it. If the reward value is high, their craving will either stay the same or even go up (because they really want it now that they've imagined having it). It goes even higher if they are hungry.

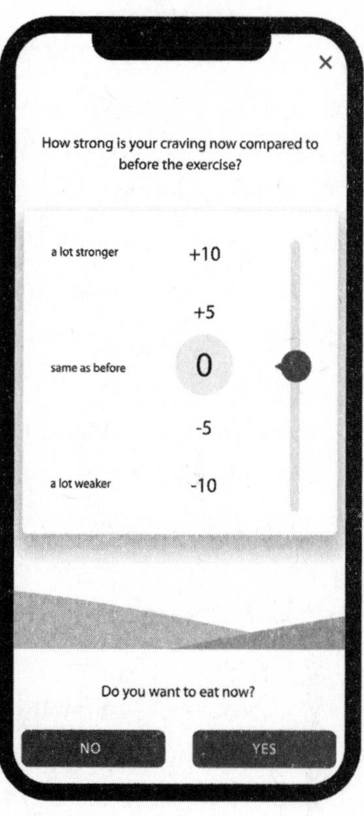

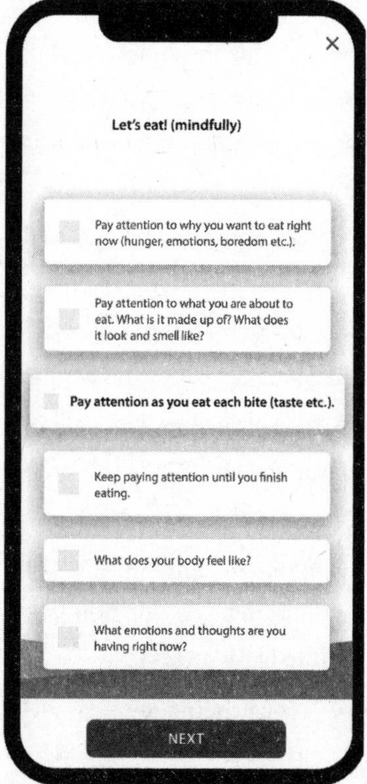

Then in Step 2, we have our subjects perform a mindful eating/smoking exercise, so that the actual outcome gets registered in their brain:

Here, if they pay careful attention when they eat three pieces of cake (instead of stopping at one), or smoke a cigarette, they see (and feel) for themselves just how rewarding the behavior actually is. We have them report on this immediately by rating how content they feel. We also have them repeat this a few minutes later in our Eat Right Now program because sometimes the full gut bomb from scarfing down a big piece of cake or a bunch of cookies doesn't register immediately. We have them repeat this each time they have a craving to make sure their brain gets accurate and updated information on how rewarding the behavior actually is, which helps to replace their old and outdated reward value memories. The more they do this, the more the new memories stick. (One person using the Craving to Quit app reported, "All of the cigarettes I smoked today were disgusting.")

Once those new reward values take hold, the next time someone is triggered to eat or smoke, simply going through Step 1 brings that value to the surface, and the craving to consume drops, which of course helps them step out of the habit loop and change their behavior.

Based on their subjective ratings (level of contentment after doing the behavior and craving to do the behavior again), we can calculate how many times it takes for the reward value of the behavior to drop. A postdoctoral fellow in my lab, Dr. Veronique Taylor, did all of the fancy Rescorla-Wagner (RW) modeling for two studies, one for smoking and one for eating. She found remarkably similar RW curves in both studies: after ten to fifteen times of someone's using the craving tool, the actual reward value dropped to close to zero.

Bringing these results together with other studies that my lab has published on brain changes in smokers after using the Craving to

Quit app for a month—together with a 40 percent reduction in craving-related eating after using the Eat Right Now app for two months—we're starting to get a much better handle on how the three-gear model works in the brain and behaviorally. Though of course there is a lot more for us to explore to firmly bring everything together.

But one thing is pretty clear from all of the math and measurement: paying attention is really important if you want to change a habit. If it's a habit that you desperately want to break, you can't tell, force, or wish it to stop, because these likely don't have an effect on its reward value. If it's a habit that you want to start in twenty-one days or twenty-one years, the chances of that happening based on reason, force, or wish are pretty slim on the same grounds.

You can't think your way out of a bad habit or into a good one. As much as we all have wishes and plans for our habits, our feeling body (which is where behavioral outcomes register) trumps our thinking mind.

See if you can hack your brain and put some of this conceptual knowledge into action by continuing to practice second gear (present moment and retrospective). See how quickly your Rescorla-Wagner curves drop from "rewarding" to "meh" to "no thanks."

Who Needs a Pep Talk?

If you are struggling at this point, don't worry. First and second gears aren't even focused on changing behavior yet. We'll come to that in Part 3. But for now let's think about a little train.

One of my favorite childhood stories was *The Little Engine That Could.*

In the book, there was a little blue train engine that started out her days as a switch engine, but when she's tasked with pulling a load of children's Christmas presents over a hill, she doesn't think she can make it up the hill.

The little engine is fighting great odds: she's got lots of devilish confidence-squashing thoughts in her head keeping her down. To combat them, she comes up with a mantra that's got a nice beat to it: "I-think-I-can. I-think-I-can. I-think-I-can. I-think-I-can."

The little engine hooks herself to the train of Christmas toys, and with trusty mantra in hand and head, starts up the mountain. "I-think-I-can. I-think-I-can." She beats back her demons, crests the hill, and descends to a hero's welcome of screaming toy-deprived kids who are now crying with joy. As she rolls down the hill, she changes her mantra to "I-thought-I-could. I-thought-I-could. I-thought-I-could."

So, what was the little engine's secret sauce? Engine oil? Elbow grease?

Actually, there's something else besides *effort* that's happening in this story. The little train is at first focused on the future (I think I can), and then on reliving the past (I thought I could). But what *really* gets her up the hill is not getting caught up in either. Instead, she's focusing on the present moment.

This is what you can take from this:

Don't trust your thoughts (especially the *shoulds*). Thoughts are just mental words and images that come and go and should be viewed with a healthy skepticism. This doesn't mean that thinking is bad. Remember, planning, problem-solving, and being creative are part of what makes us uniquely human and helps us in life. Thinking trips us up when we get caught up in worry or self-judgmental habit loops (that is to say, *should*ing—I should do this, I shouldn't do that). Those types of thoughts, especially the ones that have strong opinions, are the ones to be on the lookout for, as they just make us feel bad about ourselves.

Trust your brain. Your brain has evolved over eons to help you survive. Even though it doesn't have all of the answers and can sometimes lead you astray (e.g., worry thinking), it won't suddenly switch up the very old tried, true, and trusted mechanisms of how you learn (i.e., reward-based learning) and let you down now. The more you know how it works, and the more you see that mapping out habit loops and becoming disenchanted with old behaviors helps to move you forward, the more this trust will deepen.

Trust your body, or another way to put it, your body/mind, as the two aren't really separable. This is where reward values register. When you pay attention to the results of your actions, the actual physical sensations and feelings are what tell your OFC to update rewards.

Trust your experience. *You* are the secret sauce. Mapping out your habit loops over and over helps your brain see that you are *serious* and *committed* to changing your habits. Paying attention to that cause-and-effect relationship between your habitual behaviors and their results really does change their reward value, and really does help you become disenchanted with habits that aren't helpful and more enchanted with habits that are.

FGO: How to Work with Self-Judgment Habit Loops

Once when I was in college, I walked into the dining hall and sat down to eat lunch with some friends. There was a guy there sitting alone at a different table, and for whatever reason, I blurted out something that brought attention to the fact that he was on his own. For the life of me, I can't remember what I said, but I remember the rest of the event in vivid detail because my friends and I were so aghast at what I had just done. Even now, nearly twenty-five years later, I cringe as I write this. I wasn't a particularly mean person; I hadn't been a bully at school. We were all shocked at what had just happened, but mostly the poor kid I bullied, who could do nothing else but duck his head and finish eating his lunch.

The critical point of this story is what happens next.

If my head had been screwed on straight, I would have gotten up, gone over to the kid, and apologized. But I didn't. I was so shocked by what I'd done that instead I ducked my head, too, finished my lunch, and left.

Why can I so vividly recall this scene as though it were yesterday (heart pounding, stomach clenching—all the bells and whistles of autonomic nervous system arousal)? Because instead of flinging that hand grenade out of the room (by apologizing), I buried it deep inside me, and once in a while I'd privately take the pin out. I couldn't change what I had done, but I could beat myself up over it. Over and over.

Our survival mechanisms are set up so that we learn from our mistakes. We learn to avoid hot stoves after the first time we get burned, so that we don't have to get burned over and over. By beating ourselves up, we think we are learning because, after all, we are doing something, but that something isn't learning. It's just pulling that hand grenade pin again and again as we relive the situation, thinking that self-flagellation will magically fix the past.

Of course, I did learn from that ill-fated lunchroom moment. I haven't done anything remotely like that since, but I still carry the scars. And crucially, they are scars that don't need to be there—in fact, the injury never needed to happen in the first place. Had I apologized, I imagine we both would have nervously laughed my *What was I thinking?* brain fart off and moved on.

Over a decade later, after I'd been meditating for a number of years and had been researching the ins and outs of reward-based learning, I realized that there are two paths with every FGO (fucking growth opportunity) (props to my wife for introducing me to the phrase).

Path 1 is the "look and learn" healthy option, where we actually learn and grow. We bow to it as a teacher, looking at what happened and learning from the situation (including our own internal feedback).

> Trigger: Make a "mistake."
> Behavior: Look and learn.
> Result: Don't repeat said "mistake"; grow from the experience and move on.

Think of this as the whole-food, plant-based lunch option. It tastes good, we feel energized, and we know we're helping prevent rainforest habitat destruction in the Amazon Basin.

Path 2 is the "review and regret" option, a much less healthy one, where we get stuck in a self-judgment habit loop and don't really learn anything. We ignore or suppress the growth opportunity, focusing instead on our self-imposed self-flagellation.

Trigger: Make a "mistake."
Behavior: Judge or beat ourselves up (i.e., pick the scab off the wound).
Result: Old wound is now fresh and bleeding again.

A while ago I stumbled on the saying "Forgiveness is giving up hope of a better past." It's taken a while, but assisted by my own mindfulness practice and by the knowledge of how unrewarding "review and regret" habit loops are, I've forgiven myself, which opened the doorway so that I could really learn from that lunchroom FGO.

Trigger: Remember lunchroom brain fart.
Behavior: Notice clenching in my stomach and self-judgment start to play in my head. Give myself a mental hug and remind myself that I can't change what I did and that I have learned from it.
Result: Healed wound.

But enough about me—now it's your turn to reflect on your self-judgment habit loops. Map them out. By mapping them, you will start to be able to step out of those old habit loops and instead look and learn, not from what has happened in the past, but from how you meet yourself in the present, right at the moment when those self-judgment habit loop triggers come up. Review and regret = fixed mindset. Look and learn = growth mindset.

Can you look at the self-judgment habit loops that you mapped out (first gear) and shift into second gear, asking yourself: "What do I get from beating myself up? Can I see more clearly that self-flagellation perpetuates the process? Can I see now that paying attention to how painful it is to beat myself up can help me start to break that cycle?"

We'll build on this second-gear practice by bringing the BBO (bigger, better offer) to the FGO in Part 3.

Once you build enough momentum in second gear, really feeling that disenchantment with self-judgment and self-flagellation in your bones, you're ready to shift into third gear.

PART 3

Finding That Bigger, Better Offer for Your Brain: Third Gear

Curiosity will conquer fear even more than bravery will.

—JAMES STEPHENS

CHAPTER 15

The Bigger, Better Offer

There is a song by Henry Blossom and Victor Herbert—written in 1905, though it could have been written yesterday—called "I Want What I Want When I Want It." That title seems modern because we seem to be entering into the age of addiction. Never before has the world seen the convergence of our collective capacity to develop, refine, mass-produce, and distribute both chemical substances and experiences that are vastly more addictive than anything that's gone before. Forget cocaine—Facebook introduced the like button and we all became addicted. And this is fueled by every anxiety-provoking self-judgmental thought of "I want what s/he has" that pops up in our minds when we go online and see an algorithmically curated ad pop up about something that we did a Google search for a few days ago, or scroll through our social media feed and see a photo of someone's perfectly manicured life.

Humans have been battling cravings for millennia. There is a relief on the Parthenon in Athens, Greece, dating back to c. 440 BC that shows a rider trying to tame his wild horse. This depicts the struggle between impulses and desires (the horse) and our "restraining forces" of willpower (the rider). Modern-day approaches to behavior change have been heavily influenced, perhaps ironically, by the thinking of the Age of Enlightenment: so much emphasis in today's world is placed on individualism and reason. We believe that our strength lies in our ability to think critically. We believe that we can think our way out of behaviors driven by deep desires—forces much stronger than our prefrontal-cortex-based willpower. Knowing that a habit is bad for us isn't enough to change it. Even if we come up with the most well-reasoned plan to diet and lose weight, why is it that more often than not, we'll fall into yo-yo dieting (the endless cycle of losing weight, then gaining it back)? We are focusing too much on the rider to change habits and addictions and it's not working. In the United States alone, opioids and obesity have been described as epidemics.

Are there clues from the inadequacy of our individual, rational, and self-centric approaches that we can use as lessons for moving forward?

Our modern neural networks are still very much in hunter-gatherer (and not be hunted) mode. This means that reward-based learning shows up every time we smoke a cigarette, eat a cupcake, or check our email or news feed when we're stressed: basically, each time we reach out for something to soothe ourselves, we reinforce the learning, to the point where it becomes automatic and habitual. This is how we end up stuck in anxiety (and other) loops. As just one example, by the time one of my patients came to me to help him quit his forty-year smoking habit, he had reinforced his learning pathway roughly 293,000 times. How can willpower possibly compete?

Current psychological and behavioral approaches have relied almost exclusively on reason and willpower. For example, cognitive behavioral therapy (CBT)—which is the current National Institute on Drug Abuse's gold standard for addiction treatment, and perhaps the most widely used evidence-based therapy for mental health more generally—focuses on changing maladaptive thinking patterns and behaviors. If we again use the "horse and rider" analogy—where our desires are the horse, and our cognitive control capacities are the rider—CBT focuses largely on developing the abilities of the rider to face down stressors.

Yet, as substances and experiences become more addictive and accessible, the horse continues to get stronger and wilder. For example, in 2013, investigative reporter Michael Moss published an exposé of the food industry in *The New York Times Magazine*. Titled "The Extraordinary Science of Addictive Junk Food," the article outlined the deliberate and concerted effort of food companies to *engineer* food to be more and more addictive. The tech industry has followed suit, having millions (and in some cases billions) of users on which to test products ranging from social media platforms to video games. Products are designed to increase the user's engagement with them and to lead to further consumption of the product rather than to satisfy. Sean Parker, one of Facebook's "founding fathers," whose equity therein made him a billionaire, bluntly explained that Facebook is "a social validation feedback loop . . . exactly the kind of thing a hacker like myself would come up with, because you're exploiting a vulnerability in human psychology." He continued to explain that early in Facebook's development, the objective was "to consume as much of your time and conscious attention as possible."

Our poor brains—which, lest we forget, simply want to help us find food—are outwitted and outgunned. The primary neural structures that have been shown to be associated with cognitive control (for example, the dorsolateral prefrontal cortex) are the first structures to go off-line when faced with triggers such as stress. We've all experienced this to some degree: if we're stressed and tired late at night, we're much more likely to gravitate toward ice cream than toward broccoli.

To even the odds in our favor, if desires and cravings are fed in a process driven by reward-based learning, could we tap into that very process to train our minds, possibly without even needing to use extra time or effort?

The good news is that you've been doing the preparation work for this already. You've been building awareness by mapping out your anxiety habit loops in first gear and by bringing careful and clear awareness to the results of your behaviors in second gear. In the process, you're starting to rewire the reward values in your OFC. All of those "wax on, wax off, paint the fence" moves were preparing you for the big fight with your brain.

Awareness is also required in order to affect or change behavior: you have to become aware of or wake up to being in the middle of a habitual behavior before you can do anything about it. That's the essence of first and second gears. Plus, once the value of the behavior is registered, awareness helps you not only let go of old habits through becoming disenchanted by them (second gear) but also build healthy habits—repeated behavior moves toward automaticity as the habit loops get grooved.

This is an important point of divergence between current cognitive techniques and mindfulness practices. Reason (the rider) would say stop (and change your "stinkin' thinkin'"), yet in the majority of cases, impulse (the horse) would simply buck reason off and run free, unfettered and uncontrolled. In contrast, mindfulness would suggest paying attention: experience the consequences/results of the behavior and learn for the next time. The theory underlying mindfulness practices is directly in line with how reward-based learning works in the brain: that is, when you make sure the OFC gets accurate information, the relative value of an action can be updated, stored, and remembered for the future.

When this is fully in play, you don't have to rely on reason. Instead the relative value of the action becomes clearer and your cave person brain takes over. Remember, the survival brain is much stronger than its younger and weaker prefrontal cortical cousin. You don't try to think yourself out of a situation; the situation simply unfolds, following the natural principles underlying how your brain works to help you learn.

I hope you've developed your own evidence base for first and second gears at this point. If you have, you can probably relate to this journal entry from someone in our Eat Right Now program:

> One evening I reacted to an emotional scenario by diving into a treat. I fed the fire in an effort to quickly feel better. The momentary soothing sweetness became overridden by a body sense of a chocolate "gut bomb" and slumping in defeat and disenchantment.

If you are recognizing disenchantment pretty clearly in your own experience (not just *understanding* the concepts, but feeling them in your body), congratulations, you are ready for third gear.

Third Gear

Returning to the OFC, we know that for a behavior to be reinforced and sustained, its reward value likely must be greater than that of the behavior it is replacing. Think of the OFC like someone addicted to Tinder or some dating app. They are always swiping and swiping, looking for that bigger, better offer (BBO). When it comes to choosing behaviors, our OFC is always on the lookout for that BBO.

In fact, the OFC sets up a reward hierarchy so that you can make decisions efficiently without having to exert too much mental energy. This is especially true when you are making choices. Your OFC assigns each of your previously performed behaviors a value, and when given a choice—let's say between two behaviors—it can then choose the more valuable one. This helps you make choice decisions quickly and easily without having to think too much about them.

For example, I have performed many, many chocolate-eating behaviors, to the point where my OFC has a pretty detailed chocolate reward hierarchy set up. My hierarchy goes like this: I like 70 percent dark chocolate much more than 40 percent milk chocolate. When presented with the two, I don't have to think about it; I will always eat the 70 percent. Don't get me wrong, I'm not a monogamous 70 percent guy. I'll always try something new if it meets that 70 percent threshold (higher percentage, sea salt, a little cayenne, maybe some almonds), but rarely will I slum it into the 60s.

To break old habits and make new ones stick, you need to set up the necessary conditions.

First, you need to make sure that reward value of the old habit is updated. That's why you've been practicing second gear so much.

Second, you need to find that BBO.

For example, becoming clearly aware that smoking doesn't taste good reduces the reward value of smoking cigarettes (second gear), but people don't stand idly by on their smoke breaks doing nothing if they aren't smoking. Idleness quickly gives way to boredom and restlessness, which themselves don't feel particularly pleasant. In many paradigms for addiction treatment, the solution calls for a substitute behavior. Eating candy can occupy the time and satisfy a craving (to some degree), yet feeds the habitual process: triggered by a craving, one learns to eat candy instead of smoking, which sets up its own reward-based learning loop—and is the usual suspect for the average fifteen-pound weight gain that comes with quitting.

Third, for lasting habit change, you must find a *special type of BBO*, not just any old BBO.

You need to find a reward that is more rewarding and doesn't feed the habit loop through mere substitution of a different behavior.

Mindfulness might fit the bill. This is really important, so I'm going to repeat it: *mindfulness might actually give you more satisfying rewards*, as in a substitute that has bigger, better rewards but without the baggage of feeding the craving (more on that later).

Let's continue using stress as an example. What if instead of smoking or eating cupcakes you substituted a mindful curiosity as a new behavior? Two unique differences emerge here: (1) there is a shift from externally based behaviors (eating, smoking, etc.) to internally based ones (curiosity); and more important, (2) the reward value is materially different. You can also substitute a mindful curiosity for internally based habitual behaviors such as worrying, because curiosity feels better than anxiety.

Specifically, my lab has studied the reward value of different mental and emotional states and has found something really fascinating.

States such as meanness, stress, anxiety, and craving not only feel worse (i.e., are less rewarding) than kindness, wonder, joy, and curiosity, but they also feel more closed down while the others feel more open and even expansive. Remember, this makes sense from a survival standpoint. If you are on the run from the proverbial saber-toothed tiger and then get cornered, what do you instinctively do? You tuck yourself into a tiny ball so that you can make yourself as small a target as possible to protect your vital organs.

My lab has found that even the feeling of being closed—that mental state of contraction—lines up with activation in default mode network regions of the brain such as the posterior cingulate cortex (the one that I talked about in Part 1). In contrast, a curious awareness of present-moment experience not only correlates with the feeling of openness/expansion but decreases the activation in the same brain regions. Importantly, the latter feels better than the former—its reward value is higher.

Let's do a thirty-second experiment to illustrate this concept so that you can lock it in as wisdom based on your own experience.

Think of a time recently when you were anxious or afraid. Recall enough of the events and elements so that you can feel that emotion in your body.

Notice *where* you feel it in your body.

Now notice what it feels like. Does it feel more like a closed, contracted, or constricted feeling, or an open, expanded one?

Now think of a time recently when you were joyful. Recall enough of the events and elements so that you can feel that emotion in your body.

Notice where you feel it in your body.

Now notice what it feels like. Does it feel more like a closed, contracted, or constricted feeling or an open, expanded one?

Once you do the experiment yourself, it seems like a no-brainer, but you'd be surprised by how much of this stuff we have to confirm in my lab. So, led by a postdoctoral fellow in my lab, Dr. Edith Bonnin, we measured the reward value of a bunch of these emotional states in hundreds of subjects. We found that nearly universally, people prefer open to closed states. From doing this little experiment yourself, you might have noticed the same thing and realized that joy is an expansive feeling, while stress and anxiety are constricted ones.

Here's what mindful awareness can give you: (1) it helps you update the reward value of your old behaviors, (2) this practice is internally based (i.e., you don't have to head for the store or order more on Amazon when you run low), and (3) it's a great improvement over being stuck on that hamster wheel of a habit loop.

This is third gear in a nutshell: finding a BBO (i.e., a substitute behavior) that, because it is bigger and better, becomes a preferred behavior to your old habit. Due to its greater reward value, that BBO helps you step out of your old habit loop time after time at the beginning, and then once it gets grooved, turns into a new go-to for your brain (that is to say, a new habit).

We'll spend the rest of the book learning about and practicing different mindfulness techniques so you can get a taste for which ones fall into your 70 percent of goodness range.

If we once more go back to the horse and rider analogy, mindful awareness doesn't change the strength of one's desire, nor does it increase the strength of one's willpower. Instead, it modifies the relationship between the two. Instead of fighting to tame the horse, you as the rider can learn how to ride more skillfully. As awareness harnesses the energy and power of the harmful urge, the two harmoniously blend into one, perhaps transcending and transforming opposing dualities from a fight into something akin to a dance.

Third Gear, Defined

I'm going to give you two definitions of third gear—first a broad one and then a more specific and sustainable one. Then I will unpack them both.

> *Broad definition:* Anything that helps you step out of your old habit loop.
>
> *Specific, sustainable definition:* an internally based BBO that helps you step out of your old habit loop.

The key problem with the broad definition is the word *anything*. For example, if you were simply looking to break a bad habit—let's say, eating too much cake—and knocked yourself out with a blunt object every time you were about to do so, in theory, you would be successful. That's not the kind of habit change we're going for here.

For sustainable change, you need something that is practical and always at the ready so you can pull it out whenever it is needed (and isn't a mallet). More important, the type of reward that comes with a behavior is critical. Not only must it be more rewarding than the old behavior (BBO), but it can't reinforce the old habit loop in the process. We saw how this fails earlier, with the example of substituting candy for cigarettes, which can lead to weight gain.

To illustrate how important this is, I'll use an example from someone in our Eat Right Now program. She wrote:

> Something upset me today, and I was pretty emotional about it. Normally I would seek the biggest, sweetest, most savory meal or snack I could find to drown the emotional discomfort . . . I was standing at the bakery, staring at all the cakes, pies, cookies, considering what I might eat that I wouldn't feel too guilty about. I chose to take a moment to walk around the store before deciding. I happened upon a pack of fresh blackberries and thought that that would be a nice treat for me, even better than a pastry. So I bought the pack instead of something at the bakery, sat down in the café, and enjoyed each blackberry. Afterwards, I was quite satisfied. I left the store without any traditional dessert. As I sit here now, I still feel a bit emotional and upset about the event that occurred earlier in the day. And despite treating myself to some delicious fresh blackberries, I still have this hole I want to fill, this discomfort I want to ease. I want to fill it with something. Normally it would be food. But I don't want food. So what do I do in moments like this, in those moments of serious emotional discomfort where I've traditionally sought food to help?

This person describes her habit loop clearly: she gets triggered by emotionally upsetting events and eats as a way to drown her discomfort. Eating had become her go-to substitution for emotional discomfort. (Remember Dave? He also ate as a way to distract himself from his anxiety.) Substitute behaviors such as distraction or eating *are* BBOs, but they *still feed* the habit loop.

If you are really looking to become a Jedi master of your own mind, not to simply substitute one habit for another, not just any BBO will do. Dave figured this out on his own and kicked his substitute eating habit to the curb before going on to conquer his anxiety.

So how should this person fill those painful moments? Remember, she needs something reliable, so calling a friend or family member doesn't count. After all, what if no one picks up? And substituting cute puppy pictures is still a substitution strategy that feeds the habit loop, though it highlights another element that we haven't touched on yet: habituation.

THINK BACK TO the time before you ever had any alcohol. That first drink or two would pack quite a punch, perhaps followed by a hangover if you had too much. Your brain's reaction might have been to adjust its acetylcholine receptors to make sure it could handle such behavior if it happened again. And if you did continue to drink regularly, your brain would downregulate the number of receptors (habituation), and you would develop a tolerance to the effects of alcohol, needing to drink more over time to get the same effect.

In the same way, if you substitute Instagram puppy videos for your old habit, just as with alcohol, your brain also starts getting used to seeing cute pictures of puppies—it becomes *habituated*. In other words, your brain says, *I've already seen that*. And as was the case with requiring more drinks to get a buzz, you need more and cuter puppies to get your puppy fix. Not much of a long-term solution, is it?

In some traditions, this process is described as a hungry ghost. Picture a ghost with a huge stomach and a very long and narrow throat. No matter how much the ghost eats, it will never be satisfied

because it can't get food in its belly fast enough to fill it up—its esophagus is so long and narrow that the food that actually hits the stomach gets digested and moves on before the stomach can fill up.

Like big empty stomachs, voids don't feel good; your brain, when faced with one, thinks, *Do something! Fill this! This is terrible! I'm getting sucked into this awful pit of despair.* But you can't fill a void—by trying to fill it, you just perpetuate the habit loop.

But when you can see that this void is just made up of thoughts, emotions, and body sensations, you can step back, make sure you don't feed the loop, and let awareness do the work for you as you drive in first, second, and now third gears. Awareness is the essential driving process for each of these. In third gear, simply bringing a kind, curious awareness to those sensations and feelings will help you move from habitually feeling like you have to do something to fix a situation to simply observing your experience, watching the problems lessen and disappear on their own.

Curiosity calms the restless, driven quality of *Do something!* because, as we mentioned earlier, it feels tangibly different: it's more open and expansive. Better yet, that open and expansive sensation that comes from being curious feels good. Because curious awareness is rewarding in that way—an internally based behavior that enables you to step out of the habit loop, as well as feeling good and opening you to learning—it in itself *is* that special BBO. We'll explore more about how this affects worry and other habit loops later on, after you've had more of a chance to learn about and play with curiosity itself.

Ready for some third-gear practice?

Start by mapping out what types of BBOs you bring in as substitution strategies for your old habits. Do they feed the habit loop? Hint: do they result in restlessness, contraction, temporary fixes, and desire for more—all signs of habituation? Or do they help you step out onto a different path?

CHAPTER 16

The Science of Curiosity

I have no special talents. I am only passionately curious.

—ALBERT EINSTEIN

IN 2007, NEW York City did something radical (even though in London's subway system, this "innovation" has been around for decades, as it has in D.C., Toronto, and San Francisco)—it installed train arrival "countdown clocks" to most subway and train stations. Was it worth the investment of over $17.6 million? You bet.

The city subway planners were solving a problem for each commuter, one that links curiosity with how we learn, as a way to ease their minds and commutes.

To help you understand why and how they did this, let's start with the Internet's definition of curiosity: "a strong desire to know or learn something."

Curiosity is an innate, natural, and universal capacity that we all share, and it naturally blossoms most fully when we are children. When you can tap into your own curiosity, it helps you discover how the world works, drawing you in with a childlike wonder. Leon

Lederman, who was the second director of Fermilab and won the 1988 Nobel Prize in physics, has said:

> Children are born scientists. . . . They do everything scientists do. They test how strong things are, they measure the falling bodies, they're balancing themselves, they're doing all kinds of things to learn the physics of the world around them, so they are all perfect scientists. They ask questions, they drive parents crazy with why, why, why?

Yet not all curiosity is created equal. And curiosity wasn't always seen as a good thing.

You could argue that curiosity is what got Adam and Eve kicked out of the Garden of Eden. In the 1600s, the philosopher Thomas Hobbes described curiosity as the "lust of the mind," and Blaise Pascal in the same century added that curiosity is "only vanity."

Yet, knowing how curiosity works from a neurobiological perspective is the first step to reawakening our childlike wonder and tapping into its potential.

Curiosity Comes in Two Flavors: Pleasant and Unpleasant

In 2006, the psychologists Jordan Litman and Paul Silvia itemized two main "flavors" of curiosity, which they dubbed I-curiosity and D-curiosity. The *I* in I-curiosity stands for *interest,* the pleasurable aspects of the hunger for knowledge, while the *D* in D-curiosity stands for *deprivation,* the idea that if we have a gap in information, we go into a restless, unpleasant, need-to-know state.

In other words, curiosity—our drive for information—can either induce a pleasant state or reduce an aversive state.

Deprivation Curiosity, the Closed-Down, Restless, Need-to-Know Type: The Itch That Must Be Scratched

Deprivation curiosity is driven by a lack of information, often a specific piece of information. For example, if you see a picture of a movie star or another famous person and you can't remember her or his name, you might start racking your brain to remember who that is ("Oh, she was in that romantic comedy . . . the one where she . . . Urgh, what is her name?"). Trying to remember might even get you into a little bit of a contracted state, as though you are trying to squeeze that answer out of your brain. If the squeezing doesn't work, you google the movie that you saw the person in so you can find the answer. When you see the name, you feel a sense of relief because you are no longer deprived of the information. This extends to texting and social media as well. If you are in a meeting or out to dinner, and you feel or hear a text come into your phone, you might notice that suddenly it is really hard to pay attention because not knowing what the text says makes you restless. It's as though your phone starts burning a hole in your purse or your pocket. That fire of uncertainty is put out when you check your phone to see who texted you or read what the message says.

Here's another example. Think of what it feels like to be stuck in traffic without knowing how long the backup will last. Once you look at Google maps or Waze and see how long the delay might be, you feel a lot better. The amount of time you have to wait hasn't changed a bit, but your anxiety has been relieved simply by knowing how long you will be stuck. You've filled that knowledge gap and reduced uncertainty. This reduction of the stress of not knowing is the reason that New York City installed digital signs in their subway system that told people exactly how long they had to wait for the next train.

Riders would rather know that the next train is fifteen minutes away than not know that it is only two minutes away.

The relief of the negative state, the scratching of the itch, is in itself rewarding. That's why TV shows have cliffhangers—to drive deprivation curiosity. We have to know what happens, so we binge-watch!

Interest Curiosity: The Opened-Up, Wide-Eyed Wonder of Discovery

Interest curiosity is piqued when we become interested in learning more about something. Usually this isn't a specific piece of information (like the movie star's name), but a broader category. For example, did you know that there are animals who keep growing in size until they die? They are called indeterminate growers, and include sharks, lobsters, and even kangaroos. In fact, a twenty-pound lobster was discovered that is believed to be 140 years old, based on its size. That's one big old lobster! Isn't that fascinating?

Interest curiosity is like diving into an Internet search and realizing hours later that you've learned a whole bunch of stuff and your thirst for knowledge has been quenched. It feels good to learn something new. This is different from filling a deficit, simply because there wasn't a deficit there in the first place (that is, you didn't know you didn't know about big lobsters, but when you found out about them, you were intrigued and delighted). Unlike the D-curiosity—which is about destinations—the I-curiosity is more about the journey.

So why do we have curiosity in the first place? It turns out curiosity builds on (surprise!) reward-based learning.

Remember, reward-based learning relies on positive and negative reinforcement. You want to do more of the things that feel good and fewer of the things that feel bad. Back in cave person days, this was critical for helping us to find food and avoid danger.

This might also be the case with curiosity.

The idea that curiosity aligns with reward-based learning has been supported by a growing body of research.

One study by Matthias Gruber and his colleagues at the University of California–Davis had students review a list of trivia questions and rate their curiosity level in learning the answer. At peak curiosity, dopamine pathways in the brain fired with increased intensity and there was a stronger connection between reward centers and the hippocampus, a brain area associated with memory. Peak curiosity primed students to remember more information—not just the answers to their trivia questions.

Another study by Tommy Blanchard and his colleagues at the University of Rochester and Columbia University looked at how curiosity related to getting information is coded in the orbitofrontal cortex. (Remember that the OFC is associated with reward value and assigns value to different things [broccoli vs. cake].) In fact, in studies of primates, Blanchard's team found that primates were willing to give up rewards such as getting a drink of water in exchange for information.

Together, these studies suggest that the expression *thirst for knowledge* really is more than metaphorical. The acquisition of information follows the same basic behavioral pathways as reward-based learning and even has a literal reward value in the brain. We can add information to the list with food and water when it comes to survival. Old brain (find food, avoid danger) pairs up with new brain (get information to plan and predict the future) to help us thrive today. But when it comes to curiosity, is there such a thing as too much information?

Different Flavors, Different Rewards, Different Results

Each curiosity "flavor" has different "tastes." They fall into different categories in terms of how they feel in our bodies: deprivation feels closed, interest feels open. So what about their reward structures drives these behaviors? With deprivation curiosity, getting the answer is rewarding, but with interest curiosity, the process of being curious feels good.

This is critical for two reasons. First, with interest curiosity, you don't need something outside of yourself to get a reward—the curiosity is rewarding in and of itself—and second, because of its inherent nature, it doesn't run out.

In addition to interest curiosity's potential as a never-ending resource, it also feels better (i.e., is more rewarding) when compared to the scratchy, closed-down itch of deprivation.

So how can you use this knowledge to optimize curiosity-driven learning? First, let's graph out curiosity and knowledge in the form of an inverted U-shaped curve. Imagine curiosity on the vertical axis and knowledge on the horizontal axis. If you have very little knowledge about something, your curiosity is very low. As you start gaining knowledge, your curiosity goes up and eventually plateaus. As you gain even more knowledge, your curiosity decreases because the gaps in your information have been filled.

Put another way, curiosity seems to follow a Goldilocks rule with regard to information. Too little uncertainty about something fails to

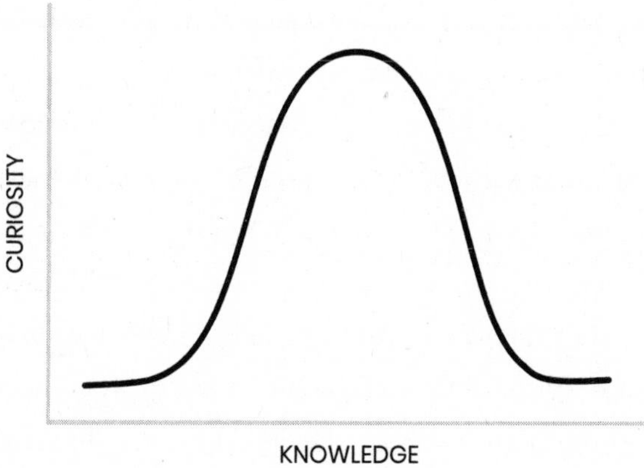

provoke curiosity (of the deprivation type); too much uncertainty provokes anxiety. Finding the sweet spot of curiosity requires staying atop the inverted U-shaped curve and having just enough information to sustain curiosity.

Using Curiosity for Habit Change and Learning

Most of us approach ourselves and the world with D-curiosity, like a problem to be solved. But we're all actually in the perfect place to build and sustain curiosity by playing deprivation and interest curiosity off each other. And you can leverage this interplay between the two to help you break old habits and build new ones. At this point in the book, you have built up some knowledge about how your mind and brain work—like learning about habit formation by identifying rewards. This helps you move up on that inverted U-shaped curiosity curve as you get more and more interested in how to harness your brain to do your bidding, rather than being a servant to your desires and habits. And yes, this links back to Carol Dweck's growth mindset—being open and interested in learning from our experiences rather than closing down at the first sign of "failure" (and sliding off the inverted U into a lack of interest or frustration).

Hopefully you've got enough conceptual information at this point to put you in the sweet spot to get even more curious about your own experience. This will allow you to move out of trying to think your way out of anxiety and into behavior change, and instead allow you to harness the power of curiosity, tapping into it as an inner resource that drives itself (because it is rewarding). You can probably already see how this primes you to stay at the top of that inverted U-shaped curve—getting more and more curious about what anxiety feels like, how it triggers worry and procrastination habit loops, instead of assuming you know everything about it and that the feeling never will change or that you have to find that magic pill or technique that will cure you of it. This will also help you work with any of your habits as well as become more and more curious about what you can learn when you get caught up in a habit loop.

As Einstein put it, "Curiosity has its own reason for existence. One cannot help but be in awe when he contemplates the mysteries of eternity, of life, of the marvelous structure of reality. It is enough if one tries merely to comprehend a little of this mystery each day. Never lose a holy curiosity."

Curiosity: Our Innate Superpower

Of all of our human capacities, curiosity is at the top of my list of most essential. From helping us learn to survive in the world to bringing the joy of discovery and wonder, curiosity really is a superpower.

In the fall of 2019, I led a seven-day silent meditation retreat for the U.S. women's Olympic water polo team. This is a group of amazing women who have won back-to-back gold medals in the past two Olympics. When they arrived at the retreat center, they were fresh off of winning the world championship *and* a gold medal at the Pan American Games. They are literally the best team in the world at water polo. What more could I teach them about being top athletes?

I was leading the retreat up in the mountains in Colorado with my good friend, Dr. Robin Boudette, with whom I often co-lead weekend workshops and retreats. About three days into the retreat, we had led the team on a hike to the top of an overlook that had an awe-inspiring view of the valley below. That's when I decided to drop the C-bomb on them. All week, Robin and I had emphasized the importance of bringing an attitude of curiosity to everything from meditation to eating, but we were saving our method for dropping into curiosity until the right time. And that time was now.

On the count of three, Robin and I both broke into the silence with a loud *hmm* (this is the type of *hmm* that we naturally emit when we're curious about something, not to be confused with the traditional mantra, *Om*). We had them repeat it with us, and a collective *hmm* reverberated its way across the rooftops of the world. This act got all of us out of our heads and into a direct experience of being curious.

Over the rest of the week the team took to this curiosity practice like fish to water. When they felt frustrated or stuck during a meditation practice, *hmm* seemed to help them explore what that felt like in their body and mind (instead of trying to fix or change it). When they got caught in a habit loop of worry or self-judgment, *hmm* could help them shift into third gear and step out of the loop. Instead of their minds spinning out of control and feeding more habitual self-judgment, they found that *hmm* could help them step back and see their habit loop component elements for what they were: thoughts and emotions.

Curiosity also helped them stay present in a nonjudgmental way to whatever their experience was. It proved to be stronger than any type of force or willpower they (habitually) used, and also brought a playful, even joyful attitude to the meditation retreat. (It is hard to take yourself too seriously when you are *hmm*-ing all day long.)

Over the years, I've found that I can teach this simple tool as a way to help people—regardless of their language, culture, or background—drop directly into their embodied experience and tap into their natural capacity to be curious. It also avoids the "head trap" of wanting to fill a knowledge gap, getting people right into that sweet spot of openness, engagement, and curiosity.

Curiosity (the interest type, not the deprivation type) fits all of the third-gear conditions perfectly: it is an internally based (and thus always available) BBO behavior that enables us to step out of our old habit loops in a sustainable way.

Here's an example of how curiosity is helpful, from a patient in our Unwinding Anxiety program:

> When I first started the program, I didn't quite buy into the benefits of curiosity. Today, I felt a wave of panic, and instead of immediate dread or fear, my automatic response was "Hmm, that's interesting." That took the wind right out of its sails! I wasn't just saying it was interesting, I actually felt it.

Sometimes I get the question "What happens if I'm *not* curious?" My response: "Use the mantra to drop right into your experience.

Hmm, what does it feel like to not be curious?" This helps them move from their thinking, fix-it mind state into a curious awareness of their direct sensations and emotions in their bodies, moving out of their thinking heads and into their feeling bodies.

How to Practice Curiosity

Let's walk through the curiosity exercise that I teach everyone on Day 1 in the Unwinding Anxiety app. This exercise works as a kind of "panic button" for when anxiety hits. It will take about two minutes.

First, find a quiet comfortable place. You can be sitting, lying down, or even standing up; you just need to be able to concentrate without being distracted.

Recall your most recent run-in or "incident" with a habit loop. See if you can remember the scene and shift right into retrospective second gear: focus in on the behavior itself.

See if you can relive that experience, focusing on what you felt right at the time when you were about to act out the habitual behavior. What did that urge to go ahead and "do it" feel like?

Now check in with your body.

What sensation can you feel most strongly right now? Here's a list of single words or phrases to choose from. *Pick only one,* the one you feel most strongly:

- ❑ tightness
- ❑ pressure
- ❑ contraction
- ❑ restlessness
- ❑ shallow breath

- ❑ burning
- ❑ tension
- ❑ clenching
- ❑ heat
- ❑ pit in stomach
- ❑ buzzing/vibration

Is it more on the right side or the left? In the front, middle, or back of your body? Where do you feel it most strongly?

Now let out your inner *hmm*—is that *hmm* on the right side or the left? In the middle, front, or back of your body?

Don't worry about what area you picked. They are all perfect.

Was there anything you noticed about being curious about what part of your body you felt the sensation in? Did being a little curious help with getting closer to this sensation?

If the sensation is still there, see if you can get curious and notice what else is there. Are there other sensations you're feeling? What happens when you get curious about them? Do they change? What happens when you get really curious about what they feel like? Follow them over the next thirty seconds, not trying to do anything to or about them, but simply observing them. Do they change at all when you observe them with an attitude of curiosity?

Here's an example from someone in our Unwinding Anxiety program:

> The Stress Test is amazing! To actually feel where in the body the stress is held and then to "drill down" into the actual sensations totally changes the experience. In the process of turning toward the stress and

> discomfort, I find they [bodily sensations] transform into sources of keen interest and lose the negative "spin" I put on them. Curiosity trumps anxiety! I have heard that many times, but to actually know it from the inside lands on a whole other level. I can see how this works, and that gives me the sense that I can do this.

This short exercise was just to give you a taste of curiosity—to support your natural capacity to be aware and even curious about what is happening in your body and mind right now, instead of getting caught up in a habit loop. If you noticed that by being curious you just gained even a microsecond of being able to be with your thoughts, emotions, and body sensations more than you have in the past, you've just taken a huge step forward.

That's third gear: it's a process of stepping out of your old habit loops and into the present moment. When you use *hmm* as a mantra, you bring out your childlike fascination, especially if you haven't used it in a while. *Hmm* helps you drop right into your direct experience, instead of getting stuck in your head trying to do something about those pesky habit loops or to fix yourself.

Whenever an urge to do a habitual behavior comes up—or even while you're in the middle of the behavior—see if you can practice shifting into third gear. Try to bring the attitude of curiosity even into second gear as you ask, *What am I getting from this?* so that you can open to the experience and move into a growth mindset (look and learn).

CHAPTER 17

Dave's Story, Part 3

HERE'S HOW DAVE supersized his curiosity to conquer fear and anxiety.

One clinic visit, Dave told me that his father had physically abused him as a kid. He'd be sitting there, minding his own business, and out of the blue, his dad would hit him. There was no apparent reason (not that there ever is a reason to hit your son); it was like Dave was simply a handy punching bag for his father. Dave realized that as a consequence of his abuse, his brain had been on constant alert since childhood—always looking out for danger. His brain had never been able to determine which environments were safe and which were legitimately dangerous, because his dad slapped him *randomly*, not systematically. (Remember the concept of intermittent reinforcement from chapter 3? It isn't limited just to getting people addicted to slot machines and social media.) Dave's brain couldn't use its reward-based learning processes to rate behaviors as safe or not safe, so it simply assumed nothing was safe (it was safer that way). He had been walking around on high alert (with high anxiety) for more than three decades.

This led Dave to an epiphany. He realized that his high alert mode was a habit he had taken on *as an identity*.

To combat this, I gave him a simple practice. I told him that when he felt as though he were on high alert, he should take a moment to get curious about what he was feeling, and he should also check to see if there actually was danger. I asked him to try it out in my office and report what his experience was. As he went through the exercise, he said, "Wow, those feelings just disappear when I go looking for them."

"Is there danger here now?" I said.

"No danger . . . calm," Dave said.

The high alert habit mode could be seen for what it was: sensations associated with danger. In the absence of danger, by simply getting curious about what those sensations felt like, Dave could see for himself that these sensations not only were inaccurate (signaling danger when there was none) but would fade on their own.

I sent him home to practice. He just needed some time and repetition to update his brain's old memory systems from "not safe" to "safe." Importantly, I wasn't trying to convince him that he was safe, nor asking him to convince himself. Instead we were training him to give his brain more accurate information.

Over time, Dave learned that he didn't need to be anxious all the time. Ironically, while he was enjoying significant calm stretches, which felt strange and different, his brain would chime in, wondering if there *was* something wrong (wearing those old habit glasses), whether he *should* be anxious.

Dave was demonstrating classic "savannah behavior." Remember, our brains evolved to take a "safety first" approach to life. If we're exploring a new part of the savannah, we have to be on the lookout for danger. We can relax only when we've mapped that territory over and over and haven't found any sign of danger. This is where the modern notion of comfort zone comes from. When we're in a place that is safe and familiar, we feel comfortable. This can be a physical place that feels safe (like our home), an activity that we're good at (e.g., playing a favorite sport or musical instrument), or even a mental space we inhabit (e.g., teaching seminars on habit change is my sweet spot, math not so much).

When we move out of our comfort zone, our survival brain starts warning us that we're moving into parts unknown—there could be danger out there. If we see the world as either safe or unsafe, the only options are comfort or danger: we're either in our comfort zone or in the danger zone (which many of my patients call the panic zone, because it feels so uncomfortable that they start panicking). That's how Dave described it to me: not being anxious was making him anxious because it was unfamiliar to him. In other words, the discomfort of being in a new mental space, even if that new place was the garden of calm, was triggering his survival brain to look out for danger. Who knows, calm could be dangerous.

Yet, there is actually another option. Going back once more to Carol Dweck's fixed vs. growth mindset, we can add a zone between comfort and danger: the proverbial growth zone. The world outside our comfort zone isn't always dangerous. We just need to check to see if it is. Whether we are exploring a new idea, an unfamiliar place, or a person we've just met, we can approach new areas with fear *or* we

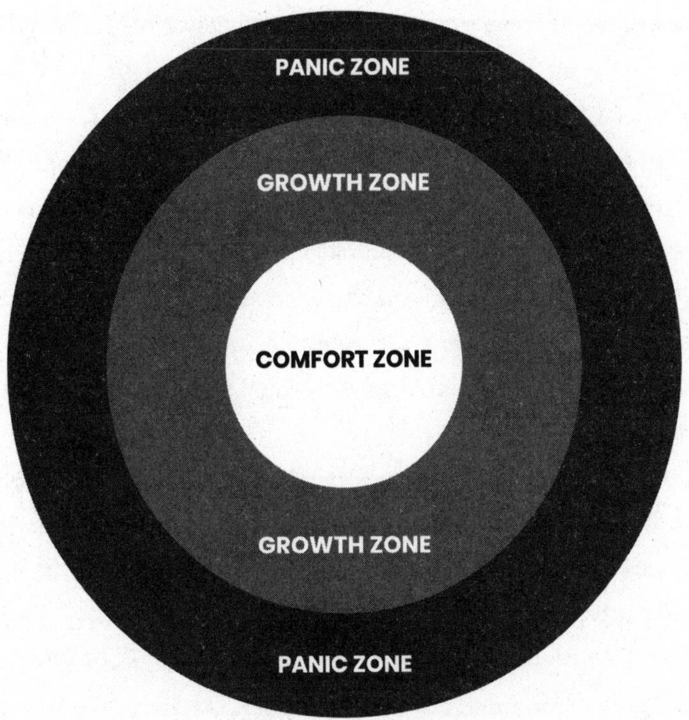

can employ an attitude of curiosity. The more curiosity we have, the more open we are to learning and growing from exploration, as compared to closing down or running back to our safe space at that first hint of discomfort. All of us need to keep this in mind: change can be scary, but it doesn't have to be. The more we can learn to lean into the discomfort of difference—recognizing that we might be nervous simply because something is new to us—the more we make ourselves at home in our growth zone. This is how we learn and grow, after all. As a bonus, the more comfortable we feel in our growth zone, the more this zone increases in size.

Dave and I discussed this in terms of a metaphor of friends.

Sometimes old friends can feel comforting because they are familiar, but they aren't necessarily good to hang around with now (like a childhood friend that was always making fun of you). Dave could bring awareness to this as well, noticing that because of its familiarity, anxiety had strangely been a comfort to him, yet he had outgrown it now. As he began to unlearn this old anxiety habit loop, Dave learned to live more and more in his growth zone, and with this, he started to learn to be more familiar and comfortable with ease, calm, and even joy. He found new friends, ones that would perhaps become lifelong companions.

Throughout this book I have emphasized curiosity. I've said that curiosity is a superpower that helps us replace old habitual behaviors with the simple "behavior" of curious awareness. With anything unpleasant (especially anxiety and panic), we tend to run away from it, which then becomes a learned behavior. Yet with curiosity, we can learn to turn toward it, or even lean into unpleasant things. All this curiosity can help us break free and step out of our old habit loops (it's amazing how comforting worrying is, isn't it?) as we learn to explore sensations in our bodies and minds and see them for what they are: thoughts and sensations that simply come and go.

Curiosity is different from willpower or grit. Grit is about resolve, but it takes a huge amount of energy, which gets depleted, leaving us at our worst (exhausted and defeated). Put simply, effort takes effort. When I go mountain biking, willpower helps me get in low gear and "grind" up a hill so I can get to the top. During a technical descent down a mountain or a tricky rock and root section, I find grinding gets me nowhere. If I simply aim my front tire at the rocks and try to power myself over them using only sheer strength, I end up falling.

Curiosity is different. When you are curious about something, it effortlessly pulls you in because it *in itself* feels good and rewarding. The more curious and open to your experiences you are, the greater your reserves of energy to explore. When mountain biking, curiosity rocks: instead of blindly throwing myself at a technical section, I can investigate all the different ways that I might creatively finesse my way through it.

When it comes to your own mental obstacles, hurdles, and habits, you have a lot of ground to cover, especially as you learn the rich and endlessly fascinating territory of your mind. So don't tire yourself out, trying to push your way forward. Let curiosity naturally move you forward, building your ability to navigate new challenges in the future and saving your strength for when you need it.

Also, curiosity naturally moves you from a fixed mindset into a growth one. The greater your curiosity and openness to your experiences, the greater the reserves of energy you have to explore. The function of curiosity is to help you learn, and you can do this only through active participation.

Over the course of a few months, Dave had discovered the power of curiosity. He wrote me an email:

> I think it's important for people to understand that I went from being terrified to even leave my bed to yesterday driving an Uber all over Rhode Island. Three weeks ago, I was too scared to drive my girlfriend to the airport. Yesterday, I did a drop-off at [the airport] with no anxiety. I don't even think about going grocery shopping now, but two months ago I couldn't even walk into Whole Foods. I've made a ton of progress, healthfully. I'm not hooked on pills or dependent on them to

> live my life. I'm changing my entire outlook and becoming a happier person.

This is not to say that Dave's anxiety has magically disappeared. Through tapping into his own curiosity and replacing his fear response with that as a BBO when anxiety comes on, rather than being driven by anxiety, Dave is back in the driver's seat, exploring life on his terms.

Take a Breath

Adults tend to be self-conscious about a lot of things, including saying *hmm* in public (or even to ourselves), even if it is soft or seemingly spontaneous. But that doesn't mean you can't start practicing curiosity in places where you feel *less* self-conscious, like in the shower, with the water running, where nobody can hear you *hmm*ing ("*hmm*, what does this soap really smell like?"). If you have kids, you can observe curiosity "in the wild" by watching three-year-olds and joining right in. But I'm also going to teach you a third-gear technique that you can use any time as a way to help you step out of old habit loops. It's a subtle, non-insecurity-inducing practice that you can do in the company of others and even at work.

Breathing Exercise

Third gear is about finding a readily available BBO that helps you step out of your old habit loop yet doesn't *feed* the habit loop process.

When we medical professionals call a code in a hospital for a patient who is down, we start at the very beginning with A-B-C.

A-B-C stands for *airway, breathing,* and *circulation.* We start with airway, because if a patient's airway is blocked, how can he or she breathe? Then we move right on to the B, for *breathing.* If you are breathing, there is a good chance that you are alive, so we medical folks can stop there without doing further damage.

If you are sitting in a meeting at work, there is a good chance that everyone there is breathing. Since everyone is breathing, if you happen to notice that you are about to get caught up in a habit loop like interrupting others or getting defensive about feedback, you can duck under the cover of normalcy and take a moment to pay attention to your own breathing as a way to step out of feeding *that* beast of a habit. You see, your breath is actually a great third-gear BBO:

1. Your breath is always available.
2. Paying attention to your breath helps you step out of your old habit loop.
3. Breathing doesn't feed the habit loop process itself.

There are a bazillion instructions and entire books dedicated to teaching you how to pay attention to your breath as a way to "anchor" you in the present moment. Feel free to read them. (One of my favorites is *Mindfulness in Plain English,* by Bhante Henepola Gunaratana.)

Here I'll give you the short version that you can use when you're in a meeting.

Sit, which you probably already are doing, or stand (if it's a standing meeting) in a comfortable posture. Do not close your eyes, or everyone will think you are sleeping. Ask yourself the question *How do I know I'm breathing?* and get curious to see where you feel the physical sensations (a silent *hmm* is appropriate here). You might notice the physical sensations of your abdomen moving in and out; you might notice your chest moving if you are a bit nervous and breathing shallowly. (If you notice that you're breathing through your nose, then you're already ahead of the game, as this can be pretty subtle.)

Once you've found where you notice your physical sensations of breathing, you can simply continue paying attention to your breathing, or if that gets boring or becomes challenging, amp up the curiosity by watching your body's natural processes that determine your breathing cycle, such as when the inhale/exhale stops and reverses course, or how long your body pauses between the in and out breaths. (Trust me—it's truly fascinating to watch yourself breathe!)

To apply the breathing practice to moments of anxiety, urges, and other things habit loop–related, try this variation.

Use your curiosity to check in and see where that anxious feeling or the urge to correct your coworker's last statement feels strongest in your body. Now slowly breathe in through your nose, right into that body part (don't worry about being anatomically correct here, just go with it). Let that breath go right into that feeling of anxiety or urge and hold it there for a few seconds before letting your breath out. If it doesn't sound too woo-woo to you, when you exhale, some of that feeling flows out with your breath. If you aren't into woo-woo, simply check to see if the offending sensation has changed with that cycle of breathing. Then do it again. Take a slow, deep breath, imagining that kind, curious breath going right into your anxiety. Let your breath wrap that feeling of anxiety in a warm blanket of curiosity and kindness for a second, and then breathe out, let it go. See if any of that feeling releases with your outbreath.

You can repeat this for just a few breath cycles, a minute or two, or until your boss gets suspicious because you look too calm and content.

Here's a real-life example of the productive use of breath awareness, from someone who was pilot-testing our Unwinding Anxiety program. This person happened to be at work:

> Found myself in a meeting feeling anxious about bringing up a difficult point. Felt my breath get a little shallow so got curious about it and noted it a little—"I wonder why" and "oh, here's anxiety"—and I rode it out and it went away! Third gear!

(That example was actually more a mix of breathing, curiosity, and a noting practice that you'll learn later, but you get the point.)

Here's another example:

> I was in a meeting today where I was getting some negative feedback that was a surprise to me. It was very interesting to feel the heat of a flush rise in my face and feel my stress reaction arising, but then step back from it. I was able to keep quiet for longer, listen better, and notice clearly the stress response happening to the other people in the meeting. Next step was being able to reach a level of calm where I can actually think clearly in that moment and formulate a coherent response!

Notice how curiosity isn't the type of superpower that magically gives you clairvoyance or on-the-spot clear and coherent responses to coworkers. It simply helps you step back and not get caught up in a habit loop.

The breath is a convenient object that you can use as a tree root to grab on to when you notice that you are starting to slide off of an anxiety habit loop cliff. Because what feels better: getting stuck in a habit loop that you've been trying to change forever (and perhaps beating yourself up over it), or stepping out of it?

You might also wonder why paying attention to your breath is not also just another distraction. Well, it's because paying attention to your breath keeps you in the present moment in an embodied way. In other words, you are staying with your direct experience, in the moment, rather than trying to escape it by going outside of yourself.

So, today, see if you can unselfconsciously play with building your mental curiosity muscles if you haven't yet, and see what it is like to add a bit of breath awareness practice to the mix. Both of these are great third-gear practices that help you step out of your old habit loops into new ones—habits that are more rewarding.

CHAPTER 18

What's Good About Rainy Days?

Before the invention of the Internet and other weapons of mass distraction, staying inside on a rainy day often meant using your imagination and discovering something to play with. For me, that often meant finding a toy that I could destroy in the name of science. Under the banner of "Let's figure out how this works," I would locate whatever hammer, screwdriver, or other tool I needed to take apart a toy to see how it ticked.

One day I was up in my room when I came upon a particularly tricky demolition problem—and I foolishly thought that tackling it required a knife. Being a Boy Scout, I had learned proper knife handling and was allowed to own (and sometimes carry) a knife or two. Sadly, as I did my dissection, I pressed too hard and the knife slipped, leaving a nice big gash in the middle of my thumb. Perhaps with the sixth sense of a future physician, I instinctively followed the basic life support protocol of "First call 911," which before the advent of cell phones consisted of running downstairs to find my mom. As I ran, I hastily applied a "tourniquet" with materials at hand: the index finger and thumb of my other hand. I must have made it to her with enough blood in my head not to faint, because I remember yelling with the sincerity of any kid who knows nothing about anatomy or medicine, "*I must have hit an artery!*" (To be fair to myself, the cut *was* deep enough that I still can make out the scar now, which nearly perfectly bisects my left thumbprint.) My mother, being a little older and wiser than I was, calmly reassured me that I hadn't hit an artery and helped me bandage it up.

What had happened? Well, I had been so caught up in dismantling whatever toy I was working on that I had *stopped paying attention* to how I was doing it.

> Trigger: Frustration with not being able to dissect toy
> Behavior: Ignore proper knife-wielding protocol; grab sharp object and push
> Result: Filet-o-thumb

And to be clear about the habit loop I mapped out above, it's not that I was in the habit of cutting my thumb open, but I did have a pretty ingrained habit of getting caught up in wanting to get something done, to the point that I wouldn't slow down, take a breath, and collect the right tools needed for a job, whether it was a loose screw somewhere in the house or a new gadget that required assembly.

> Trigger: Frustration with not wanting to stop doing something to get the right tool for the job

Behavior: Keep using the end of a fork to try to tighten the loose screw in the kitchen cabinet

Result: Stripped screw that now needs to be removed and replaced

I was pretty far along into adulthood before I recognized *that* habit pattern. And what helped me break it was seeing all of the screws and bolts I stripped by grabbing whatever utensil was at hand (second gear), and how much faster and cleaner I could get the job done when I took the thirty seconds to go to the garage and get the right tool (third gear).

Rules go out the window when we get caught up in habit loops. Haven't you tried using rules to change habits before, like "no sugar" or "always be nice" or "a drink of alcohol only if the Cleveland Browns win the Super Bowl"? How well have those worked? After three days of not having any sugar, you find yourself in serious sugar withdrawal, irritably snapping at everyone to get out of the way as you head for the liquor cabinet, knowing damn well that you were drunk when you made the Cleveland deal with yourself, so it doesn't count.

The problem is that rules are made to be broken, especially by kids who deem them to be "dumb." Why? Because kids haven't learned from experience. The prefrontal cortex can tell the limbic system that knives are dangerous, but the limbic system doesn't respond to reason. It has to *feel the pain* of the wound to learn its lesson. Which of course is exactly what happened to me: I didn't need to be told to pay closer attention when using knives in the future. I learned my lesson with that one fateful cut, and ever since then have followed the commonsense rule of paying attention when using knives.

Getting caught up in a habit loop and not paying attention can lead to the not-very-good combination of freaking out (I cut myself and I see blood, so it must be pretty bad) and jumping to conclusions (I've hit an artery). Here's another story that illustrates how important it is to pay attention and how to keep your cool when blood is involved.

One evening while I was a third-year medical student all hopped up with the excitement of actually being in the hospital taking care of patients, things were pretty quiet on the wards, so my attending physician (our team leader) gathered the medical students and resident physicians around him for a team-bonding "teachable moment." Teachable moments often involve some hands-on procedure that involves gloves and feces and rites of passage, so I braced myself for what might be about to happen.

But instead of making one of us do some character-building procedure, to my surprise, he told us a story about when he had been a young hotshot resident physician himself. Before continuing, he told us to remember the sentence "If someone dies, first take your own pulse."

As a young resident physician, this doctor had been sitting in the ICU minding his own business when he heard the heart monitor of one of his patients switch from the usual *beep, beep, beep,* "patient alive, all good" sound to the *beeeeeeeep,* "patient might be dead" sound. The doctor flew across the room, and in what must have been milliseconds, landed his fist right on the bull's-eye of that patient's chest, administering a potentially lifesaving precordial thump. (Precordial thump is the technical term for giving someone a big blow to the chest, which perhaps counterintuitively is a great way to get a stopped heart beating again.)

To his surprise, the patient said, "Hey, what did you do *that* for?" Doing the postmortem on the sequence of events (because the patient was obviously alive), my now very embarrassed professor realized that the heart rate monitor had merely slipped off his patient while he was sleeping . . . and from across the room, if you don't check the vital signs, it is pretty easy to mistake a slumbering patient for a dead one.

The doctor went on to explain how he (1) had been paying attention to something else (not this patient), (2) had freaked out, and as a result (3) had jumped to a conclusion, instead of remembering to check the vitals. Therefore (4) he had taken the wrong action *and* had potentially harmed his poor patient.

Had the doctor first taken his own pulse, he might have looked around and realized that his patient had a pulse and that his heart monitor had simply slipped off. Then without stress or his prefrontal cortex going off-line, the doctor could have reasoned that he should quietly and gently put the monitor back on his hopefully still sleeping patient.

Fortunately, the only thing that was damaged was my professor's ego.

Often, trying to break a bad habit can be all-consuming. In fact we might be willing to do whatever it takes to get the job done. This win-at-all-costs approach can actually have significant costs, including increased frustration and stress when brute force doesn't work. If this is the case for you, finding ways to help yourself pay attention and ride those waves of stressful urges instead of getting sucked into frustration habit loops can help keep your prefrontal cortex online so that you don't make things worse. Curiosity is a great attitude, and third-gear practice to foster that can help in situations similar to the one the doctor faced. A few cycles of paying attention to your breathing is another way to keep your prefrontal cortex online so you can do the proverbial pulse-taking for a millisecond or two, avoiding damaging consequences. Here's another third-gear practice that can be particularly helpful with pesky things like urges and cravings, not to mention full-blown panic attacks.

RAIN Practice

Cravings and anxiety sneak up on you, and before you know it, you're completely sucked into one habit loop or another. But you don't have to be slaves to those habit loops. The more you become aware that urges and cravings are just body sensations taking you for a ride, the more you can learn to ride them out.

Here's an acronym that helps you stay present so that you don't freak out when an anxiety loop hits. (Michele McDonald, an American meditation teacher, first came up with this decades ago. I've adapted it slightly, based on noting practice, which was popularized by the late Mahasi Sayadaw, a Burmese meditation teacher.)

RECOGNIZE/RELAX into what is arising (e.g., your craving).

ACCEPT/ALLOW it to be there.
INVESTIGATE bodily sensations, emotions, and thoughts.
NOTE what is happening from moment to moment.

The noting part is similar to the observer effect in the field of physics, in which the act of observation changes the phenomenon being observed. In other words, when we notice (and note) the physical sensations that are arising in our body that make up a craving, we are already less caught up in it, simply through that observation. I'll give you specific instructions on noting as a stand-alone practice in a later chapter.

Here's the basic RAIN practice:

First, RECOGNIZE that the stress is coming on and RELAX into it.

Don't grit your teeth and brace for impact! Just let go and feel it come on, since you have no control over it anyway. It's even okay if you smile a little. Really.

ALLOW and ACCEPT this wave as it is. Don't try to push it away or ignore it.

Don't distract yourself or try to do something about it. This is your experience. Here it comes.

To catch the wave of anxiety, you have to study it carefully, INVESTIGATING it as it builds. Be curious. Do this by asking, "What is going on in my body right now?" Don't go looking for it. See what arises in your awareness most prominently. Let it come to you.

Get curious. Where does the feeling originate in your body?

What does it really feel like?

Is it tightness in your chest? Is it a burning feeling in your belly? Is it a restlessness that urges you to do something—like run away?

Finally, NOTE the experience. This keeps you here now, curious and focused, riding the wave. Keep it simple by using short phrases or single words. This helps you stay out of thinking or figuring-out mode, and instead will keep you in the direct experience of what is happening to you. For example, you might note clenching, rising, burning, heat, restlessness as the feelings come on and peak, and then vibration, tightness, tingling, lessening, relaxing, relief, and expanding as they subside. If thoughts arise, simply note "thinking" and don't get caught up in analysis or fix-it mode! Note your actual experience.

Follow that wave until it completely subsides. If you get distracted or your mind shifts to something else, simply return to the investigation. Be curious and ask, "What is going on in my body right now?" Ride the feeling until it is completely gone.

You might notice that RAIN builds on the curiosity practice that you've already learned. Investigating your feelings helps you focus and get curious about your moment-to-moment experience. As you tap into your curiosity and get better at this practice, you might find that it even can be a little fun (really!).

Here's an example from a participant in our Unwinding Anxiety program.

First, she maps out her mind so she can be more aware of her habit loops (first gear), and even explores the results (second gear):

> I reflected more on the Habit Loops I have, trying to observe them throughout the day. I mostly focused on triggers at work. One that I noticed was that in a meeting, when one of my supervisors talks after me, I feel like they see me as not explaining myself well enough. This

then begins the reaction of fearing that I don't add value anymore on projects and being self-conscious about what I say. This makes me nervous about saying more things. Sometimes, I shut down and just don't say anything. Other times, I try to "redeem" myself by saying something else, which I then regret and makes me even more self-conscious about saying something.

Then she shifts into third gear using RAIN:

I had an interesting experience with RAIN today. I had to attend and participate in a meeting where I knew someone would be there that I was dreading seeing. We used to be friends, but then he blew me off, so I feel a lot of pain and negative feelings when I think about him and see him. I could feel myself dreading the meeting, and I got curious about what that dread felt like. I also decided that, knowing feelings of anxiety were going to arise during the meeting, I should just try my best to note the sensations internally. And it worked pretty well! I was able to note "tightening," or "heart beating faster." At first, I had concerns that the noting would be hard, since I also had to facilitate in the discussion, but since noting only takes an instant, it wasn't hard at all. In fact, I think it might have helped, because in order to note I had to stay present in the discussion, rather than getting lost in a thought loop of self-judgment and hurt. So, while the meeting wasn't a picnic, I was proud of how I handled it. I was also able to take that success and appreciate it, which helped my outlook on the day.

Notice how her prefrontal cortical function stays online after a few moments of the RAIN practice. She's able to stay present and facilitate the discussion instead of getting lost in a self-judgmental habit loop.

The next time you notice a habit loop wave building, see if you can try the RAIN practice.

Below is a card-sized version of the RAIN practice that you can photocopy or take a picture of with your phone, so you can carry it with you for easy reference.

RAIN

Recognize what is happening right now.

Allow/Accept it: Don't push it away or try to change it.

Investigate body sensations, emotions, thoughts: Ask, "*Hmm,* what is going on in my body right now?"

Note what is happening in your experience.

CHAPTER 19

All You Need Is Love

A WHILE AGO, I met a thirty-year-old woman who was referred to me to help her with her binge-eating disorder (BED). She fell into the extremely obese category, with a body mass index (BMI) greater than 40 (normal is between 18.5 and 25), and met all of the criteria for BED: eating much more rapidly than normal; eating until feeling uncomfortably full; eating large amounts of food when not feeling physically hungry; feeling disgusted, depressed, or guilty after overeating.

When I took her history, she described how her mother had begun to abuse her emotionally when she was eight. As a result of this chronic trauma, over time she learned that she could "numb herself" from the unpleasant emotions by eating. By the time she came to see me, she was bingeing on entire large pizzas twenty out of thirty days a month, sometimes multiple times a day.

Let's pause and map out what's going on:

Trigger: Unpleasant emotion
Behavior: Binge-eat
Result: Brief relief in the form of numbing herself

But for her and for many others, as soon as the bad feelings go away and her prefrontal cortex comes back online, there is guilt and recrimination at the unwanted behavior, which itself is a trigger for more negative emotions, making it go off-line again, and bringing her cave person brain back online to repeat the binge behavior. Think of this as an "echo" habit loop—one triggered by the original binge habit loop.

She would get stuck in an echo habit loop because her old brain works like a one-trick pony: it knows only how to survive, even though her thinking brain, the prefrontal cortex, knows her behavior is highly irrational. Her willpower couldn't keep up. Just being able to map out the habit loop process with her was a big step forward. There was no doctor "preaching at her" or making her feel bad about her lack of willpower (and potentially retriggering her). Instead she gained insight into one of her deepest insecurities, *and* she saw that I understood where she was coming from. That empathy helped open the door for trust and the following steps.

I followed up with her in my clinic for a number of months, helping her map out these habit loops, seeing what she was getting from them and learning mindfulness practices as a way to step out of them. But the reason I bring her up here is because of that echo habit loop:

Trigger: Feel guilty about bingeing (unpleasant emotion)
Behavior: Binge-eat (again)
Result: Brief relief in the form of re-numbing herself

As she started to see that this habit loop was not helpful, her binges started to decrease in intensity, frequency, and duration. More important, as part of this healing process, she recognized another habit loop: one of self-judgment. She realized that nearly every time she looked in the mirror, she would judge herself for being too fat or unattractive. This was affecting other aspects of her life, including going out in public and dating. That self-judgment habit loop spiraled as she became more isolated and depressed. Even though she was bingeing less, her whole self wasn't healing.

The next step was to introduce her to a mindfulness practice called loving kindness.

Loving Kindness

Loving kindness practice (also known as *metta,* from the ancient Pali language) can help us start to soften and to accept both others and ourselves as we are. This helps us let go of what has happened in the past and learn from it so we can move forward in the present.

Loving kindness isn't positive self-talk or a pat on the back when we're feeling down. Instead, loving kindness is a capacity that we all have and can draw upon at any time (a condition for sustainable BBOs). It is based on a genuine well-wishing that we offer to ourselves and others. As I've written about previously, my lab has shown that loving kindness can even decrease activity in the self-judgmental habit loop parts of the brain such as the posterior cingulate cortex. When we practice loving kindness, we also learn to see more clearly when we're doing the opposite—that is, when we're judging ourselves. And when we see more clearly how the judgment is not helpful, we'll tend to drop it, because kindness feels better.

There are three parts to the loving kindness practice:

1. The use of some loving kindness phrases to help you stay centered
2. Seeing the image of the being to whom you are sending loving kindness
3. Recognizing a feeling of kindness that arises in your body as you do the practice

To begin with, sit in a comfortable position in a quiet place and let your mind just rest on the feeling of your body breathing. (As a reminder, no driving!)

Now—and as a contrast to loving kindness—bring to mind a situation that made you stressed or anxious recently. Notice what it feels like in your body. Does it feel contracted or expanded? Note the sensations that arise for a few moments.

Now imagine a dear friend coming through the door—someone that you haven't seen in a long time. What does this feel like?

Notice any differences between this feeling and the feelings that arose when you remembered the situation that made you anxious. Which one feels more clenched or contracted? Which one feels more warm, open, or even expanded?

Now bring to mind this dear friend again, or perhaps someone who has been a role model in your life, or someone who has been unconditionally loving, generous, or wise. This can even be a family pet; pets are really good at displaying unconditional love.

Now think about their loving qualities and kindness toward you. Notice if there is a feeling that arises in your body. Warmth, expansion, perhaps in the chest/heart?

(If you don't notice anything immediately, that's okay too—just keep checking in with your body as we do this exercise.)

Now pick a few phrases of well-wishing to offer to this figure. Here are some suggestions (but be sure to pick phrases that really speak to you, or drop the phrases altogether and simply anchor in the feeling in your heart):

"May you be happy," breathe it in; "may you be happy," breathe it throughout your body.

"May you be healthy," breathe it in; "may you be healthy," breathe it throughout your body.

"May you be free from harm," breathe it in; "may you be free from harm," breathe it throughout your body.

"May you care for yourself with kindness," breathe it in; "may you care for yourself with kindness," breathe it throughout your body.

Repeat these phrases silently at your own pace for the next minute or so. Use the phrases and the feeling of unconditional love in your body as anchors to keep you in the present moment. If the feeling seems weak or forced right now, just relax and focus on the phrases. As you reawaken this natural capacity, it will strengthen with time; don't try to force it.

Also, if your mind wanders, just note where it has gone off to and return to repeating the phrases and anchoring on the feeling of unconditional love if it is there in your chest.

Now bring *yourself* to mind. Bring to mind some of your own good qualities. Notice if there is some closing down or resistance to doing this. Yes, we're good at judging ourselves as not worthy. Just notice what this feels like and see if you can place it off to the side for now. You can certainly go back and judge yourself later if you'd like!

Offer yourself the same phrases you offered to others:

"May I be happy," breathe it in; "may I be happy," breathe it throughout your body.

"May I be healthy," breathe it in; "may I be healthy," breathe it throughout your body.

"May I be free from harm," breathe it in; "may I be free from harm," breathe it throughout your body.

"May I care for myself with kindness," breathe it in; "may I care for myself with kindness," breathe it throughout your body.

As before, repeat these phrases silently at your own pace. Use the phrases and the feeling of warm, expanding, unconditional love in your body as anchors to keep you in the present moment. When your mind wanders, just note where it has gone off to and return to repeating the phrases and noticing any feeling of warmth or expanding in your chest. If you notice resistance or tightness or other body sensations, get curious, *hmm*, tightness, interesting. Simply note these and return to repeating the phrases.

And now bring this guided practice to an end.

You can extend this exercise not only to yourself and loved ones, but to people you meet, and even difficult people in your life. Eventually you may find that the practice of letting go of contraction and moving into the warm, open qualities will open your heart to kindness.

Loving Kindness Isn't Always a Walk in the Park

Practicing loving kindness can be challenging at first.

I was very resistant to practicing loving kindness when I first learned it because it seemed too touchy-feely—my kumbaya meter was off the charts. It took me years of practice before I saw how helpful and valuable it is.

At the time I started my residency training, I had been meditating for about ten years, with only a few years of loving kindness under my belt. I was starting to notice a warmth in my chest, a loosening up of some type of contraction in my body when I was doing it. Not all the time, but sometimes. Back then, I lived a few miles from the hospital, so I rode my bicycle to work. When commuting on my bike, I definitely felt a contraction when someone honked or yelled at me. I noticed that I had been getting into a weird habit loop:

Trigger: Get honked at
Behavior: Yell, give them the universal sign of displeasure, or purposefully ride in front of the car
Result: Feel self-righteous

The problem was that I would bring that contracted self-righteousness into the hospital.

Noticing that I wasn't exactly bringing good cheer to my patients, I started testing what would happen to my contraction (and attitude) if, instead of yelling at the cars, I used their honks as a trigger to practice loving kindness. First, a phrase to myself, "May I be happy," and then a phrase to the driver, "May you be happy." This helped break the habit loop cycle of self-righteousness and the contracted feeling that went along with it.

Trigger: Get honked at
Behavior: Offer a twofer of loving kindness: one phrase to myself, one to the driver
Result: Feel lighter, more open

Pretty quickly I noticed that I was arriving at work in a much lighter state. The contractedness was gone. Then it hit me: I didn't have to wait until someone honked at me to practice wishing people well. I could do it with anyone I met. I tried this and started arriving at work joyful on most days. Seeing that difference between the results of those two habit loops—the closed-down contraction in the former and the opened-up joyful expansion in the latter—helped me see that loving kindness was the more rewarding way to be. It no longer feels like a struggle.

Like me, you might find that practicing loving kindness might be hard to start. You might judge the practice, judge yourself, or worry that you can't do it, can't do it correctly, or are too broken to be able to do it at all. If this is the case for you, I'll paraphrase a verse from the singer Leonard Cohen's song "Anthem": Don't worry about being perfect. That crack we all have and think is a flaw or weakness is actually our strength.

Resolution

In the case of my binge-eating patient, I introduced loving kindness to her as that one BBO that might help pull her out of the downward spiral of isolation and depression. It took a little bit of practice, but after a while, she started using it as her go-to when she would be triggered and tempted to judge herself. More often than not, she was able to pull out of her depressive rumination, and eventually she stopped binge-eating almost entirely, to the point where I discharged her from my clinic because she didn't need my help anymore.

She came back to my clinic for a follow-up visit about four months later, just to make sure everything was still going well. She had lost forty pounds, but more important, she told me this: "I'm grateful for this approach because I feel like I have my life back. I can eat a single piece of pizza and actually enjoy it."

Notice how she didn't have to resort to avoidance or some other strategy to break her habit loop(s). And what she was describing was not a miracle—it was simply bringing all three gears together and applying them in real life. She was able to map out her habit loops (first gear), see that poking herself in the eye was painful (second gear), and bring in the BBO of loving kindness (third gear), to step out of them and into something beautiful: herself.

So give loving kindness a shot in your life. Start exploring how curiosity and kindness can help you act in ways that benefit both yourself and others. It can move you into a better space for solving problems and interacting with the world. You can practice it formally while sitting in a chair or on a meditation cushion, or while you are lying down to go to sleep. You can even do it as you're walking down the street—offering these phrases to yourself and anyone who walks by. The more you practice them, instead of judging yourself or beating yourself up, the more you'll get in the habit of opening, being present, allowing yourself to simply be human, and the more you'll tap into those natural rewards that are available right within you: warmth, expansion, peace, or whatever describes your experience.

CHAPTER 20

The Why Habit Loop

AMY (NOT HER real name) is a patient of mine. She's in her late thirties, is happily married, and has three teenage kids. She's pretty busy, tackling the seemingly impossible juggling act that so many women face: being the primary caretaker of her children (and husband) while working at the same time. Many women have it worse than she—my mom (who is my hero!) raised four kids by herself while going to law school at night—but Amy had come to me with some pretty severe anxiety over trying to juggle it all.

When I started working with Amy, at the end of her first visit, I sent her home with the instruction to start mapping out her habit loops. It's helpful if my patients do a bit of homework between visits. When they clearly map out habit loops in the context of their real lives, not in a therapeutic setting, not only do they get a better sense of what's going on, but we make more efficient progress during treatment. When they come to their next visit, we can jump right in with the habit loops themselves instead of taking precious clinic time to go through and try to figure things out, based on their recall of what happened over the past week or month.

On a recent visit, Amy came in looking flustered. She wasted no time; as soon as she sat down, she launched right in. She described how every little thing was tipping her into a debilitating anxiety. She had a lot of responsibilities—that in itself wasn't a big deal—but lately everything seemed huge, to the point that she was snapping at her kids and husband for no reason (not that there is ever a reason to snap at our loved ones). She also said that though she liked her job and it wasn't stressful, just the thought of driving to work made her anxious. With her increasing anxiety, her to-do list was becoming mountainous because instead of ticking things off, she'd get worried looking at the list, feel exhausted from the stress, and find herself napping a good bit of the day—only to wake up and repeat the process all over again. She wasn't using her energy in productive ways. Her anxiety was siphoning it off; she was flaming out, sparked by the tiniest of triggers.

In that session, Amy made a comment that gave me a big clue as to where she was stuck: "I feel anxiety come over me and I keep wondering why I'm anxious," she said.

Amy said anxiety would just pop up randomly, not triggered by anything in particular. On top of this, her well-meaning husband and friends would ask what was wrong, and then say, "Aren't you seeing a psychiatrist?"

I asked her, "Are they saying, 'Why aren't you fixed yet?'"

"YES!"

Amy continued, "If I could just figure out why . . ."

Amy had fallen into a mental trap, just like way too many other people. They think that if they can just figure out why they are anxious, that discovery will magically fix their anxiety. This works just fine when it comes to fixing cars and dishwashers, but our minds can't be fixed like appliances.

That's the trap. We get stuck in this mindset that psychiatrists are like mechanics: we go to them to get our anxiety fixed. More often than not, that "fixing" comes in the form of trying to figure out what caused the problem. And once we become aware of what caused it, we'll be healed.

Triggers are the result of us having learned a behavior that we then associate with a stimulus. That trigger can be anything. Seeing something, feeling something, or even having a simple thought can trigger a habitual reaction that then sets a habit loop in motion. Naturally, we think that if we can identify those triggers, we can either avoid them in the future, or better yet, fix them. Thus we're getting stuck trying to fix the past. But we can't change it—we can only learn from it and change our habitual behaviors in the present, which sets up new habit loops going forward.

Amy had gone down the rabbit hole of *why*. She was desperately trying to figure out why she was anxious, thinking that when she got the answer, she could fix it and her anxiety would go away. Ironically, in the process, she was getting more and more caught up in a why habit loop:

Trigger: Anxiety
Behavior: Try to figure out why she's anxious (and fail)
Result: Get more anxious

During the first ten minutes of this visit, she had already gotten stuck three times in her why habit loop, just in the act of trying to describe to me *what* she was struggling with. (Nothing like demonstrating the problem right in front of your doctor for him or her to get a really clear picture of what is going on!)

After that third time, I asked her, "What does it feel like when you can't figure out why?"

"It makes it worse," Amy said.

Even if she could clearly identify a trigger, the trigger wasn't the problem. Her problem was actually the very act of asking why. The first thing I did was have her take a deep breath to calm down. Then we mapped that why habit loop out together. Just doing that made her visibly less anxious because she could see how she was fueling her anxiety right in that moment. I then leaned in and suggested something radical.

I asked, "What if the *why* doesn't matter?"

"What?" she said, looking confused.

It doesn't matter what triggers worry or anxiety, but it *does* matter how you react to it. If Amy gets caught up in a why habit loop, she just adds fuel to the fire, making it worse. If she can learn to step out of the loop, she can not only put out that anxiety fire, but at the same time learn how to avoid starting another in the future. With mindfulness training, the why/what distinction is critical. Instead of getting caught in the why, anxious people learn to focus on what is happening right in that moment. What thoughts are they having? What emotions are they feeling? What sensations are showing up in their bodies?

I gave Amy some homework.

"Whenever you notice a why habit loop developing, take three deep breaths. Breathe in deeply, and on the exhale, say to yourself, *Why doesn't matter.*"

The aim of this was to help her notice when anxiety was coming on, focus on what was happening in that moment, and not get caught up in that why habit loop. We practiced the breathing exercise together to make sure she could do it, and with a simple yet concrete tool to help her step out of her why habit loops, Amy headed home to practice.

We all get caught up in mechanic mode from time to time, thinking that our brains are like cars. And of course, if there is some physiological problem (e.g., a brain tumor), Western medicine is fantastic at doing the fixing. Yet trying to fix something from the past that set up a habit loop will never work, because the past is the past. This is where that adage about forgiveness that I mentioned in chapter 14 comes in: "Forgiveness is giving up hope of a better past." If we take the approach of trying to avoid triggers, not only is it nearly impossible (though it hasn't stopped my patients from trying!), but it doesn't get at the root cause of the problem. We have to learn to let go of the past and focus on the present, because we can work only with what is here *right now*: habit loops that we are acting out in the present moment. Each time we get caught in a why habit loop, we burn ourselves while at the same time adding more fuel to the fire.

See if you have a why habit loop (or two) and notice what it feels like to get burned. Then focus on the what (not the why); see what happens when you map it and step out of the loop using something simple like the breathing exercise I taught Amy (reminding yourself that *why doesn't matter*). And see what happens next.

Your Eyes Are a Window into Your Soul (Or at Least Your Emotions)

Have you ever wondered why many professional poker players wear dark sunglasses during tournaments? It's so that their eyes don't give away their schemes. The worst thing a poker player can do is have a tell—a change in behavior or demeanor that provides clues to the cards being held in a hand.

It's really hard to stop or mask involuntary eye movements and expressions—hence the shades.

Your eyes really can be a window into your current emotional state. By first understanding how your eyes connect to your emotions, you can then apply a simple practice based on this to help you work with anxiety, fear, frustration, and other emotional states. At the same time, this practice will help you build the habit of curiosity itself. Ready to explore this a bit? Let's dive right in.

Let's start with some science. When we're afraid, our eyes instinctively open really wide. Back in the 1800s, Charles Darwin theorized that in the face of uncertainty, we open our eyes wider to gather a greater amount of visual sensory information about whether there is danger "out there." Eye widening, when combined with other facial expressions of fear, also serves as a social signal to let others know that we are afraid. The contrast between the sclera (the outer white coat of the eyeball) and the rest of the eye makes this particularly pronounced in humans. Someone can look at our face and quickly read, *Hey, there may be danger out there,* without our saying a word.

In fact, this involuntary widening of the eyes can increase the cognitive processing of environmental events in both the person widening his/her eyes and the person seeing this happen. This was demonstrated in an elegant experiment done by psychologists Daniel Lee, Joshua Susskind, and Adam Anderson back in 2013. The first thing they asked participants to do was to pose as though afraid, then with a neutral facial expression, then with disgust. What the researchers found was that posing as though afraid, in particular, enhanced the participants' ability to accurately perform a perceptual cognitive task, while posing as though disgusted (which narrows the eyes) thwarted their ability to do the task.

In a second experiment, the researchers focused on whether or not eye fear responses transmitted cognitive benefits to onlookers. Sure enough, simply seeing pictures of eyes opened wide (i.e., with more sclera showing) improved one's performance on a cognitive task.

Opening our eyes really wide isn't just out of fear—it happens with other types of information gathering as well. When we're really interested in learning something, our eyes tend to get big and wide. In an interesting twist to the study, the researchers turned the pictures of the wide eyes upside down so that participants couldn't read the expression as fear but would simply see how wide the eyes were. Here they found that fear wasn't driving the enhancement of perceptual processing; the iris-to-sclera ratio (i.e., wider eyes = showing more white parts of the eyes) explained the associated improvement in task performance, not the perceived emotionality (i.e., fear) of the eye expressions.

Darwin's hunch, now borne out by research, has important implications for learning in general, and can give you specific tips and brain tricks to help you change habits.

Let's start with associative learning. This is how we learn to pair body sensations and positions with emotions. From a survival standpoint, if you are in danger, you instinctively tuck in your body, making yourself as small as possible and also using your arms and legs to shield and protect your head and vital organs.

When we pair a body posture or a facial expression with an emotion over and over, eventually the two become inseparable. In other words, it's hard to have one without the other. For example, if you tighten your shoulders and raise them toward your ears, you might notice that this makes you feel a little stressed. That's because many times in our lives, we've tightened our shoulders up toward our ears when stressed. (When we're happy, we tend to have a more relaxed body posture.) This process is called *somatic memory formation* because we are forming memories that associate body sensations (soma = body) with thoughts and emotions.

You can even play with this. Check to see if you are holding any tension in your shoulders from today or the past week (or the past year!). Now take a deep breath, hold it for three seconds, and when you exhale, relax your shoulders. Do you feel more stressed or more relaxed?

Your eyes do the same thing. We've learned to associate the literal openness of our eyes with taking in new information. When you open your eyes wide in fear or wonder, this signals to your brain that you are in a good place to take in new information. If you narrow your eyes in disgust or anger, this may signal to your brain that you aren't open to learning right now—instead, you're primed to act.

Let's play with this:

Open your eyes really wide and think of something that made you feel disgusted, frustrated, or angry. Try to keep your eyes really wide and see how disgusted (frustrated or angry) you can get. "Oh, I'm really disgusted!" Or, "Oh, I'm really angry!" How well did that work? Not well, I bet. Just as is true with disgust, when we're angry, we don't think, *Hmm, what happened? Should I really be angry? Let me gather more information . . .* Our brain is not in information-gathering mode—instead, it's intent on acting on whatever provoked the anger, and our eyes narrow with laser-like focus. This narrowed-eye expression of anger is so locked in that when you open your eyes and try to get angry, your brain says *does not compute* to itself, because there is a mismatch between your facial expression and your emotions. It's very hard to get angry with your eyes wide open.

Now let's do another exercise. Narrow your eyes as much as you can and then try to get really curious. Again, no dice: your brain is used to pairing your eyes being really wide open with curiosity and wonder. Remember, with curiosity, you're in information-gathering mode. Another mismatch: your brain says, *Hey, wait a minute. If you're really curious, your eyes should be open. Are you sure you're curious?*

The eyes are a great tell for emotional expressions in general. We've linked eye expressions with emotions for so long that the two are really tightly coupled. Knowing this, we can hack this simple system to help us move from frustration and anxiety into curiosity. Here's how:

The next time you are frustrated or anxious, try this.

1. Stop and simply name the emotion (e.g., "Oh, that's X emotion").
2. Check to see how narrow or wide your eyes are.

3. Open your eyes wide (and perhaps add in a *hmm*) as a way to jump-start your curiosity. Keep them wide for ten seconds and notice what happens to the anxiety (or whatever difficult emotion you've just identified). Does it get stronger or weaker? Does it change in character, or shift in some other way?

Once you get the hang of this, see how often you can repeat this exercise throughout the day. Whenever a difficult emotion arises, see if this exercise can open you up to leaning into the emotion and learning from it (and about yourself), while at the same time working to solidify the habit of being curious.

CHAPTER 21

Even Doctors Get Panic Attacks

So far our mindfulness toolbox includes lots of tools that you can use to hack your brain to shift from first and second gears into third gear. Curiosity is foundational, loving kindness helps you step out of self-judgmental habit loops, and RAIN helps you ride out urges for late-night snacks.

How about a tool that you can practice in short bursts at any time during the day?

We often talk about mindfulness practice as a way to learn how to *respond* rather than to *react* in life. The urge to do something quickly is often a reaction to something unpleasant. If you aren't paying attention, you habitually react to make that unpleasant feeling go away. That's like driving on autopilot, or as someone in one of our programs put it, "driving with your eyes shut." You don't know where you're going, but you can bet it isn't in the right direction.

If you pay attention and bring an accepting, curious awareness to your unpleasant feelings, your eyes will open, and you will find the space to respond rather than react. RAIN helps open that space because you aren't caught up in habitual reactivity.

One of our community members said that she felt like a "human *doing* rather than a human *being*." She explained that she was doing, doing, doing as a way to try to make herself feel better; but she had gotten lost in the process of doing and had stopped being.

With a little space, you, too, can *be* rather than *do*. If you map out your inveterate reactions to unpleasant emotions like fear and anxiety (first gear), and explore what the results are when you habitually react (e.g., worry, avoid, procrastinate, etc., second gear), you now have the speed to shift into third gear and start creating the room for a different behavior, such as getting curious or practicing RAIN. In fact, curiosity may be all you need to get up on your surfboard and ride.

Being curious helps you hack your reward-based learning system, replacing habitual reactions with awareness and flipping the reward from "contracted, feel a little better," to "expanded curiosity, feels pretty good." Because curiosity feels better than anxiety (it is, after all, that bigger, better offer), reflecting on how it feels to be curious (relative to anxious) will naturally reinforce it as the new behavior. Best of all, you won't get bored being curious. As the American writer Ellen Parr put it, "Curiosity is the cure for boredom. There is no cure for curiosity."

Let's take a moment to see what it's been like playing with the RAIN practice. Focus on your mental attitude. Have you found yourself trying (and yes, I mean trying, as in *forcing* yourself) to ride out urges? As in, I'm doing RAIN, so why isn't this urge going away?

This is an example of forcing yourself to shift from first to third gear too quickly. Remember, you can't think your way into changing a habit; otherwise you would already have done so. Just like trying to force yourself to relax, trying to force an urge or another negative feeling to simply go away through RAIN merely adds fuel to the fire. You run the risk of getting caught in another loop: if I practice RAIN, then I will feel better! Stress then triggers you to try to *force* RAIN:

Trigger: Unpleasant feeling or urge
Behavior: Do RAIN
Result: Frustration that RAIN didn't make it go away

You can't force acceptance, just as you can't force curiosity. That's why we've been spending so much time on supporting your curiosity before shifting into third gear. Any time things feel forced or using RAIN feels like one more thing you have to do, right in that moment get curious and note what contraction or forced feels like. And if you get sucked into some reactivity pattern or your thoughts spiral out of control, you can shift back into second gear and ask yourself, *What do I get from this?*

Third Gear Isn't Better

Don't forget: *third gear isn't better than second or first gear.* You need all of these gears to drive. Some days you're driving up a big hill, and all you've got is first gear. And that's okay. Other days, the road is flatter or has fewer curves, so you can drive in second and third gears. All of the gears move you forward. This is really important. *No matter what gear you're in, you're moving forward.*

Check in with yourself from time to time to see if you're beating yourself up for not always driving in second or third gears. Perhaps you're saying to yourself, "I should be in third gear by now," or "I should be free of that bad habit by now." But maybe that's a habit loop of its own? Maybe you should stop *should*ing on yourself and MAP THAT OUT?

Noting Practice

Let's try another exercise.

Let's zoom in on the N in the RAIN exercise. As you know from RAIN, noting is an important practice to help you step out of autopilot mode. But did you know that you can practice noting even when you're not about to get swallowed whole by a habit loop whale? This will help strengthen your skills so that you can be more fully present with your experience of life each moment.

Start with your five senses—sight, hearing, touch, smell, and taste. Now add two more: feeling physical sensations in your body (i.e., interoception) and thinking. Notice which one is most predominant at any moment.

If you're walking down the street, a motion might catch your eye, so you can just note "seeing" to yourself. A moment later, you might hear a bird, so you'd note "hearing." If a thought pops up—*oh, that's a bird singing*—you'd now note "thinking," because that's most predominant in your experience at that point. Pretty simple.

Perhaps the singing makes you happy, so you'd now just note

"feeling," because that happy feeling is most predominant. Each time you note your experience, it keeps you in the present moment, rather than your being lost in thought or on autopilot.

When you're on autopilot, it is easy to drift on in life. For example, that bird you heard chirping might lead you to think, *Oh, that bird is singing . . . It's so wonderful . . . I wonder what type of bird that is—maybe a warbler? Didn't I see a show on warblers on the Discovery Channel, about how their natural habitat was being destroyed? . . . I can't believe people don't take care of the environment more . . . My neighbor doesn't even recycle . . . I can't believe that jerk.* And on and on.

One moment you're happily listening to a bird's song, and the next moment you're angry at your neighbor. How did that happen? Autopilot. An untrained mind is going to drive off in any direction that it wants, usually steering itself into trouble along the way.

Noting practice helps train your mindfulness muscle. It helps keep you from adding fuel to the fire, whether it's anger, fear, or some other damaging emotion. When your mind starts running off, you just note "thinking, feeling, or even fear." Successfully using noting (and other third-gear practices) will rewire your brain to change old habits into new ones.

So take thirty seconds right now. Drop into paying attention and note whatever is most predominant in your experience: seeing, hearing, thinking, feeling, smelling, or tasting.

Afterward, notice the difference between doing this and being lost in thought or carried away by an emotion. That's the difference between watching a fire burn down to embers and letting it flare up and spread.

One person in our program talked about her stress-eating habit loop this way:

> In the past I've been so anxious that I'll go out of my way to get food, just to calm the storm of tightness in my chest and throat, even if it means being late to something. That's how uncomfortable it's been before . . . And noticing when those feelings come up is empowering. I can see it and think, *Hey, you're not hunger, you're stress*, and then decide what to do from there.

Can you see how just noticing gives that little mindful pause, that space that enables you to see what is actually going on? It keeps you from getting sucked into an emotion or urge to do something to make it go away.

Noting practice is relatively simple. Like a surfboard that keeps you afloat in the ocean, it helps you stay in the present moment, rather than getting clobbered by a strong wave of emotion and drowning. If you are already fully present in the moment, there will be no need to add the noting because you're already there.

As you begin the noting practice, it can feel like work. Don't worry about that. It will get easier the more you get used to doing it. Do it *for short periods, many times throughout the day*. I'm italicizing this so you'll remember it; it is important for forming a new habit. This will help groove a new brain pathway that will make noting your new habit. Keep an eye out for that habit loop of "I must be perfect" or "This is too hard, I must be doing something wrong. I'm a failure. I might as well give up and go check social media or eat some ice cream instead" and simply note that as "thinking."

As you build your mindfulness muscles through RAIN, noting, and other exercises, you will begin to see your habit loops more clearly. Over time, they will eventually stop coming—on their own, without your having to chase them away.

Try practicing noting today, not only when you use RAIN, but when you're walking down the street, sitting on your couch, or even riding in a car. Remember, it's short moments, many times throughout the day, that work to set a new solid habit.

Even Doctors Get Panic Attacks

When I was in medical school, there was an unspoken code that students had to be tough, almost superhuman. That meant never being tired or hungry; we couldn't even admit we needed to go to the bathroom. This approach was called "armoring up." Thus we were never taught how to properly manage stress or anxiety.

I was particularly good at suppressing the stress, so it was no surprise, then, that during my later residency I started waking up with full-blown panic attacks in the middle of the night. My heart would race and I would have tunnel vision, shortness of breath, a strong feeling of impending doom.

I had started meditating back in medical school, so I had about ten years of practice under my belt when these panic attacks began. At the time, I had been doing a lot of noting practice. Luckily, the first time I woke up with an attack, the noting practice kicked in—it was habitual by this point—so I simply noted "tightness," "can't breathe," "tunnel vision," "heart racing," and so on. When the panic attack was over, I went down my mental diagnostic checklist and was able to realize that yes, I had experienced a full-blown panic attack.

Here's the kicker. It wasn't like, "Oh *no*, I had a panic attack." Instead, my mind had simply noted what had happened without adding spin or commentary. The spin and commentary are what turn panic symptoms/attacks into a panic disorder: we start worrying about the next time we will worry; we start getting anxious that we might get anxious.

Panic attacks can have all of the telltale symptoms of panic, including a pounding or racing heart, sweating, trembling, feeling short of breath or faint, having a strong fear of dying. But for someone to be diagnosed with panic disorder, their panic attacks "must be associated with longer than one month of subsequent persistent worry about: (1) having another attack or consequences of the attack, or (2) significant maladaptive behavioral changes related to the attack." This is a critical distinction that I hadn't realized back when I was a resident physician and was having my own panic attacks. Panic attacks are just panic attacks (which doesn't diminish how horrible they can feel at those moments). It is only when we start to get worried about having another attack that this becomes a problem and affects how we live our lives. Dave had first come to me because he was so worried about having a panic attack while driving that he had significantly curtailed his driving: he didn't drive on the highway and barely left his house to drive to the grocery store. Dave had formed maladaptive habit loops to avoid panic triggers:

Trigger(s): Driving (especially on the highway)
Behavior: Avoid driving
Result: No panic attacks!

Don't forget, our brains are set up to survive. They try their best to help us avoid danger, and panic attacks sure feel like danger. Some of the most extreme symptoms I can remember from my own panic attacks are feeling as if I was suffocating and going to die. Dave's brain was that one-trick pony: if *X* causes a panic attack, avoid doing *X*.

Fortunately for Dave, he learned that his brain was much more adaptable. By understanding how his brain learns, he could teach it new tricks. One of the critical insights Dave had was that worrying about future panic attacks was just a story he was telling himself. It wasn't reality. It was simply a story.

The story of fear or worry that we tell ourselves can take on a life of its own. Each time we retell it to ourselves—*oh, no, I might have a panic attack if I drive*—it gets reified and solidified in our brain to the point that we believe it is true. Not only do we believe the thoughts, but we also learn to associate them with certain emotions, to the point that having a thought (*will I have a panic attack?*) can trigger a certain emotion (fear, worry, etc.). Remember that bit about somatic memory formation that I introduced earlier? That applies here, too.

Earlier in the book, I spoke of someone who had become so identified with the habit loop of being anxious that she described it as being "etched in [her] bones." We can become identified with more than just habit loops; we can even become so wrapped up in our own thoughts, emotions, and stories that we can't see what is real anymore. Wound up tight as a spring, we fall into a rage or dissolve in a puddle of tears, triggered by a coworker or family member tapping us on the shoulder or doing something completely innocuous.

During my medical school and residency training, mindfulness had taught me that I was not my thoughts; I was not my emotions; I was not my bodily sensations. I didn't have to be identified with any of these. Our habitual tendency is to push away anything that is unpleasant. When I was having panic attacks, by noting the sensations, emotions, and thoughts, I could simply observe and watch them come and go instead of pushing them away. This helped me avoid spinning a tale of worry and woe, enabling me to end the episodes without embellishing them or editorializing about them. Thus I avoided dragging things out or making them be something beyond what was really there. This also helped me not to form associative somatic memories between physiological experiences, such as feeling my heart racing and thinking that I'm about to have a panic attack. Experiencing my heart beating faster after I walk quickly up a flight of stairs doesn't need to trigger panic; it can simply be a sign that my heart is doing the right thing: pumping more blood to my muscles.

Because of my mindfulness practice, I was able to avoid going over the event horizon into the black hole of panic disorder. Knowing how my mind worked helped me deal with it. I did not become identified with panic or develop the habit loop of worrying that I might have another panic attack. I ended up enduring several more panic attacks that year, but they all ended the same way. And with each subsequent one, my curiosity and confidence grew. I knew that I could work with my mind.

Now you might think, *Well, he'd been practicing hard-core mindfulness meditation for ten years. I can't do that!* And I'm here to bear witness to the fact that whatever the habit is, no matter how old, deep, or entrenched it is, in fact you can. You build good mindfulness habits through short moments of practice, many times throughout the day. As Dave did within a few months, we all can learn how to work with our minds. It's all about setting *good* habits, like curiosity as our go-to.

Setting Good Habits

If you've been playing with the practices I've suggested in this book, you've been discovering for yourself, from your own experience, bigger, better offers such as curiosity and kindness. You can add RAIN and noting practice to this list of third-gear practices because, as you've seen from my experience, forming the habit of noting is certainly more rewarding than having a panic attack and then worrying about it so much that one goes on to develop a panic disorder.

For all of these practices—and for any third-gear practice, for that matter—you must see and feel really clearly just how rewarding they are. You can reinforce this by downshifting into second gear after you've done a third-gear practice (or even had a third-gear moment). Simply ask yourself, *What did I get from this [third-gear practice/moment]?* and savor how good it feels. I call this turbocharging second gear, because it really revs you up to do more third-gear practices in the future. Importantly, this also solidifies the greater reward value of the practice in your brain. This is especially important for habitual self-doubters (and the rest of us) who quickly move on from those rewarding moments. Because of our overscheduled and hectic lives, when we lack danger at our doorstep, we often quickly move on from the good, so it doesn't register in our brains. In psychology, our tendency to register and continue to ruminate on negative stimuli and events more than positive ones is known as *negativity bias* (aka *positive-negative asymmetry*). That's why the sting of a rebuke is felt more powerfully than the joy of praise. And you can also see how turbocharging second gear can help equal the playing field. Mindfulness helps us feel the negative and the positive fully, not get caught up in one or the other.

Hopefully you've already figured out that habits such as being kind and curious are good habits unto themselves. To be clear, curiosity and kindness won't suddenly or magically drag you to the mental gym or force you to work out, like some drill sergeant screaming in your ear. They work their magic in a different way, naturally drawing you in because they feel good. And if you have been stuck in old drill sergeant self-motivation habits, hopefully you've seen from your own experience how well the inner screaming bit *actually* works (it doesn't), so you can let go of those as well.

Taking a larger view, you might be seeing that gyms are good for training, yet you can't spend your entire life in the gym. Sitting down and dedicating some time each day to more "formal" meditation practices, which simply mean making the time and space to meditate (e.g., breath awareness, noting practice) in an uninterrupted way can be helpful—similar to going to the gym to do weight training. More important, as you build your mental muscles, you can take these tools like RAIN and noting into your daily life. Eventually, you can merge the formal and the informal as you realize that the entire world is your mental gym. Just as you can be active throughout the day by taking the stairs instead of the elevator, you can "work out" every moment of the day by bringing awareness and curiosity to bear. As you keep working the gears to refine your brain's reward value hierarchy, unrewarding habits drop lower and lower on the list (e.g., being sedentary, eating junk food, worrying), and rewarding ones keep moving up (e.g., being active, eating healthfully, being curious). Remember, the way to build good habits of being mindful is short moments, many times throughout the day.

So if you are trying to motivate yourself to get to the proverbial gym for longer than a week after you set your New Year's resolution, instead of forcing yourself, try using the tools from this book. Can you find mental and physical exercises that you actually enjoy doing, paying attention to their rewards so that they lock into your brain as a BBO? For example, my wife, when not motivated to go for a run, reminds herself of how good it felt after the last time she ran. That memory more often than not leads to a grin, which pulls her right out the front door at a running pace. And when it comes to mental exercise, a great way to motivate practicing kindness is to remember an act of kindness and recall how good it felt (it sure works for me).

Can you find the sweetness that comes with eating healthy food, exercising, volunteering, or whatever the habit it is that you're looking to foster?

CHAPTER 22

Evidence-Based Faith

You are nearing the end of the book. How are things going? Like the beat-boxing little engine who found that she could, did you find a good mantra or reminder phrase that you can say to yourself as a way to drop into being mindful and start working the gears? Can your trigger du jour become that mindfulness bell—*ding!*—that triggers shifting into third gear and a new behavior, the reward of which is bigger and better than your old habit?

If you are like many of the patients and students I've worked with, you might be wondering, "Am I going to be able to make lasting change?" Honestly, it's just a matter of settling in and doing the work. It's like taking a test—if you haven't studied as hard as you think you could or should have, don't worry, just keep studying and you'll get there.

These mental skills aren't hard to learn; they just need to be practiced a lot so they become your new habits. Training your mind takes practice: you practice mapping out your habit loops; you practice looking more and more closely at the results of your behaviors; you practice riding out those urges to do something so that you can learn to be with whatever thoughts and emotions arise. And with all of this practice, you learn to calibrate your system so that you can clearly recognize the feelings of contraction or constriction that come with itches, urges, and worries, as well as their opposite—the expansion that comes with kindness and curiosity. You learn the difference between external rewards (needing to get something to feel better) and internal rewards (feeling the relief that comes with being curious and kind).

Faith

One of the most important elements of learning a new skill is trusting yourself, having the faith that you can do it.

There are two basic types of faith. The first is that leap you take without having done something before but believing that it will work out because you've seen others do it or because your intuition says it's the way to go. This leap of faith is often the scariest because you are going into unknown territory. You may have taken this leap the first time you completely rode out an urge or craving using RAIN.

The second type of faith builds on the first one. I call it evidence-based faith.

In the medical field, we look at the evidence that a treatment works before we can say that it does. If you are getting a medication to lower your blood pressure, you want some evidence showing that it actually does what it says it will. Medical researchers (like me) perform research that provides this evidence. This is where the term *evidence-based medicine* comes from.

For example, my lab conducted clinical studies to see if teaching mindfulness to people who wanted to quit smoking, stop overeating, or stop getting caught up in anxiety would work. Though first tested by delivering treatment to individuals in person and then in clinical trials using digital therapeutics (an app), our methods used the same type of training that you are getting from this book, and they actually worked.

Remember, in one study, we found that mindfulness training was *five times* better than the current leading treatment in helping people quit smoking. And smoking is the hardest chemical addiction to quit—yes, harder than cocaine, alcohol, or heroin.*

I also mentioned the studies that we've done with overeating (e.g., a 40 percent reduction in craving-related eating and reward value reduction), and anxiety (e.g., a 57 percent reduction in anxiety in physicians, and a 63 percent reduction in anxiety in people with Generalized Anxiety Disorder). And it's not just my lab that has found evidence supporting mindfulness training. There are now hundreds of published scientific papers on the clinical efficacy and even the neuroscience behind mindfulness.

As I've already mentioned, my lab scanned people's brains while they were meditating and found that with practice, meditation changes our default brain activity patterns. Other researchers have found that it can even change the size of your brain. The evidence base supporting mindfulness training is growing larger each day.

But I'm not asking you to trust me or put blind faith into this training just because it has been shown to work in others. I want you

* This is due to a number of factors, including that when you smoke cigarettes, the nicotine gets absorbed into your bloodstream really fast, which jacks up the dopamine in your brain more and gets you even more addicted.

to collect evidence *from your own experience* along the way. How many times have you dropped in and gotten really curious about what anxiety feels like in your body? How many times have you been able to map out your triggers and habitual behaviors? How much have you driven in all the different gears?

Each time you breathe into that urge, ride out a craving using RAIN, feel the warmth of kindness, or are able to let go of destructive thought patterns using noting practice, you're collecting data, building your own evidence base. Each time you become aware (as compared to being lost), you see the results in real time. You've been gathering the evidence all along to show that this actually works for you.

Take a moment and reflect on all of the evidence you've collected over the course of reading this book. Consider it carefully. If you've been practicing, you should have quite a bit of data at this point. Now bring all of this evidence together to build your evidence-based faith in this program. When doubt or skepticism comes up, first note these as "doubt" or "skepticism." Remind yourself that you've got a huge pile of evidence to base your faith on. Evidenced-based, not blind faith. You can do this. Just relax and keep doing it.

Someone in our Eat Right Now program made the following reflection:

> We need to have faith that we can keep up these practices, and this faith can be strengthened by the personal evidence we've collected . . . I have seen this program working and the benefit of these practices when I practice them well. I have also seen how easy it is to return to my old habits when I let these practices slide. Diligence is necessary to

> really ingrain these as new habits. Part of that will take faith that I can make these practices my new habits, so that I don't just give up and go back to my old ways.

Wise words indeed. Just as when you learn to play a musical instrument, you have to practice to keep your skills strong.

So keep practicing and building that evidence-based faith, note "doubt" when it arises, and notice the joy of letting it go instead of being caught up in it.

Why not try to be mindful and curious throughout the day? See if you can be mindful while you wait for your coffee to brew, when you walk from your home to your car or the bus, or even while you're using the bathroom. How much can these short moments, practiced many times, help you to drive in first, second, and even third gears, building your confidence and momentum?

My Procrastination Habit Loop

Growing up, as a kid on a mission, I could be pretty focused. If I wanted to do something, I was hell-bent on getting it done. Yet that focus came at an expense. As my knife incident highlighted, I could get so caught up in what I was doing that I wouldn't stop to see *what* I was doing (or about to do). This focus was driven by interest. When I was interested in something, it took little effort to do it. When I wasn't interested, I had to be dragged, kicking and screaming. And even then I would do only the minimum necessary to check that box of the job's being "done."

When I was a kid, my mom quickly learned that instead of

dragging me to do whatever needed to be done, it was much easier to get me interested in doing it. When interested, I would not only do the job but do it well. When I was in my twenties, with no mom checking in on me, whenever I had a task that I had to do but wasn't that interested in doing, I would find ways to distract myself.

Trigger: Deadline for writing a paper
Behavior: Check the *New York Times* website (again)
Result: Felt up on the news, behind on the work

Over the years, as I practiced meditation, studied neuroscience, and started working with patients, I learned a great deal about how my own mind worked. I started to see how unrewarding procrastination was. I also started seeing *why* I procrastinated. For example, when I had to write a scientific review paper because it was "good for my career," I would sit down to start and notice this big white-hot twisting ball of contracting dread show up in my stomach. I quickly learned that the proper pain reliever was checking the *New York Times* website to make sure the world hadn't fallen apart since the last time I had checked (five minutes earlier). This follows a simple formula that everyone from doctors to parents to marketing firms knows:

Trigger: Pain
Behavior: Take a pain reliever
Result: Relief from pain

It took me a while, but I figured out that a lot of my stomach pain came from not knowing the subject matter well enough to know what to write. Not knowing enough about my subject left me with just two unhappy options: (1) Sit there, searing pain in stomach, staring at my unfinished paper on the computer screen; or (2) check the *New York Times* website (again). But once I understood that my habit loop wasn't helping, I learned that if I carefully did my research before sitting down to write, my checking behavior diminished and my writing behavior increased.

And then I figured out something that turbocharged the whole process: *actual experience.*

Here is my pain-relieving formula for procrastination: interest + knowledge + experience = enjoyment in writing + good product = flow.*

In other words, if I could find a subject matter that was of interest to me and make sure I knew enough about the topic to stave off the tummy tightness, I could write and have fun while doing it. For example, I was *interested* in mindfulness and helping people change habits. Over the years, I learned and gathered more and more *knowledge* about reward-based learning and neuroscience and had gained *experience* through my own meditation practice, working in the clinic and developing treatments. When I brought these together, not only could I sit down and write, but I *enjoyed* the process.

I literally stumbled upon this formula one fateful Saturday morning back in 2013. It was a bright, cold winter morning. I came downstairs relatively early with this strange sense that I needed to write something. I grabbed my resources, sat down at the dining room

* Also known as being "in the zone," flow is the mental state in which a person is fully immersed in an activity, experiencing a feeling of energized focus, full involvement, and enjoyment in the process.

table, opened up my laptop, and three timeless and uninterrupted hours later, a paper entitled "Why Is It So Hard to Pay Attention, or Is It? Mindfulness, the Factors of Awakening and Reward-Based Learning" was finished. And by *finished*, I really mean complete.

Usually peer-reviewed papers take a lot of editing, going back and forth with reviewers over details and so on. Not this one. I sent it off to two potential coauthors to make sure it was sound, and with very few edits, submitted it for publication (where it was accepted with very few suggested edits—unusual for the scientific publication process). Looking back on this experience, I realized this all came together because I had been practicing, studying, and teaching about this topic for long enough that the paper was in that supersaturated solution stage and simply needed a seed crystal to set off the chain reaction of crystallization. For me, that seed crystal had been a recent conversation with someone about how mindfulness might fit with reward-based learning.

I had been playing with the concept and experience of flow but hadn't realized that I could get into flow when writing. As any good scientist would do, I tested to see if this experiment was repeatable. I started with some pilot studies (papers, blogs, and such) and then went for the big conclusive experiment: Could I write an entire book while being in flow?

I checked to see if I had the proper background:

1. Interest: I was interested in writing a book on the science of mindfulness and addictions.
2. Knowledge: I had been studying mindfulness for about twenty years, and addictions for about ten years.

3. Experience: I had been practicing mindfulness for about twenty years, and treating patients with addictions for about nine years.

Since these were all in place, I then set up the proper conditions:

1. Food
2. No distractions
3. Mental massage

I figured that to give me the best shot at writing a book while in flow, I needed not to be hungry, or to have things like the *New York Times* website easily available. What I needed was something to massage out those balls of heat should my stomach start contracting with writer's-cramp-inducing thoughts of *What am I supposed to write next?*

So, late in December 2015, I set up those conditions by going on a two-week self-meditation retreat at my home—with all technology turned off and nobody to distract me except my cats. My wife agreed to help with this "experiment" by heading to the West Coast to see relatives for the holidays. Before starting, I cooked and froze away enough food so that when hungry, I could just pop something into the microwave and heat it up.

After everything was set, I gave myself the simple instructions: sit, walk, write, repeat, but write only when in flow. I would do my regular meditation "thing" by practicing a lot of sitting and walking meditation and would sit down to write only if moved to do so. And most important, I would immediately get up from writing and return to meditation if I felt the slightest bit of contraction, which signaled a movement out of flow and into some type of striving. (My aim was to have meditation massage out any writer's cramps.)

Two weeks later, a solid draft of my first book, *The Craving Mind*, was finished. The experiment had worked! My hypothesis had been proven. And it was a really enjoyable process. But replication is the hallmark of science. You have to replicate an experiment to see if it is true.

So in late December 2019, my wife flew off to the West Coast to see relatives for the holidays, leaving me alone with our cats so that I could go on a self-retreat. (See, I even kept the time of year, the cats, and all the rest the same, so as not to confound the experiment.) I went on retreat for only nine days and didn't intentionally go in with the aspiration to write a book—I was going to put together a consumer-oriented deck of cards with short practices for habit change, based on the three gears—so this wasn't a perfect replication of my experiment, but it was good enough.

I started the retreat and sat and walked for three and a half days, not being inspired to write in the least. Whenever the thought of *Should I write something?* came up, that pain in the pit of my stomach followed. So I went on walking and sitting. And then, the next morning came, which happened to be Tuesday, December 24. That day I didn't feel that pain in the pit of my stomach, so I sat down to see what would happen. I wasn't sure if I was ready to write something or not, so I just turned the spigot on a little. It was only a card deck, after all. Not a book or anything, so no big deal. Yet there must have been some pressure backed up in the system, because all of the bits and pieces from my experience and previous writings came gushing out onto my computer screen. It's Monday, December 30, 2019, seven days later. I'm finishing this final chapter now.*

Does that count as replication?

It certainly suggests that the interest + knowledge + experience = enjoyment in writing = flow part of the equation is true.

The experience was yet again enjoyable for me. Only time will tell whether that final piece of the equation holds: good product. And that part will be up to you as you go along your journey. If you feel that you need more than these three gears to develop your own evidence-based faith that you can do it—perhaps wishing you could find that magic pill that could suddenly make your anxiety vanish forever or miraculously fix your other habits—ask yourself honestly, "How many non-Disney wishes come true?"

If you'd rather lean into the science and trust your own experience, look at how far you've come already, simply from learning how your mind works, and working with your mind. Keep building your own faith, one moment at a time.

* Actually, this ended up being the penultimate chapter, as I was inspired to add a new chapter at the beginning based on the COVID-19 craziness and a concluding chapter after all that was revealed by and transpired after George Floyd's murder, but close enough.

CHAPTER 23

Anxiety Sobriety

Every week, I co-lead a live online video group for people who struggle with anxiety and other habits they are trying to change. For years now, people from all over the world have joined Dr. Robin Boudette (my co-facilitator) and me for an hour of in-depth discussion via the Zoom video-conferencing platform. In the spirit of reality TV (but really real—this is about helping people, not ratings), instead of setting a specific agenda of wisdom that we want to impart from on high, Robin and I invite our participants to bring topics forward. Then we dive into an exploration of what ails them, where they're stuck, and what they might do to get un-stuck. This keeps it real, and also keeps Robin and me on our toes. We never know who will show up to ask a question or what they will want to discuss.

This is far from group therapy, for it's hard to imagine what that would look like with 150-plus people in a two-dimensional space. We use simple methods of inquiry to understand their "problem," and after a bit of back-and-forth, with the *Mission Impossible* encouragement of "your mission, should you choose to accept it," give them a few tips to try out over the next week. The kicker: we try to cover each conversation in under ten minutes, so that we can get to as many topics as possible, and we work with the constraints of modern-day attention spans, where people have their weapons of mass distraction at their fingertips and just offscreen. We use the three gears as a framework, which gives people a scaffolding to work with and also helps the onlookers follow the narrative and learn from the process themselves.

One week, a thirty-something looking gentleman brought up a struggle that he was having: he could use the "third-gear" practice of RAIN or other mindfulness tools to help him cool his anxiety when it flared up in that moment, but he couldn't imagine being calm the rest of the day. After confirming that he could use the practices, and yes, they were helpful, he would immediately flip into worrying about the future. As he put it, "But what about the next twenty-four hours?"

His quandary reminded me of my clinic patients—not those with anxiety per se, but those struggling to stay sober. Many of my patients are in Alcoholics Anonymous or some other 12-step program to help them with their chemical or behavioral dependency. In AA, the process involves admitting that one can't control one's behavior (revolutionary for a program that started in the 1930s, bucking centuries of philosophers who claimed that willpower was king), examining past errors, making amends for these errors, and helping others who suffer from the same affliction. Perhaps the most famous AA saying is "One day at a time."

When patients come to me after decades of uncontrolled drinking, they can't imagine what it would look like to be sober in a month. Usually they can't even imagine what sobriety in a week would be like, because one of the other habits they've developed is telling themselves that they'll quit tomorrow. They swear to themselves that this is it, their last drink, and tomorrow they'll drive down sober road, without a glance in the rearview mirror of their (previously) alcoholic life. They are not unlike my patients who aim to have their last cigarette or ice cream binge, in that tomorrow beckons with promise and ease, because today has been stressful or too much of a train wreck already, and they deserve this little indulgence. Their minds somehow convince them that while quitting is the best and kindest thing they can do for themselves, imbibing today is also the kindest thing they can be doing right now. (As an aside, Mary Karr's memoir *Lit*, which beautifully and movingly tells her story of her struggles with drinking, describes the "tomorrow" mantra to a tee.)

Of course, when tomorrow comes around, the urge to drink far outweighs any clarity my patient had the night before, when they swore to themselves that they'd quit pickling their liver. They ask themselves some version of "Did I say that?" Well, too much has happened between yesterday and today. In fact, too much can happen between this morning and this afternoon. Going for a couple of hours without a drink can feel like forever for someone whose brain is getting itchy and antsy as their blood alcohol levels drop. That's where "one day at a time" comes from.

Once someone manages to get a few days of sobriety under their belt, the "one day at a time" mantra becomes a lifesaver. If someone is sober in this moment and tomorrow seems like an eternity away, too much of a mouthful, they can break it down into bite-size pieces, and take it not just one day, but one hour, ten minutes, and even one moment at a time. When my patients are sitting in my office saying how they can't possibly stay sober tomorrow, I can inquire, "Well, how about right now? You're sober now. Do you think you can *not* drink for the next five minutes?" This is, of course, a trick question, because they're in my office, and I'm not asking them at the end of the session.

After they mull over if I'm asking a trick question or not, they typically reply, "Yes, I can do that."

"Okay, how about when you leave. Do you think you can stay sober for the next hour?"

With the help of coping skills, meeting schedules, and sponsors' phone numbers, most of my patients can generally get by. A critical aspect of "one day at a time"—indeed, perhaps all of its power—lies in not looking too far into the future. Remember, our brains hate uncertainty. The further something is in the future, the more that can happen between now and then. For many of my patients, who have sworn sobriety up and down on a stack of Bibles, they have had every conceivable sobriety-busting thing happen between now and tomorrow. For their brains, tomorrow equals a lot of uncertainty. *Which one of a thousand things can and will go wrong?* their minds start thinking, as they start adding up the minutes between now and bedtime. But the possibility of calamity or error between now and an hour from now is much smaller, and thus their path to sobriety is more certain (and contains many fewer minutes). And between now and five minutes even more so. With certainty comes a reduction in anxiety, because you don't have to worry about that "uncertain outcome" baked right into the definition of anxiety. My patients can take a deep breath and plan for today—hence taking it one day at a time. If that feels too scary, they can take it one hour or even moment at a time. Stringing moments together leads to hours of sobriety. Stringing hours together leads to days of sobriety, and so on. Yet this all rides on taking it one moment at a time.

Which brings this back to my Zoom caller, who was giving me

flashbacks of my clinic patients when he was swearing up and down on a stack of Bibles that he couldn't work with his anxiety. He couldn't imagine not being anxious tomorrow, even if he could be calm right now. So I described to him how my clinic patients get sober. I described how they don't think about tomorrow, because that "stinkin' thinkin'" gets them in trouble. Once he was nodding along, showing that he understood, I asked him whether he thought he could apply this same principle to anxiety. Could he get some "anxiety sobriety" under his belt? Not tomorrow or this afternoon, but right now. He nodded that he could. He knew that he could use his mindfulness skills to calm his anxiety for five minutes. Most important, he saw how thinking about being anxious tomorrow was making him anxious right now—and that he could step out of that loop, in that moment. So I sent him off with his mission (which he chose to accept): get some anxiety sobriety under your belt, not tomorrow, but right now. If you find yourself worrying about tomorrow, bring in your mindfulness skills to notice the future thinking, and go from there.

This is a critical concept for anyone struggling with anxiety (or any habit, for that matter). It is true that past behavior is likely the best predictor of future behavior (hence habit formation), but what we do in the present moment, not what we did in the past, will determine the likelihood of continuing or changing that trajectory. As clichéd as it sounds, we live only in this moment. As is true in assembling a beaded necklace, time is a concept that strings together "this moment" that just happened a second ago to the "this moment" of the present. As the bead from this moment passes into the past, that narrative necklace gets longer, stringing together the story of our lives. In the same way, we also look into the future, searching for beads that we might add to the necklace. Working from past experience, our brain projects what might happen next. Yet we can only look forward, in the present moment, because the future is entirely in our minds. In other words, we're thinking (and often worrying) about the future in this moment—the present. As the musician Randy Armstrong put it, "Worrying does not take away tomorrow's troubles. It takes away today's peace."

So yes, all we have is now. And what we make of this moment creates that bead that we add to our necklace. Past predicts the future in the present. This is important so I'm going to repeat it: what we do in the present sets our course in life. If we're anxious now, we create a bead of anxiety. If we do this a lot, we make an anxiety necklace that we wear (sometimes with pride) and take with us wherever we go. If in this moment, we step out of an anxiety habit loop, we don't add that bead to the necklace and have the opportunity to add a different bead instead. We can create curiosity necklaces. We can create kindness necklaces. And with these BBOs in hand, we can put our old necklaces down.

Taking Extremism to the Extreme

I'm an extremist.

My wife jokes that I have two speeds: fast and off. As you saw with my knife-wielding incident as a kid, I have somewhat of a tendency to take things at the all-or-none level. When I was six or so, I wanted to be a cowboy. I wore cowboy boots, a holster plus a toy gun, a bandanna, and a cowboy hat to my group violin lessons because I wanted to be a cowboy. When I was in grade school, I would try to complete all of my homework on the bus, so that when the bus got to my stop, I could devote my energy to more important pursuits, like playing in the woods. A few years later, when I was a paperboy, I competed with myself to see how infinitely small I could roll the newspapers before rubber-banding them for delivery (to the chagrin of my customers) and how fast I could complete my route. In high school, I got on a no-sugar kick (to improve my sports performance), and while my classmates enjoyed ice cream and other treats, I counted my days of sugar sobriety. Perhaps as that cherry-on-top summary of all of this, my favorite saying in grad school was "go big or go home"—why settle for an MD or a PhD when both are possible?

Looking back, I could chalk this up to passion and focus. But really, this is an example of what all of our brains do to one degree or another: they find something rewarding and seek it out again and again. This is fine—until it isn't. Our drive to survive can be seen as both perk and limit: reward-based learning has gotten us humans into some less-than-survivable situations.

While we neuroscientists have barely scratched the surface in terms of our understanding of how the brain works, all of our very human survival mechanisms aren't going to get selected out in some Darwinian fashion any time soon. If I try to take myself as a case study or look more broadly, the research into extremism is far from a sure science. Yet clearly people become extremists using the same learning mechanisms as we use for tying our shoes: just like not tripping when we walk, some behavior alleviated some ache and got reinforced until we can't imagine doing anything else. In fact, there's a vast social experiment happening right now (without our signing consent forms to be part of the study): every time we go on social media or news sites that algorithmically use our click preferences to selectively show us items in our feed, we're unknowingly casting our vote for tailored and computer-curated content, which becomes familiar and thus reinforces our preferences for future clicks.

The more we click, the more likely we are to develop extreme views, simply because the ambiguity of having to figure something out, or consider a number of facts or opinions feels worse than the in-group feel of a shared view or a single perspective (black and white have very little uncertainty compared to shades of gray). A simple example of this is how feedback on social media is binary and quantitative (number of likes and retweets) as compared to the complex ambiguity of reading body language and interpreting tone of voice during an in-person conversation. No wonder we see teenagers sitting right next to each other yet communicating through their phones—uncertainty is scary.

But the feeling of in-group certainty and security comes at a significant cost. Not only do extreme views get reinforced; at the same time, they obscure the view of our feelings and actions toward others. Racism, sexism, and classism have significant costs: they cause stress, anxiety, and trauma for those who are "othered."

Yet with regard to the learning that is critical for survival, Charles Darwin made an interesting observation—one that was more of a footnote to his theory of evolution. Evolution can be pithily summed up in a tweet: "survival of the fittest." But Darwin noticed that something more than simple fighting to rule the roost was a driver of survival. In *The Descent of Man and Selection in Relation to Sex,* he wrote that "those communities which include the greatest number of the most sympathetic members, would flourish best, and rear the greatest number of offspring." This can be interpreted as kindness trumping meanness, even when it comes to survival. Can this view be taken to an extreme?

In 2004, Dacher Keltner, a researcher at the University of California–Berkeley and the founder of the Greater Good Science Center, wrote an article entitled "The Compassionate Instinct," in which he summarized a huge amount of work supporting a biological basis for compassion. Examples of this include brain regions associated with positive emotions lighting up in mothers looking at pictures of their babies, and similar regions lighting up when research subjects contemplated harm being done to others. Keltner concluded: "This consistency strongly suggests that compassion isn't simply a fickle or irrational emotion, but rather an innate human response embedded into the folds of our brains." Still, a bridge between survival and compassion seemed to be missing: if reward value drives behavior, what links it with prosocial behavior? And further, how could this explain extremism?

I was curious to see how closely emotional states lined up with reward value, so my lab set up an experiment in which we could ask people from around the world to simply rank their preference of fourteen different mental states—preference being a marker of reward value, as we naturally prefer behaviors and states that are more rewarding. After collecting data from hundreds of subjects who answered a short online survey, we found that individuals consistently and significantly preferred mental states such as feeling kind, curious, and connected to those of feeling anxious, fearful, and angry. These results fit with philosophical arguments suggesting that paying attention to how it feels to be nasty as opposed to how it feels to be kind may provide a stronger foundation for ethical conduct than the reason-based theories of Kant and Hume. (I wrote an entire chapter in *The Craving Mind* on "learning to be mean and nice," and it was good to see we could now back this up with data.)

In other words, as much as self-righteous anger may feel empowering in the moment, being kind feels better and more empowering than being mean, especially when you look at what actions these opposing emotions lead to and their results (e.g., no buildings get burned or people injured during a "kindness riot"). Abraham Lincoln, when once asked about his faith, pithily responded, "When I do good, I feel good. When I do bad, I feel bad. And that's my religion." If Honest Abe were alive today, he could have tweeted that in response to the vitriol out there, summarizing my lab's study with extra character space to spare. Maybe he would have added a hashtag such as #AwarenessMakesItHardToBeAHater.

Let's go back to the old saying that "research is me-search." My lab's results also fit pretty squarely with my own experience. I learned the hard way that judgment and anger feel painful not just for me but for those at whom I have directed my emotions. (In fact, if Malcolm Gladwell's rule of 10,000 hours of practice has any basis, I became an expert in judging others before I graduated from college.) And in my self-imposed "anger rehab" of meditation practice, I have learned unambiguously that kindness trumps meanness every time. It is unequivocally the BBO.

If that sounds like extremism, I would agree. You see, similar to my patients and program participants who see so clearly that smoking tastes like shit, overeating feels much worse than stopping when they're full, or that curiosity kicks anxiety's ass (in a nice way, of course), I'm now a kindness extremist. In other words, when I'm fully aware, I can't force myself to purposefully be mean to someone else. Why? Imagining the results of my actions (i.e., being mean to someone) puts a big pain in the pit of my stomach. It feels awful simply to imagine doing it. My brain has become completely disenchanted with meanness and all jacked up on kindness. Yes, sounds extreme, but believe me, I'd rather be addicted to kindness than cocaine. Darwin was right.

In a world of extremism, whether political or ideological, when it comes to survival, I'm going with kind-ism over racism, sexism, and tribalism. I think we've all seen enough hatred and violence to last lifetimes. And while I grew up without much money, raised by a single mom in Indiana, my gender and skin color have protected me where others have suffered on a daily basis, whether through micro aggressions, hostility, or overt abuse. As the Reverend Dr. Martin Luther King Jr. wrote in his letter from a Birmingham jail (1963): "So the question is not whether we will be extremists, but what kind of extremists we will be. Will we be extremists for hate or for love? Will we be extremists for the preservation of injustice or for the extension of justice?"

In a world set up for and moving more and more toward extremes, my rallying call of "Who's with me?!" comes back to what Dr. Martin Luther King Jr. and so many others have tried to get into our thick skulls: use your brain. What kind of extremist will you be? Can you tap into your innate capacities of curiosity and kindness to build a better life and world? Or will you get swept up in the tide of fear and self-interest? If you don't want to get washed out to sea, leaving a trail of tears in your wake (whether knowingly or unknowingly), remember your anchor of awareness and pay attention to the results of your actions. You've got all of the understanding and tools that you need to build your speed and momentum as you unwind your anxiety and move forward in your journey toward a happier, kinder, and more connected life.

EPILOGUE

Six Years and Five Minutes

In 2013, I was invited to give a TEDx talk on flow. I gave the talk in a quaint 1920s-style theater in Alexandria, Virginia, just on the other side of the Potomac River from Washington, D.C. The talk went well (I felt like I was in flow while giving it, so it felt great to me!), but serendipitously, my team had just completed an early version of our Craving to Quit app. We had worked on it for a long time, and back then app-based mindfulness training was such a novel concept that I was dying to have people try it out to see if it worked. Nearly twenty years had passed since I was first introduced to mindfulness, and we had something that could potentially scale to help many people—basically anyone with a smartphone. To put it mildly, my phone was burning a hole in my pocket.

Since I was near the nation's capital, I paid a visit to Tim Ryan (D), who represents Ohio's 13th district in Congress. He's a friend and a big mindfulness proponent (he even wrote a book called *A*

Mindful Nation), so who better to talk to about improving our nation's healthcare with low-cost solutions?

Tim and I are only four months apart in age, and first met at a party at a contemplative science research conference the year before. When I arrived at his office, he ushered me in and immediately asked for an update on the latest research. Tim impressed me with his desire to understand the facts and science behind something before he supports it.

As Tim and I talked, I mentioned our recent findings with mindfulness and smoking cessation, and that we'd just developed an app to deliver the training digitally. I pulled out my phone and started showing him the program's features. He got this wild look in his eyes and suddenly cut me off. He got up and yelled out to one of his young staff members in the other room, "Hey, Michael, come in here!" I can only imagine what it is like to be "on call" all the time as a staff member of a congressperson. Michael came in looking like he didn't know what to expect. "You smoke, don't you?" Tim asked—more of a command than a question. Hesitantly and somewhat quietly, he replied, "Yes." "Well, you don't have to quit, but try this app out and tell me if it's any good," Tim commanded and summarily dismissed him. Michael nodded. Looking somewhat confused, he left the room to await further instructions.

On my train ride home that afternoon, I sent Michael an email. "Thanks for volunteering (or being volunteered by Congressman Ryan) to help test out our Craving to Quit program," it began, and then gave him the details on how to get started. Two days later, he started the program. The following week, he wrote me an email to update me on his progress. He ended it with: "Thank you again for giving me this opportunity, I was not planning on quitting, but now that I am doing the program I figure now is as good a time as any." The next month, I received a follow-up email from Michael: "I began this program a skeptic, but saw its benefits almost immediately. I went from smoking 10 cigarettes a day, literally afraid to leave the house without a pack and a lighter, and after 21 days I have been able to stop smoking altogether. This would have never been possible without Craving to Quit." As I read this, tears streamed down my face. My wife asked what happened, and I stammered, "This may actually work."

Over a year later, Anderson Cooper was visiting my lab at the Center for Mindfulness to film a story for CBS's *60 Minutes*. He had just come from interviewing Congressman Ryan. I asked Denise Cetta, the show's producer, about Michael. Yes, she remembered him—and mentioned that he told her he was still smoke-free.

Nice.

In the fall of 2019, Tim and I were giving back-to-back talks at a conference. Just before I got up to give my talk, Tim leaned over and whispered in my ear, "Hey, do you remember that guy that works for me that quit smoking?"

"Yes, of course."

"He's still smoke-free," Tim said, a big grin spreading across his face.

Wow, six years later, after a five-minute conversation, a guy who was "voluntold" to give mindfulness a try had kicked his smoking habit for good.

Nice indeed. I love my job.

Feedback

Just like anyone else who has a brain, I learn from feedback. I have tried to write an honest account of the simple ways in which my lab's science has come together with my clinical work (both in person and through app-based digital therapeutics). Feel free to offer feedback via email—you can reach me at www.drjud.com. I'd love to hear anything that I missed, got wrong, or could have done better. It would also be lovely to hear things that you liked, found helpful, and so on. This is a continual learning process for me. The more I learn, the more I can make these tools better for others.

Acknowledgments

If you flip back to the dedication page, you'll see that I dedicated this book to someone named Amazon Addict. I don't actually know this person's name. I know only that this person identifies as a woman. And I know this because she wrote a three-star review on Amazon about my first book, *The Craving Mind*. The title of her review was "Intentionally withholds information."

So why did I dedicate the book to her, and not to my wife, or at least to someone whose name I know? (My wife is a brilliant scholar, has a heart of gold committed to improving the world, and is my best friend. She doesn't need me to dedicate a book to her to show how much I love her.)

Amazon Addict had an attention-grabbing title to her review but, more important, as with many things on the Internet that might have been innocently posted and then gain a life of their own, her review got enough "likes" that it went to the top of the reviews, where it is the first one viewed on the site. And because of this prime placement, it will likely stay there for eternity. This is a great reminder to me that the universe has a sense of humor. She wrote:

> In his discussion of the research into cravings, the book really shines. As someone who has both taken graduate school–level neuroscience classes, and spent some "time on the cushion" (meditating), it was a fascinating book. However, it was deeply disappointing in one important sense, and unfortunately I am not able to recommend it. The critical problem is that it doesn't fulfill the second half of its title, "How We Can Break Bad Habits." . . . The author comes across as a genuinely caring human being, and it is puzzling to me that he doesn't offer people the help he's spent his adult life researching.

Amazon Addict's words were like a punch or a kick that I didn't see coming. I had mistakenly thought that people would read *The Craving Mind* and be able to apply the concepts to their own lives to break free from habits and addictions. While I have received a number of emails from people who were able to kick hard-core addictions to the curb after reading *The Craving Mind,* Amazon Addict helped wake me up to the fact that most people need more than a map and compass. They need a guide. I wasn't ready to be that guide back when I wrote the book. I didn't have enough experience working as an addiction psychiatrist and hadn't done the research that you've just read about in the preceding chapters. (*The Craving Mind* mostly focuses on all the different ways that we get addicted, and the neuroscience behind how mindfulness helps.) Over the years, seeing that review sticking at the number one slot must have subconsciously left an impression in my brain, like the small dent in your car that triggers you to relive the "dent moment" each time you see it and then prompts you to rub your fingers over it, as though that action will somehow magically make it go away. When the conditions were right, that dent in my brain became a seed crystal for *this* book. So thank you, Amazon Addict, whoever you are, for that well-placed kick.

I am forever indebted to the many individuals who volunteered for my lab's research studies, and to my current and former lab members who, with a shared vision of making the world a better place, formed a great team to carry out our work, including Alex(andra) Roy, Prasanta Pal, Veronique Taylor, Isabelle Moseley, Bill Nardi, Shufang Sun, Vera Ludwig, Lindsey Krill, May Gao, Remko van Lutterveld, Susan Druker, Edith Bonnin, Alana Deluty, Pablo Abrante, Katie Garrison, and others. My patients are a constant source of inspiration and humility, and have taught me more about the practice of psychiatry and medicine than any textbook ever could.

A big thanks to my editor, Caroline Sutton, who among other very insightful observations had the brilliant idea to have anxiety be the central focus of this book, and to Luke Dempsey who, through his Socratic method of editing, helped bring my writing to a higher level. Josh Roman has expertly helped me shape ideas and their expression for years, many of which have formed chapters of this book. Caitlin Stulberg did a fantastic job of finding places of unclarity as well as providing general copyediting.

I'd like to thank my wife, Mahri Leonard-Fleckman, who, in addition to being the best life partner I can imagine, came up with the phrase "unwinding anxiety." I'm also indebted to my agent, Melissa Flashman, who has been instrumental in all things promotional.

I have been fortunate enough to get to work closely with Robin Boudette and Jacqui Barnett, to help people overcome unhelpful habits and discover their inner superpowers of curiosity and kindness. I have learned a great deal from our work together. I'd like to thank Rob Suhoza with whom I had a number of illuminating conversations which provided color and insight that helped bring a number of concepts to life for this book. My hikes and bikes with Coleman Lindsley have helped bring forward and express my approach to life (and a particular walk around Walden Pond was instrumental in helping me articulate the similarities and differences between stress and anxiety).

A number of people volunteered to not only read various drafts of this book, but carefully crafted comments and suggestions, including Alice Brewer, Vivienne Keegan, Mark Mitchnick, Michael Irish, Brad Stulberg, Kevin Hawkins, Amy Burke, Michaella Baker, Abigail Tisch, Mitch Abblett, Jennifer Banks, Leigh Brasington, Jaime Mello, and others that I may have inadvertently forgotten to mention.

I would like to thank Julia Miroshnichenko for producing the artwork for figures and graphics.

Notes

Chapter 1. Anxiety Goes Viral

12. **the evils which have never happened.** *The Letters of Thomas Jefferson 1743–1826*; http://www.let.rug.nl/usa/presidents/thomas-jefferson/letters-of-thomas-jefferson/jefl242.php.
12. **enslaved more than six hundred people over his lifetime:** T. Jefferson, *letter to John Homles*, April 22, 1820; T. Jefferson, *letter to Thomas Cooper*, September 10, 1814; T. Jefferson, *letter to William Short*, September 8, 1823.
12. **264 million people worldwide had an anxiety disorder:** Anxiety and Depression Association of America, "Managing Stress and Anxiety"; https://adaa.org/living-with-anxiety/managing-anxiety.
12. **19 percent of the population had an anxiety disorder within the past year:** National Institute of Mental Health, "Any Anxiety Disorder," 2017; https://www.nimh.nih.gov/health/statistics/any-anxiety-disorder.shtml.
12. **had the same level of anxiety as the last year:** APA Public Opinion Poll, 2018; https://www.psychiatry.org/newsroom/apa-public-opinion-poll-annual-meeting-2018.
13. **at the lowest point they can remember in history:** "By the Numbers: Our Stressed-Out Nation"; https://www.apa.org/monitor/2017/12/numbers.
13. **rates of Generalized Anxiety Disorder across the globe:** A. M. Ruscio et al., "Cross-Sectional Comparison of the Epidemiology of DSM-5 Generalized Anxiety Disorder Across the Globe." *JAMA Psychiatry* 74, no. 5 (2017): 465–75; doi: 10.1001/jamapsychiatry.2017.0056.
14. **grand scheme of the pandemic:** Y. Huang and N. Zhao, "Generalized Anxiety Disorder, Depressive Symptoms and Sleep Quality During COVID-19 Outbreak in China: A Web-Based Cross-Sectional Survey." *Psychiatry Research* 2020:112954; doi: 1.1016/j.psychres.2020.112954.
14. **compared with pre-COVID-19 trends:** M. Pierce et al., "Mental Health Before and During the COVID-19 Pandemic: A Longitudinal Probability Sample Survey

of the UK Population." *The Lancet Psychiatry*, July 21, 2020; doi: 10.1016/S2215-0366(20)30308-4.

14. **reported severe psychological distress:** E. E. McGinty et al., "Psychological Distress and Loneliness Reported by US Adults in 2018 and April 2020." *JAMA* 324, no. 1 (2020): 93–94; doi: 10.1001/jama.2020.9740.
14. **alcohol use after the 9/11 attack back in 2001:** D. Vlahov et al., "Sustained Increased Consumption of Cigarettes, Alcohol, and Marijuana Among Manhattan Residents After September 11, 2001." *American Journal of Public Health* 94, no. 2 (2004): 253–54; doi: 10.2105/ajph.94.2.253.
14. **19.8 percent in Generalized Anxiety Disorder symptoms:** V. I. Agyapong et al., "Prevalence Rates and Predictors of Generalized Anxiety Disorder Symptoms in Residents of Fort McMurray Six Months After a Wildfire." *Frontiers in Psychiatry* 9 (2018): 345; doi: 10.3389/fpsyt.2018.00345.

Chapter 2. The Birth of Anxiety

19. **some type of physical exercise:** This merits a longer discussion, one beyond the scope of this book. If you're interested in learning more about the underlying science, I would recommend Robert M. Sapolsky's *Why Zebras Don't Get Ulcers*, 3rd ed. (New York: Holt, 2004). To learn how this relates to trauma and to get some pragmatic tips and tools on safely discharging energy, check out *The Body Keeps the Score* by Bessel van der Kolk (New York: Penguin, 2015) and *My Grandmother's Hands* by Resmaa Menakem (Las Vegas, NV: Central Recovery Press, 2017).
20. **and (surprise!) higher uncertainty:** A. Chernev, U. Böckenholt, and J. Goodman, "Choice Overload: A Conceptual Review and Meta-Analysis." *Journal of Consumer Psychology* 25, no. 2 (2015): 333–58; doi: 10.1016/j.jcps.2014.08.002.
25. **twenty-six times an hour:** Y. L. A. Kwok, J. Gralton, and M.-L. McLaws, "Face Touching: A Frequent Habit That Has Implications for Hand Hygiene." *American Journal of Infection Control* 43, no. 2 (2015): 112–14; doi: 10.1016/j.ajic.2014.10.015.

Chapter 6. Why Your Previous Anti-Anxiety (and Anti-Habit) Strategies Failed

67. **recent research:** B. Resnick, "Why Willpower Is Overrated." *Vox*, January 2, 2020.
67. **willpower is itself a myth:** D. Engber, "Everything Is Crumbling." *Slate*, March 16, 2016.
67. **the more depleted they felt:** M. Milyavskaya and M. Inzlicht, "What's So Great About Self-Control? Examining the Importance of Effortful Self-Control and Temptation in Predicting Real-Life Depletion and Goal Attainment." *Social Psychological and Personality Science* 8, no. 6 (2017): 603–11; doi: 10.1177/1948550616679237.
68. **basically shutting the latter down until the stress is gone:** A. F. T. Arnsten, "Stress Signalling Pathways That Impair Prefrontal Cortex Structure and Function." *Nature Reviews Neuroscience* 10, no. 6 (2009): 410–22; doi: 10.1038/nrn2648; A. F. T. Arnsten, "Stress Weakens Prefrontal Networks: Molecular Insults to Higher Cognition." *Nature Neuroscience* 18, no. 10 (2015): 1376–85; doi: 10.1038/nn.4087; A. F. T. Arnsten et al., "The Effects of Stress Exposure on Prefrontal Cortex: Translating Basic Research into Successful Treatments for Post-Traumatic Stress Disorder." *Neurobiology of Stress* 1 (2015): 89–99; doi: 10.1016/j.ynstr.2014.10.002.

70. **self-control decisions in the first place:** B. M. Galla and A. L. Duckworth, "More Than Resisting Temptation: Beneficial Habits Mediate the Relationship Between Self-Control and Positive Life Outcomes." *Journal of Personality and Social Psychology* 109, no. 3 (2015): 508–25; doi: 10.1037/pspp0000026.
72. ***fixed* and *growth mindsets*:** C. S. Dweck, *Mindset: The New Psychology of Success* (New York: Random House Digital, 2006).
73. **current gold-standard treatment:** J. A. Brewer et al. "Mindfulness Training for Smoking Cessation: Results from a Randomized Controlled Trial." *Drug and Alcohol Dependence* 119, no. 1–2 (2011): 72–80; doi: 10.1016/j.drugalcdep.2011.05.027.

Chapter 7. Dave's Story, Part 1

80. **Rapidity of Habit Formation:** R. M. Yerkes and J. D. Dodson, "The Relation of Strength of Stimulus to Rapidity of Habit Formation." *Journal of Comparative Neurology and Psychology* 18, no. 5 (1908): 459–82; doi: 10.1002/cne.920180503.
81. **improve a subject's task performance:** H. J. Eysenck, "A Dynamic Theory of Anxiety and Hysteria." *Journal of Mental Science* 101, no. 422 (1955): 28–51; doi: 10.1192/bjp.101.422.28.
81. **slightly dropped off again:** P. L. Broadhurst, "Emotionality and the Yerkes-Dodson Law." *Journal of Experimental Psychology* 54, no. 5 (1957): 345–52; doi: 10.1037/h0049114.
82. **level of stress inhibits performance:** L. A. Muse, S. G. Harris, and H. S. Feild, "Has the Inverted-U Theory of Stress and Job Performance Had a Fair Test?" *Human Performance* 16, no. 4 (2003): 349–64; doi: 10.1207/S15327043HUP1604_2.

Chapter 8. A Brief Word on Mindfulness

86. **50 percent of our waking lives:** M. A. Killingsworth and D. T. Gilbert, "A Wandering Mind Is an Unhappy Mind." *Science* 330, no. 6006 (2010): 932; doi: 10.1126/science.1192439.
87. **not engaged in a specific task:** M. E. Raichle et al., "A Default Mode of Brain Function." *Proceedings of the National Academy of Sciences of the United States of America* 98, no. 2 (2001): 676–82; doi: 10.1073/pnas.98.2.676.
87. **triggers for their addictions:** J. A. Brewer, K. A. Garrison, and S. Whitfield-Gabrieli, "What About the 'Self' Is Processed in the Posterior Cingulate Cortex?" *Frontiers in Human Neuroscience* 7 (2013): 647; doi: 10.3389/fnhum.2013.00647; J. A. Brewer, *The Craving Mind: From Cigarettes to Smartphones to Love—Why We Get Hooked and How We Can Break Bad Habits* (New Haven, CT: Yale University Press, 2017).
89. **staying in it:** Y. Millgram et al., "Sad as a Matter of Choice? Emotion-Regulation Goals in Depression." *Psychological Science* 26, no. 8 (2015): 1216–28; doi: 10.1177/0956797615583295.
91. **main hubs of the DMN:** J. A. Brewer et al., "Meditation Experience Is Associated with Differences in Default Mode Network Activity and Connectivity." *Proceedings of the National Academy of Sciences of the United States of America* 108, no. 50 (2011): 20254–59; doi: 10.1073/pnas.1112029108.
91. **instead of being caught up in them:** K. A. Garrison et al., "Effortless Awareness: Using Real Time Neurofeedback to Investigate Correlates of Posterior

Cingulate Cortex Activity in Meditators' Self-Report." *Frontiers in Human Neuroscience* 7 (2013): 440; doi:10.3389/fnhum.2013.00440; K. A. Garrison et al., "Real-Time fMRI Links Subjective Experience with Brain Activity During Focused Attention." *Neuroimage* 81 (2013): 110–18; doi: 10.1016/j.neuroimage.2013.05.030.

91. cut down on smoking: A. C. Janes et al., "Quitting Starts in the Brain: A Randomized Controlled Trial of App-Based Mindfulness Shows Decreases in Neural Responses to Smoking Cues That Predict Reductions in Smoking." *Neuropsychopharmacology* 44 (2019): 1631–38; doi: 10.1038/s41386-019-0403-y.

Chapter 9. What Is Your Mindfulness Personality Type?

94. fight, flight, or freeze buckets: N. T. Van Dam et al., "Development and Validation of the Behavioral Tendencies Questionnaire." *PLoS One* 10, no. 11 (2015): e0140867; doi: 10.1371/journal.pone.0140867.

94. "May temperament be recognized": B. Buddhaghosa, *The Path of Purification*, trans. B. Ñāṇamoli (Onalaska, WA: BPS Pariyatti Publishing, 1991), 104.

Chapter 10. How Your Brain Makes Decisions (Why We Prefer Cake to Broccoli)

108. the food hits our stomach: S. E. Thanarajah et al., "Food Intake Recruits Orosensory and Post-Ingestive Dopaminergic Circuits to Affect Eating Desire in Humans." *Cell Metabolism* 29, no. 3 (2019): 695–706.e4; doi: 10.1016/j.cmet.2018.12.006.

108. behavioral information gets integrated: M. L. Kringelbach and E. T. Rolls, "The Functional Neuroanatomy of the Human Orbitofrontal Cortex: Evidence from Neuroimaging and Neuropsychology." *Progress in Neurobiology* 72, no. 5 (2004): 341–72; doi: 10.1016/j.pneurobio.2004.03.006; J. O'Doherty et al., "Abstract Reward and Punishment Representations in the Human Orbitofrontal Cortex." *Nature Neuroscience* 4, no. 1 (2001): 95–102; doi: 10.1038/82959.

109. automatic and habitual response: M. L. Kringelbach, "The Human Orbitofrontal Cortex: Linking Reward to Hedonic Experience." *Nature Reviews Neuroscience* 6, no. 9 (2005): 691–702; doi: 10.1038/nrn1747.

109. is to update its reward value: J. A. Brewer, "Mindfulness Training for Addictions: Has Neuroscience Revealed a Brain Hack by Which Awareness Subverts the Addictive Process?" *Current Opinion in Psychology* 28 (2019): 198–203; doi: 10.1016/j.copsyc.2019.01.014.

110. no fewer than four Marlboro men have died from COPD: https://www.latimes.com/nation/nationnow/la-na-nn-marlboro-men-20140127-story.html.

Chapter 12. Learning (and Growing) from the Past

132. "repair their own confidence": C. S. Dweck, *Mindset: The New Psychology of Success* (New York: Random House Digital, 2006), 179–80.

Chapter 13. Fixing the Fix: Dana Small's Chocolate Experiment

136. when people ate chocolate: D. M. Small et al., "Changes in Brain Activity Related to Eating Chocolate: From Pleasure to Aversion." *Brain* 124, no. 9 (2001): 1720–33; doi: 10.1093/brain/124.9.1720.

138. our mindful eating program: A. L. Beccia et al. "Women's Experiences with a Mindful Eating Program for Binge and Emotional Eating: A Qualitative Investigation into the Process of Behavioral Change." *Journal of Alternative and Complementary Medicine*, online ahead of print July 14, 2020; doi: 10.1089/acm.2019.0318.

138. overindulging or overeating: J. A. Brewer et al., "Can Mindfulness Address Maladaptive Eating Behaviors? Why Traditional Diet Plans Fail and How New Mechanistic Insights May Lead to Novel Interventions." *Frontiers in Psychology* 9 (2018): 1418; doi: 10.3389/fpsyg.2018.01418.

Chapter 14. How Long Does It Take to Change a Habit?

144. to reach "automaticity": P. Lally et al., "How Are Habits Formed: Modelling Habit Formation in the Real World." *European Journal of Social Psychology* 40, no. 6 (2010): 998–1009; doi: 10.1002/ejsp.674.

144. In the 1970s, two researchers: M. A. McDannald et al., "Model-Based Learning and the Contribution of the Orbitofrontal Cortex to the Model-Free World." *European Journal of Neuroscience* 35, no. 7 (2012): 991–96; doi: 10.1111/j.1460-9568.2011.07982.x; R. A. Rescorla and A. R. Wagner, "A Theory of Pavlovian Conditioning: Variations in the Effectiveness of Reinforcement and Nonreinforcement," in A. H. Black and W. F. Prokasy, eds., *Classical Conditioning II: Current Research and Theory* (New York: Appleton-Century-Crofts: 1972), 64–99.

148. one for smoking and one for eating: V. Taylor et al., "Awareness Drives Changes in Reward Value and Predicts Behavior Change: Probing Reinforcement Learning Using Experience Sampling from Mobile Mindfulness Training for Maladaptive Eating," in press.

149. works in the brain and behaviorally: A. E. Mason et al., "Testing a Mobile Mindful Eating Intervention Targeting Craving-Related Eating: Feasibility and Proof of Concept." *Journal of Behavioral Medicine* 41, no. 2 (2018): 160–73; doi: 10.1007/s10865-017-9884-5; V. U. Ludwig, K. W. Brown, and J. A. Brewer. "Self-Regulation Without Force: Can Awareness Leverage Reward to Drive Behavior Change?" *Perspectives on Psychological Science* (2020); doi: 10.1177/1745691620931460; A. C. Janes et al., "Quitting Starts in the Brain: A Randomized Controlled Trial of App-Based Mindfulness Shows Decreases in Neural Responses to Smoking Cues That Predict Reductions in Smoking." *Neuropsychopharmacology* 44 (2019): 1631–38; doi: 10.1038/s41386-019-0403-y.

Chapter 15. The Bigger, Better Offer

160. individualism and reason: W. Hofmann and L. Van Dillen, "Desire: The New Hot Spot in Self-Control Research." *Current Directions in Psychological Science* 21, no. 5 (2012): 317–22; doi: 10.1177/0963721412453587.

161. thinking patterns and behaviors: Wikipedia, "Cognitive Behavioral Therapy," https://en.wikipedia.org/wiki/Cognitive_behavioral_therapy.

161. CBT focuses largely: Hofmann and Van Dillen, "Desire: The New Hot Spot in Self-Control Research."

161. food to be more and more addictive: M. Moss, "The Extraordinary Science of Addictive Junk Food." *New York Times Magazine*, February 20, 2013; https://www.nytimes.com/2013/02/24/magazine/the-extraordinary-science-of-junk-food.html.

161. your time and conscious attention as possible: O. Solon, "Ex-Facebook President Sean Parker: Site Made to Exploit Human 'Vulnerability.'" *The Guardian*,

November 9, 2017; https://www.theguardian.com/technology/2017/nov/09/facebook-sean-parker-vulnerability-brain-psychology.

162. **triggers such as stress:** A. F. T. Arnsten, "Stress Weakens Prefrontal Networks: Molecular Insults to Higher Cognition." *Nature Neuroscience* 18, no. 10 (2015): 1376–85; doi: 10.1038/nn.4087; A. F. T. Arnsten, "Stress Signalling Pathways That Impair Prefrontal Cortex Structure and Function." *Nature Reviews Neuroscience* 10 (2009): 410–22; doi: 10.1038/nrn2648.

162. **needing to use extra time or effort?** J. A. Brewer, "Feeling Is Believing: The Convergence of Buddhist Theory and Modern Scientific Evidence Supporting How Self Is Formed and Perpetuated Through Feeling Tone (*Vedanā*)." *Contemporary Buddhism* 19, no. 1 (2018): 113–26; doi: 10.1080/14639947.2018.1443553; J. A. Brewer, "Mindfulness Training for Addictions: Has Neuroscience Revealed a Brain Hack by Which Awareness Subverts the Addictive Process?" *Current Opinion in Psychology* 28 (2019): 198–203; doi: 10.1016/j.copsyc.2019.01.014.

166. **feeling of being closed:** K. A. Garrison et al., "Effortless Awareness: Using Real Time Neurofeedback to Investigate Correlates of Posterior Cingulate Cortex Activity in Meditators' Self-Report." *Frontiers in Human Neuroscience* 7 (2013): 440; doi: 10.3389/fnhum.2013.00440.

Chapter 16. The Science of Curiosity

173. **most subway and train stations:** W. Neuman, "How Long Till Next Train? The Answer Is Up in Lights." *New York Times*, February 17, 2007.

174. **Children are born scientists:** Transcript from an interview with Leon Lederman by Joanna Rose, December 7, 2001; https://www.nobelprize.org/prizes/physics/1988/lederman/26243-interview-transcript-1988-3.

174. **I-curiosity and D-curiosity:** J. A. Litman and P. J. Silvia, "The Latent Structure of Trait Curiosity: Evidence for Interest and Deprivation Curiosity Dimensions." *Journal of Personality Assessment* 86, no. 3 (2006): 318–28; doi: 10.1207/s15327752jpa8603_07.

177. **level in learning the answer:** M. J. Gruber, B. D. Gelman, and C. Ranganath, "States of Curiosity Modulate Hippocampus-Dependent Learning Via the Dopaminergic Circuit." *Neuron* 84, no. 2 (2014): 486–96; doi: 10.1016/j.neuron.2014.08.060.

177. **information is coded in the orbitofrontal cortex:** T. C. Blanchard, B. Y. Hayden, and E. S. Bromberg-Martin, "Orbitofrontal Cortex Uses Distinct Codes for Different Choice Attributes in Decisions Motivated by Curiosity." *Neuron* 85, no. 3 (2015): 602–14; doi: 10.1016/j.neuron.2014.12.050.

180. **"Never lose a holy curiosity":** Albert Einstein, "Old Man's Advice to Youth: 'Never Lose a Holy Curiosity.'" Life, May 2, 1955, p. 64.

Chapter 19. All You Need Is Love

209. **self-judgmental habit loop parts of the brain such as the posterior cingulate cortex:** J. A. Brewer, *The Craving Mind: From Cigarettes to Smartphones to Love—Why We Get Hooked and How We Can Break Bad Habits* (New Haven, CT: Yale University Press, 2017); K. A. Garrison et al., "BOLD Signal and Functional Connectivity Associated with Loving Kindness Meditation." *Brain and Behavior* 4, no. 3 (2014); doi: 10.1002/brb3.219.

Chapter 20. The Why Habit Loop

221. **about whether there is danger "out there":** C. Darwin, *The Expression of the Emotions in Man and Animals* (New York: Oxford University Press, 1998).

222. **Adam Anderson back in 2013:** D. H. Lee, J. M. Susskind, and A. K. Anderson, "Social Transmission of the Sensory Benefits of Eye Widening in Fear Expressions." *Psychological Science* 24, no. 6 (2013): 957–65; doi: 10.1177/0956797612464500.

Chapter 21. Even Doctors Get Panic Attacks

233. **"changes related to the attack":** American Psychiatric Association, *Diagnostic and Statistical Manual of Mental Disorders (DSM-5)* (Washington, D.C.: American Psychiatric Association Publishing, 2013).

Chapter 23. Anxiety Sobriety

257. **"greatest number of offspring":** C. Darwin, *The Descent of Man and Selection in Relation to Sex*, vol. 1 (New York: D. Appleton, 1896), 72.

258. **biological basis for compassion:** D. Keltner, "The Compassionate Instinct." *Greater Good Magazine*, March 1, 2004.

260. **"for the extension of justice?":** *Diagnostic and Statistical Manual of Mental Disorders (DSM-5)*. Dr. Martin Luther King Jr., "Letter from Birmingham Jail," https://www.africa.upenn.edu/Articles_Gen/Letter_Birmingham.html.

Index

Page numbers in *italics* indicate figures; those followed by "n" indicate notes.